Who Put th
In the Bury Net?

By

Mark Wellington

RB
Rossendale Books

Published by Lulu Enterprises Inc.
3101 Hillsborough Street
Suite 210
Raleigh, NC 27607-5436
United States of America

Published in paperback 2013
Category: Reference
Copyright Mark Wellington © 2013
ISBN : 978-1-291-43197-1

All rights reserved, Copyright under Berne Copyright Convention and Pan American Convention. No part of this book may be reproduced, stored in a retrieval system, or transmitted in any form or by any means, electronic, mechanical, photocopying, recording or otherwise, without prior permission of the author.

The author's moral rights have been asserted.

Dedication

For Dad

Acknowledgements

I would to take this opportunity to thank those people who have assisted in helping with the book; it as all been greatly appreciated: The Echo newspaper for the photos used, Southend-on-Sea library and Paul Boreham. The following Wellington's: Paul, Kelly, Abby & Emily whose contributions have been a big help and, of course, Paul Clark for writing the foreword as well as his generous assistance with some of the images.

Also, I would like to mention my Dad and Grandads -Don and Norm - who first introduced me to football and Southend United. Going to games at a young age with my family gave me 'the bug' that meant I was always going to be a Shrimper and I wouldn't want it to be any other way.

Up the Blues!

'Up The Blues!'

Contents

Foreword by Paul Clark 7

Introduction 9

Pre-Season 13

August 1990 35

September 1990 43

October 1990 64

November 1990 84

December 1990 105

January 1991 130

Photographs & Illustrations 156

February 1991 163

March 1991 186

April 1991 215

May 1991 - End of Season 247

What It Meant to Me 268

Southend United: Results & Stats 1990/1991 272

'Up The Blues!'

Foreword

"It was a good goal, not stunning, but what it eventually meant was history making..."

4th May 1991 Gigg Lane, Bury. Second half down to ten men and David Martin wins yet another header and the ball falls to Andy Ansah. Off he goes on a mazy run skilfully turning between two defenders then a lucky bounce off a defender gives him the ball on the right wing. He cuts back onto his left foot and puts in either a miss-hit cross or an astute, accurate pass with 'unbelievable tekkers' depending on who's telling the tale. Whichever is the truth the ball lands at the feet of Ian Benjamin, 12 yards out and with his back to goal and a defender tight behind. Benji controls, swivels and swings his left foot and...

It was a good goal, not stunning, but what it eventually meant was history making.

In their entire history up until that day Southend Utd had alternated with some frequency on the bottom two rungs of English league football. Despite many really good players coming from clubs in higher divisions, many others moving from Southend to play at the higher levels and some outstanding teams who had won promotion from the bottom tier, they had never had a team who could break through that 'glass ceiling' and win promotion to the second tier of English football.

The blues had won promotion the year before and manager David Webb had made a bold statement. Not for him the tried and trusted mantra of 'we want to consolidate in this new league'. David stated before the season started 'we want to win promotion again'. He then set about selling our top scorer of the last two years, replacing him with an unknown. He had already replaced plenty of experience with young keen talented lads from non-league and reserves from

'Up The Blues!'

other clubs so his boast could be described as wishful thinking. But here we were, on the threshold of fulfilling that prediction.

Was it easy? Of course not. Plain sailing? No promotion ever is. There were highs and lows along the way, ups and downs, unexplained defeats and surprising victories. And following all the drama is the long suffering supporter. The people whose hopes and dreams lay in the hands, or feet, of a group of strangers who have been brought to their club. They hope these players want success as much as they do. Many will have seen their team flatter to deceive before, had their hopes built up only to be dashed yet again. Maybe this time though. Maybe this set of strangers who they have come to know can deliver their dreams. They offer support home and away and just want to be able to say with pride that they support Southend United. So they listen at home or they stand on the away terraces at Gigg Lane, Bury in 1991 and at the far end the ball lands at the feet of Ian Benjamin and...

This is the story of that historic season through the eyes of a supporter. The rollercoaster of emotions and the ebbing and flowing of belief but always the hope of reaching the common goal.

When the ball landed at Benji's feet I was 50 yards away defending in our own half watching the making of Southend Utd history. If you're a Blues supporter old enough to remember you'll know exactly where you were too and this book will recall many more memories, good and bad, of that fateful season.

Paul Clark

'Up The Blues!'

Introduction

"I would not have signed on at this stage of my career unless I believed that Southend were going to progress."
– Paul Sansome

Southend United had been somewhat of a yoyo club between English football's bottom two divisions since the football league did away with the old system of splitting Division Three into a north / south divide at the beginning of the 1958-59 campaign.

Ever since the four national divisions were introduced Southend had started twenty seasons in the Third Division and twelve in Division Four.

With that in mind, it hardly came as a surprise when relegation once more darkened the corridors at Roots Hall as the 1988-89 campaign drew to a close and The Blues, almost inevitably, fell back down to England's basement division. The manager who couldn't halt that slide was former Chelsea legend, David Webb.

He was back in charge of Southend for a second spell after his first ended in the spring of 1987 following a reported clash with Chairman Vic Jobson over the lack of money made available for potential new signings.

Webb then re-joined the club in December of the following year after both he and Jobson managed to sort out their differences, but the team was already struggling towards the bottom end of the table and relegation was confirmed in spite of a last day home win over Chester City due to results going against them elsewhere.

What the club needed was stability and with Webb's second stint as Blues boss being their fourth different manager in three miserable years, Jobson acted quickly to state that Webb was his man to lead Southend forwards.

"David is under contract and I have no intention of letting him go," The Blues Chairman declared. "He only returned to us five months ago and given time I know he can do a good job for us. Its times like these he needs the support of everyone who has the club at heart and I have every confidence in his ability to plot a quick return to the Third Division."

Jobson's backing of his manager proved to be a wise move as Webb's team went into the last day of the '89 – '90 season knowing a win at Peterborough United would seal promotion back into the Third Division at the first attempt.

Throughout the majority of the year, Southend had been in pole position, but a run of only ten points from a possible twenty-four meant that there was now a chance of The Blues dropping out of the automatic promotion positions and slipping into the dreaded play offs.

However, Webb was in confident mood ahead of the final day's drama and even promised that his team would "sweat blood to see that they get the result we want." That was evident from the first minute to the last in a game that was played in ridiculously hot conditions.

Peterborough, themselves with an outside chance of making the play-offs, were determined to give Southend as many problems as they possibly could but, David Crown continued in the vein he had been in all year with two very well taken goals to make promotion a very realistic possibility after only twenty minutes of play.

The heat was obviously going to play a part eventually, and after a magnificent effort from Southend's rear-guard, they had held on to take a two goal lead into the interval.

Just five minutes into the second half Peterborough scored to half Blues lead through Mick Halsall and with the incredible heat beginning to take its toll on the players, all of a sudden there was an air of concern on the away terrace.

There was clearly going to be some nervy moments from thereon in and in true Southend United style, it was edge of the seat stuff as the Peterborough attacks just seemed to come in wave after wave.

Somehow, Blues managed to hold on and keep their precious one goal advantage in tact for the next forty minutes – plus the incredible seven minutes of injury time played – to seal promotion and bounce back with an immediate return to Division Three.

The hero that day, and not for the first time that season, was of course striker David Crown whose impressive brace took his tally to twenty-three goals for the season. His goals had won crucial points for The Blues over the course of the forty six games and Crown delivered yet again when it mattered most.

However, ask any of the fifteen hundred travelling fans who were in attendance at London Road that day who they were indebted to for the vital win and the overwhelming answer you will receive would surely be goalkeeper Paul Sansome.

Sammy made save after great save as Peterborough looked for an equaliser and, of course, every player played a part in getting the win, it was Sansome who really stood out with a truly outstanding display of goalkeeping.

So, twelve months on after relegation was confirmed it was now a very different story as Webb repaid Jobson's faith in him and led Southend back into the familiar territory of Division Three at the first time of asking. For The Blues boss though, his thoughts would straight away turn to next season and building a side that could cope with the step up in class.

His first decision with that in mind wasn't exactly the recruitment of a new face, but more a case of securing an important player at the club for the immediate future. The decision to offer a two year contract extension to twenty-eight year old Sansome underlined Webb's desire to be a success at a higher level. It was an offer that a delighted Sammy more than happy to sign, "I would not have signed on at this stage of my career unless I believed that Southend were going to progress," he said. "I know it has all been said before, but I honestly believe that the club is on the verge of much bigger days and it would be nice to be in on that from the start."

It was the first piece of business Webb managed to conclude that summer and although there was much more transfer activity to come, the talk from the club continued to be about pushing on once more in the 1990-91 season.

While many fans gave a wry smile at the thought of Southend challenging for promotion to the Second Division for the first time in their eighty-five year history, Sansome was clearly of the belief that under David Webb good things was about to happen at Roots Hall. That belief was proved to have foundation from very early on as it was clear things were to be different this time around as Webb looked to plot his way to the summit of Division Three.

'Up The Blues!'

This is the story of a dream realised for the staff, management, players and fans alike of a small team in Essex. A dream that many never thought possible and a journey which would result in long suffering supporters crying tears of absolute joy as Southend United Football Club set about to re-write history and escape the lower leagues of English football.

'Up The Blues!'

Pre-Season

"We want to make our mark in the Third Division next term."
– David Webb

David Webb was born in Stratford, East London on April 9th 1946. His football career took off at local side Leyton Orient in 1964 after an unsuccessful spell at West Ham as a youth player. Webb went on to figure in The O's first team for almost two seasons before attracting the interest of Southampton who signed the defender in March 1966. It proved a great move for Webb as The Saints clinched promotion to the top division for the first time in their history.

He was a main feature during Southampton's inaugural campaign in Division One alongside Saints legends such as Mick Channon and the future England international Terry Paine. Despite competing against the odds, Southampton managed to avoid relegation and survive their first season in Division One after finishing in nineteenth position.

Webb's impressive performances in defence hadn't gone unnoticed and in February 1968 he returned to the capital when Chelsea come calling. It was at Stamford Bridge where he had his best spell during his career. Playing in a side that boasted the likes of Peter Osgood, Ron 'Chopper' Harris, Peter Bonetti and John Hollins - Webb went on to claim his first major honour by scoring the winning goal in the infamous 1970 F.A. Cup final replay over Leeds United.

Chelsea followed that up with a second major trophy in as many years with victory over Spanish giants Real Madrid in the European Cup Winners Cup final in Athens.

Webb had written himself into Chelsea history and had become one of the legends of Kings Road of the early 70's, but by

1974 he was once again on the move, this time to Chelsea's neighbours Queens Park Rangers in a deal worth £120,000.

At Q.P.R., he once again proved what a good player he was as he was part of the team that finished runners up in Division One to Liverpool in 1976. That Rangers team is still regarded by many as their greatest ever with Gerry Francis, Frank McLintock and Stan Bowles key figures during that campaign.

Webb's career at Loftus Road came to an end the following year as he moved to the midlands and joined Leicester City for a short spell before yet another move to Derby County where he stayed for seventeen months before joining up with AFC Bournemouth in Division Four. It was at Dean Court where he cut his teeth in management at only 34 years of age, combining the role with that of still being registered as a player.

Aside from Southend, his time at Bournemouth was to be his only other promotion on his C.V. as he took The Cherries up into Division Three in his first full season in charge during in 1982. Despite this success, he was dismissed the following season after struggling with the step up. A humiliating 9-0 defeat at the hands of Lincoln City in December of that year spelt the end for Webb at Dean Court after exactly twenty-four months in charge.

Not to be discouraged from his experience at Bournemouth, Webb returned to management in 1984 when took the up the reigns of Devon club Torquay United. Things didn't go as planned as during his first full season in charge – '84-'85 – they finished bottom of Division Four and only retained their league status after having to re-apply for their right to stay as a member of the football league.

The season that followed, he decided to move into a managing director role at Torquay and appointed novice Stuart Morgan as manager, but another successive season where survival was obtained through re-election to the league meant Webb left Plainmoor, his overall spell there being a huge disappointment.

Southend United were Webb's next port of call as he began his first spell at the Essex club in 1986 and, although the two had parted company by the time The Blues had secured promotion to Division Three in 1987, it was the work he had done prior to his departure that spring that had led to the successful ending to the season.

The Shrimpers had on two occasions gone with central defender Paul Clark, first as caretaker and then the second as permanent player manager either side of a calamitous spell for Dick Bate who lasted a mere three months in the hot-seat. Eventually though – and with the ill feeling between Jobson & Webb finally put to bed – the path was clear for a return to the hot seat in December '88.

The 1990 promotion brought Southend United back into Division Three, but this time there wasn't talk of just simply surviving, Webb believed he was on the verge of something at Southend and went about getting his squad finalised for the challenges that lay ahead.

Webb went straight to work and within days of the season ending, he released the names of six players who would not be kept on at Roots Hall. Defenders Paul Roberts, Paul Brush & Andy Dixon, midfielder Nicky Smith and young wingers Ian O'Connell & Matt Jones were all deemed surplus to requirements.

There were also five first team players who were out of contract and all were offered deals by the club, but surprisingly, four of those five rejected the offers on the table almost immediately. Dave Martin, David Crown, Peter Butler and Paul Clark all turned down the proposed new deals while winger Martin Ling would eventually do the same.

A concerned Webb explained, "Obviously I am disappointed that the four lads have turned down what I considered were very fair contracts – it will be interesting to see if they can get better elsewhere. I have had several meetings with them, but my powers of persuasion were not good enough."

"We will not be letting any of them go for nothing. If other clubs can satisfy their demands then we will require decent fees for all of them," he explained before Webb then underlined his desire to add to the current squad. "I have already spoken to several players and will be stepping things up in the next week or so."

"Even if the four whose contracts are up had decided to stay we would still need to get new players in to improve the squad. Crown, Clark and co. may not get new clubs and decide to stay with us, but I cannot gamble on that – it's important that we strike as soon as possible. We want to make our mark in the Third Division next term and need some quality men to pep up competition at the club"

The first of those out of contract to resolve his situation was star striker David Crown, 32. The fan favourite opted to turn down the club's offer of a new contract to follow the security of a three year deal at Fourth Division outfit Gillingham.

Crown, who boasted an outstanding sixty-nine goal return in one hundred and thirty two appearances for The Blues, was seemingly departing with a slight bitter feeling towards his former employees. "The last thing I want is to become involved in a slanging match with Southend, but I was disappointed by their take it or leave it stance when offered a new contract," he stated.

"There was no attempt to sit down and negotiate a deal. Only three months ago Chairman Vic Jobson was quoted as saying I was the best striker Blues had had in thirty years. It was a flattering remark, but certainly one that was never reflected in the contract they expected me to sign. I was even offered a better package by Colchester – and they have now joined the non-league ranks after finishing bottom of the Fourth Division last season."

"I have a wife and family to support and I have to do my best for them. Part of the deal is that I must move house to Gillingham, but it will be a wrench to leave Southend, particularly after the way the fans have treated me. They've been great, but unfortunately Blues did not come up with the type of offer I could take seriously – let's leave it that."

Southend made use of their right of reply and that came courtesy of the Chairman. "I have gone on record saying that Crown is one of the best strikers we have ever had at this club," Jobson said. "We very much wanted to keep him at Southend and offered him the best contract any striker has had at this club. It would have made him one of the best paid players in the Third Division, just as he was one of the top earners in the Fourth Division last season."

"I note that Crown has accused us of being mean, something I strongly deny, but we don't want to get into a slanging match with him. I don't think it would be right to reveal what sort of deal he wanted or what we were ready to play. That's something which should remain private," he added, before issuing a last parting shot at Crown. "He did well during his time at Southend and we wish him well in his new challenge in the Fourth Division." Ouch!

Crown's departure would obviously leave a big hole in the team and did little to appease the fans concerns about the size of the squad. With Webb still unsure as to the futures of Messrs' Clark, Butler, Ling and Martin it was clear that he needed to get some new faces in and as soon as possible.

"I know the type of people I want here, players with drive and enthusiasm and desperate to do well for themselves and the club. People who want to earn their cash rewards by producing the goods out on the pitch," Webb explained.

"We feel we have a good blend of youth and experience already at the club and with the injection of the right sort of signings we can make an impact in the Third Division. I would ask our fans to be a little patient. I am convinced they will be more than delighted with some of the players I intend to bring here."

The first new arrival through the Roots Hall door that fitted Webb's description was six foot four central defender, Peter Cawley. Cawley, signed from Bristol Rovers, had a reputation as a no nonsense defender who enjoyed a physical battle and simply loved to defend. Webb commented that Cawley would, "certainly bring competition for defensive places," before again promising that more new faces would soon follow.

All being well, Peter Cawley's debut in a Southend shirt would come in the pre-season friendly against local amateur side Basildon United on July 30th. That game would kick off Blues fixtures in preparation for the big kick off that would come on August 25th with the rest of the warm up games giving Southend a real test that culminated in three home games against West Ham United, Ipswich Town and Tottenham. Prior to those three very attractive games were matches away at Dover Athletic, St. Albans, Aylesbury and Colchester United.

It was a tough pre-season that Webb wanted and he certainly had arranged that. His single mindedness in how best to prepare his team for the season ahead was both impressive and encouraging as was the way in which he was trying to get his squad in place for the new campaign.

Things had been a little slow as far as the incomings were concerned, but Webb was hardly helped by four key players still not having put pen to paper on new deals. In fact, he felt that following those further discussions with those concerned, all four were keen to go. "I get the impression those players have made such a big stance to get away that they will find it difficult not to go."

"I've had them in and it's not just a question of money, some feel they just want to get away from the club and move on to another challenge. They continue to express a determination to get away."

A result of that determination was the club's controversial decision to not allow midfield duo Martin Ling and Peter Butler to train with the rest of the squad after the summer break. It seemed as though their reluctance to sign the contract offer that was on the table infuriated Webb to the point of him taking the stance he had.

Obviously, with the season fast approaching, Webb needed to get in place his team for the new campaign and with key players still not committing to the club the Southend manager looked to have made the bold move of alienating both players. It was a decision that both baffled and angered Butler whose future looked more than ever to be away from Roots Hall.

"I just cannot understand their attitude," groaned the tenacious midfielder. "I was amazed to read David Webb saying we were still training with the rest of the lads, that's completely untrue. We haven't been allowed to"

"Both he (Webb) and Chairman Vic Jobson told me in no uncertain terms I was barred from pre-season training and to keep away from the club. My training schedule is confined to running around Hockley Woods with Martin Ling to keep fit. Blues attitude simply doesn't make sense. They are continuing to pay us on a weekly basis so it seems stupid they won't let us join in their pre-season work outs."

"I can only think they are determined to mess us about simply because we have dug our heels in about signing new contracts. All we are doing is exercising our rights, everyone is entitled to try and better himself and that's all I have been trying to do. It's not a question of being greedy. As far as I'm concerned Southend have not come up with a good enough offer – it's as simple as that."

Butler also rubbished the notion that he would be anything other than fully focused on his job in spite of his contractual problems, "I don't go along with the view that because a player is not tied to a club for a length of time he isn't committed to their cause. I'll always give one hundred and ten per cent whether I'm paid on a weekly basis or on a ten year contract. That's why I find it so sad and childish that I'm banned from training with them."

Webb countered Butler's comments and explained his decision by saying, "As for Butler and Ling we must write them out of our plans because they are determined to leave us."

It was a real concern for fans that such players were at odds with the club coming off such a successful season, but there was good news around the corner with new signings arriving and confirmed rumours of another that lay in the balance.

The beginning of a fruitful few days at Roots Hall first saw nineteen year old midfielder Adam Locke arrive through the doors at Roots Hall. Locke put pen to paper in a free transfer from Crystal Palace after he was deemed surplus to requirements at Selhurst Park by Eagles manager Steve Coppell. The promising youngster never made a first team appearance in his two year spell at the South London club, but that didn't deter David Webb from recognising his potential.

Webb was obviously pleased with his second signing of the summer and promised more action very soon, "I have spent hours on the phone over the last day or so trying to finalise deals and things are slowly falling into place," he said.

"I have made strides in bringing other new faces to Roots Hall, including two new strikers and an experienced midfield player and hopefully things will all be sorted out over the next day or so."

One player Webb confirmed he had been in for was left back Chris Powell, another player on Crystal Palace's books. However, Blues boss revealed that the Powell had turned The Shrimpers down after he was after more money than Southend wanted offer. He added that in regards to Powell the "door is still open should he change his mind."

The second, and without doubt most significant signing of the summer, was the deal that brought in David Crown's replacement, Brett Angell from Stockport County. The six foot two inch forward started his career at Portsmouth, but never featured in the first team before he moved to non-league Cheltenham Town. It was at Cheltenham where league clubs began to take notice of Angell as he hit an impressive twenty-four goals in thirty-seven starts during the '87-'88 season.

Derby County was his next port of call, but much like his time at Pompey, he never really got near the first team and Angell ended his short stay at The Baseball Ground by completing a move to

Stockport where he again began to find the net with consistency – hitting a total of twenty-eight goals in seventy appearances.

While Southend United sealed promotion in May 1990, they only finished a point above Angell's Stockport and the Greater Manchester club were unfortunate to miss out on promotion via the play offs. But, the tough luck encountered by Stockport was capitalised on by The Blues and the lure of Division Three football was enough to secure the services of the prolific young striker.

Many had wondered the reasoning behind Southend's seemingly strange decision to allow the prolific Crown to leave The Blues without putting up too much of a fight. It was clear that he wanted to stay and surely would have done so had the club made a better offer than the one on the table, but any speculation about the club's lack of ambition quickly disappeared with the arrival of Angell.

An overjoyed Webb beamed, "To say I am delighted at getting Angell would be an understatement. Brett is the biggest signing I have been involved in during my time at Southend. He is a vital piece in our re-building for next season, the icing on top of the cake."

The fee for Angell couldn't be agreed on between the two clubs and so it would have to be decided by a tribunal. Southend offered a reported £80,000, but County were holding out for £275,000. However, Webb was sure he'd found a gem and was convinced he'd be an instant hit with supporters.

"He is potentially the most exciting young striker around at the moment and for him to choose to come to Southend proves that we are a club with real ambition. We have been negotiating with him for some weeks now and although Brett was impressed with the set up here, he was slightly worried about moving down south with the high cost of living and accommodation."

"But we have finally wrapped everything up and I am sure our fans will be delighted with the news. They were understandably disappointed and upset by Crown's departure; Angell's arrival should go a long way to healing those wounds."

During the previous season for Stockport, Angell won the Division Four Golden Boot with an impressive thirty-one league goals. At only twenty-one, the potential was clear for all to see and by securing his signature it was suggested that maybe it was Webb's thinking all along that the signing of Angell was the way forwards for

Southend United and, as harsh as it may have seemed, Crown's best years were behind him.

The quick fire news of confirmed and potential signings didn't stop with Angell. On the same day as Southend welcomed their new striker to the club, Webb confirmed that a deal for Swindon Town utility man, John Cornwell could well be forthcoming. A confident Blues boss said, "I am still negotiating with Swindon and am hoping to finalise the deal before the weekend."

It was a busy few days and the recent activity in the transfer market certainly underlined the clubs ambition for the upcoming Third Division campaign. Webb himself once again spoke of his intent, "If everything goes according to plan then we should we should have a set of players who will be more than capable of launching a real determined assault on the Third Division next season. We're not playing at it, we mean business!"

The 'business' would get under way on August 25th with an away trip to Huddersfield Town before opening their home account by entertaining Crewe Alexandra the following weekend. Inbetween those two league fixtures would be the first of a two legged League Cup tie against Aldershot at Roots Hall, the return game would come a week later.

Before then however, Southend's pre-season would get under way with that trip to Basildon United. The game would see new signings Locke, Cawley and Angell all feature for The Blues, but there was to be one notable absentee from the game and that was Dean Austin. Austin, a £12,000 capture from St. Albans in March of that year, had played in all the last seven league games at right back, culminating in the promotion win at Peterborough. The relative ease and comfort that he immediately showed in the first team was highly impressive and at the tender age of twenty-one, big things were expected from Austin in the future.

The reason for his absence was explained by Dave Webb, "Dean had been complaining about a troublesome knee and we sent him to see a specialist who immediately diagnosed cartilage problems," said Blues boss.

"He went straight into hospital for an operation and now faces physio treatment to build up the muscles again. It's probably as well that the problem has been dealt with now rather than when the season had got underway."

A cartilage operation meant there was a real doubt as to whether Austin would be fit in time for the opening round of league fixtures and that would be a tough break for the young full back who was looking to hit the ground running in which would be his first full season as a professional.

That left Webb a man down in what was already a small squad for the start of the pre-season fixtures and with key first team members still stalling on their futures, he knew he's have to step up his search for new players immediately.

"If you take out the four contract rebels – Butler, Clark, Martin and Ling – then there are only fifteen players on the staff and that is certainly nowhere near enough," he explained.

Webb's use of the word 'rebels' seemed harsh, especially to fans who found the popular player's stance hard to take, but there was beginning to be one or two rumours that talks had reopened with both Martin and Clark about staying at Southend. Was Webb's man-management skills and use of the media beginning to turn the tide back into his favour? There was more than a suggestion, particularly with the aforementioned duo, that that could well be the case.

On the day of The Blues game with Basildon United, Dave Webb confirmed he was still in for Swindon's John Cornwell, but the two clubs were a still having trouble agreeing a price for the twenty-five year old. It was believed Cornwell's employers were after £60,000, matching the fee they paid Newcastle United for him in December 1988, but The Shrimpers boss' valuation was somewhat lower.

With attention now switching to that evenings friendly, Webb confirmed he would making the most of his squad, "I expect I shall end up giving everyone a run out at some stage in the match which is bound to be pretty competitive as always at Basildon," the Blues Boss said. "It's their (Basildon's) little cup final and a chance to pit themselves against full-time pros."

"At the moment I am looking to build up towards match sharpness and fitness. That's more important at this stage than the result, although I am sure all the lads are looking forwards to their first competitive match."

It was a most certainly a competitive ninety minutes for Southend as the home side gave their all, but still it was The Blues who controlled the game and the pace of it with a fair degree of comfort.

There were a few efforts that the visitors that cleared off the line and Blues also hit the woodwork more than once.

A goal, however, was forthcoming and it came midway through the second half when new striker Brett Angell opened up his body to place the ball into the far corner of the net after beating the offside trap. It was a clinical finish and one that Southend fans could get used to seeing in the upcoming months.

Supporters who attended the game at Basildon United would have also been pleasantly surprised to see Dave Martin feature for The Blues. That only fuelled speculation that he could be on the verge of completing a u turn and re-sign for Southend as well as the experienced defender Paul Clark who watched the game from the stands.

After the win, Dave Webb confirmed the suggested good news surrounding the futures of both players, "I am hopeful that both David and Paul will finally put pen to paper. They are both thinking over our latest offer and I hope to have some positive news by the weekend."

Webb then went on to speak about the victory over Basildon, "That was our first competitive game and I was more interested in using it for fitness than getting a result," he said. "The lads looked pretty sharp and with a little luck could easily have ended up with four or five goals. Full marks to Basildon for giving us a good match on what was a hard, bumpy pitch which made passing and control difficult."

Featuring in the friendly was the returning Spencer Prior. It was Prior's first game since breaking his league in the home game with Peterborough United the previous November. The young central defender had broken into the first team at just seventeen years of age and was hailed by many as the best prospect to come through the club's ranks for many a year.

Prior, now nineteen, had put in extra training all through the summer months in the attempt to be fit for the start of the new season by swimming regularly, completing a specific weight training course and even running along Southend's seafront long before his teammates reported back for pre-season training in July.

Seeing him on back in action on the pitch with the rest of the first team was very encouraging and it was hoped Prior would suffer no setback as he looked to regain his match sharpness in time for the season's kick off at Huddersfield.

There was more transfer news involving The Blues before their next friendly at Dover Athletic. Manager Dave Webb admitted that he had been in contact with Leeds United about the availability of experienced forward Vince Hilaire.

"I have been interested in Hilaire for quite a while now, but kept quiet for fear of alerting other people, but Leeds tell me that at least three other clubs are having talks with him so there seems little point in being secretive," revealed Webb.

"Hilaire is just the type of player I am looking for to bring much needed experience into what is basically a young set of players at Roots Hall. I have had talks with Hilaire and he is definitely interested in coming here, it seems simply a case of whether we can match what the other clubs are offering."

"I am anxious to boost our squad and if we could land a player of Hilaire's quality then it would be a gigantic shot in the arm for what we all hope will be a successful season ahead."

Despite the belief that Hilaire could be enticed to Essex, it came as quite a shock when, a few days later, Webb - who was expecting to meet the player for further talks -found out that Hilaire had already signed for Second Division side Bristol City for £100,000.

It appeared that City had stolen the march on Southend in the race for Hilaire's signature, but a perplexed Webb was after confirmation from Leeds as to what exactly was going on, but reassured fans that "If we don't get him (Hilaire) then I will definitely have to step up my search for new faces."

One man who he didn't let escape was John Cornwell. After weeks of talks with first the club and then the player, the green light was given for Southend to conclude the deal.

"He is just the type of player I desperately need here at the moment. We have a number of young, very promising players by lack people with that little bit of know how," said a happy Dave Webb. "A player like Cornwell will be more than capable of organising things and help steady us down a bit. I have said for weeks now that we lack experienced heads at Roots Hall at the moment."

"I have been pursuing Cornwell ever since I heard that he was available. Swindon at first demanded what I considered to be a crazy fee, but have since come down to a more realistic amount. We have signed him on three year contract and I'm sure it won't be long before he becomes a firm favourite with our supporters."

That size of the transfer fee that finally got Blues their man was £45,000. Webb had, once again, managed to agree terms so that he got the best deal possible for Southend United. Cornwell's versatility was a real asset to have at the club as he could comfortably play anywhere on the right side as well as both central defence and centre midfield.

The Blues boss was also conscious of keeping the supporters in the loop about what was going on at the club. He'd worked extremely hard at bringing in new faces and as soon as the Brett Angell deal was announced, there was a feeling that the words that kept on being re-iterated about making a real go of it in this upcoming campaign wasn't just talk – Webb believed it and it appeared the players were buying into his vision of where his team were heading.

Despite Cornwell signing before the friendly at Dover, he didn't feature in the game played down on the South Coast. It was again game that was more geared towards fitness and match sharpness, but even with that in mind a Mario Walsh strike was unable to prevent a 3-1 defeat at the hands of their non-league opponents.

Two days after the defeat at Dover, Southend were in action again, this time at St. Albans, the side that Dean Austin had joined from earlier in the calendar year. The Blues failed to win for the second successive match against non-league opposition, only managing a 1-1 draw.

Again, two days later, Southend carried on their hectic pre-season schedule with a trip to Aylesbury Town. The Ducks, as they were also known, had knocked The Blues out of the previous seasons F.A. Cup by a solitary goal to nil, so there was more than a hint of revenge on their minds.

However, frustratingly for Webb and his team, they fared no better on this visit to Aylesbury as the home side ran out comfortable 3-1 winners with midfielder Paul Smith netting the goal for The Shrimpers.

Boss Dave Webb was aware of the reasons for his team shipping seven goals in three games against teams from outside the football league after this disappointing result saying, "We are making some stupid, elementary mistakes at the back," he moaned.

To reinforce the defence, Webb acted quickly to reignite the deal for Crystal Palace left back Chris Powell and after he was granted permission to speak to the player he was quick to agree personal terms, the only stumbling block would yet again the transfer fee involved.

Palace wanted around £25,000 for Powell, but the shrewd Webb thought that was far too high and wanted to sign the young full back for nothing. Palace then suggested the price of £10,000, but still Webb wanted the free transfer he originally went in with. Powell, though, had been allowed leave The Eagles and once the personal terms with Southend were agreed the move would be completed as soon as an independent tribunal had come to a decision at the end of August to decide the fee. Until then, the player was left in limbo as he was unable to feature in games for The Blues even though he was training with his new club.

The continuing saga surrounding Blues contract rebels then took yet another twist. Paul Clark dramatically opted to return to training with Southend and, along with Dave Martin, he was expected to sign the new offer that was on the table.

As for Peter Butler and Martin Ling, they were still left on the periphery of the club as they continued to train alone, but Webb offered a lifeline to both players. "I have said all along that Clark and Martin were the players I wanted to keep, but my door is also open should Butler and Ling want to talk."

"I have never shut them out, but merely said there was no point in players who did not see their long term future at the club training with the rest of the squad. Should they have a change of heart then I am always ready to speak to them. The ball is in their court," he explained.

Then news broke that Brentford were after securing the services of winger Martin Ling and that possible deal might involve a straight swap for ex Southend United striker Richard Cadette. Cadette was a prolific forward during his time with The Blues scoring a highly impressive fifty-six goals in one hundred and four starts during a two year spell with the club that started in 1985.

Any chance that he may return to the club that still hold him in such high regard would be more than welcomed, especially by then fans who adored him for his explosive strike rate. All David Webb would say on the matter was, "I have got nothing to tell you about any moves like that. Cadette was a very popular figure, but I have not heard anything from Brentford. If they contact me then I would be happy to talk, but at the moment any talk like that is pure speculation."

And that was that. The rumour seemed to die as quickly as it came about, but it did reaffirm that Ling wanted away and was actively seeking other clubs for employment.

Southend's next friendly was away at Layer Road, home of Essex rivals Colchester United. The U's had suffered relegation to the Conference after finishing bottom of Division Four at the end of the season, but it was always going to be a competitive game with local bragging rights at stake.

On the day of the game an elated Dave Webb confirmed that Paul Clark had indeed decided to put pen to paper on a new one year deal to stay at the club. It was hoped that Clark's decision to end his exile from the club would lead the others to follow suit. Rumours suggested that an agreement to tie Dave Martin to the club was expected to be completed in the days that followed.

"We have had more talks and Paul has agreed to a new one year deal," announced Webb. "I have always wanted Clarky to stay because he is another experienced head who finished last season in tremendous style. He will give us a big boost," he added.

Clark's decision to stay at Roots Hall was a major boost for the whole club. A favourite amongst the fans, he was revered for his tough tackling and leadership qualities that would prove vital over the months that lay ahead.

He had a long history with the club having made his debut in a 2-1 win over Watford in August 1976. Clark then left and joined Brighton in the autumn of '77 where stayed for almost five years before being persuaded to re-join The Blues by then manager, Dave Smith.

Late in the '86-'87 campaign, Clarky was asked to take over the managerial reins and steer Southend over the finish line to promotion following Webb's decision to walk out. Back to back wins in their last two games of the season meant it was mission accomplished for the caretaker player-manager who was still only 28 years old.

Many expected that accomplishment to earn him the job on a full time basis, but Vic Jobson decided to go in a different direction and Dick Bate was appointed that summer. However, Bate made a disastrous start to the new season and was sacked in September leaving the door open for Clark to step in once more – only this time the position was made permanent.

Southend managed to avoid relegation that year and also performed a giant killing act by dumping First Division side Derby County out of the Littlewoods Cup. But, after an indifferent start to the following season, Webb was once more re-united to the club, first as General Manager, before taking over team affairs in December of that year.

Clark was retained as a player and also club captain and such was the professionalism of the man that his performances never suffered as a result. If proof was needed of this then his superb defensive display against Wolves' Steve Bull in the spring of that campaign was all the evidence required. He was simply outstanding that night as Southend trounced their opponents by three goals to one.

Now that he had signed on for at least another year, Clark could once more concentrate solely on football and he went straight into the squad for the short trip to Colchester for a pre-season fixture. New signing John Cornwell was also pencilled in to make his first appearance in a Southend shirt at Layer Road.

There was a change in goal for The Shrimpers for this 'friendly' with trialist Jimmy Jones getting his chance as Paul Sansome had to miss due to a back injury. Unfortunately for the young keeper, he didn't have the best of games and was at fault for two of Colchester's three goals.

Cornwell and Clark played a central defensive pair, but elsewhere the team was littered with young players as the likes of Christian Hyslop, Peter Daley and Andy Edwards all were given a chance to stake their claim for a place in the first team.

There was very little on offer in terms of creating goal scoring chances for Southend and in their only real opportunity to net, Andy Ansah did just that to make the final score 3-1 in favour of The Blues rivals.

Up next was Division Two opposition at Roots Hall with Billy Bonds bringing his West Ham side into town for a high profile friendly. The game was incredibly Southend's sixth game in eleven busy days and it would be the first pre-season match in which The Blues played at home.

It underlined the work that was going on behind the scenes at the club with the extremely busy fixture schedule and the constant attempts in trying to improve the playing staff at the club. An example of this was the news that inbetween the defeat at Colchester and the home match with The Hammers, Webb managed to tie up another exiled player to Southend United. Peter Butler had had a change of heart and put pen to paper initially on a month to month contract, but The Blue boss was confident a longer deal would be sorted out at a later date.

That initial short term deal didn't concern Webb in the slightest when asked about Butler's commitment to the club, "Peter is ready to pledge himself to our cause and that's good enough for me. What has happened in the past is all water under the bridge," he said, before adding, "I have told him that I'm not the type to bear grudge. If he does his stuff out on the pitch then he will get a fair crack of the whip."

"Peter has always been an enthusiastic type who gives one hundred and one per cent and if he continues to do that then I cannot ask for more. We need people with Peter's experience at the moment and I am confident that he will return with all his old appetite for the game."

Butler signed from Cambridge United for £70,000 in 1988 and was now the third of the original five contract outcasts to have a change of heart. It was another clever move by Webb to play the situation just right. He was indeed an important part of the team that won promotion the previous season and his energy, drive and dynamism would have been sorely missed he been allowed to leave the club.

David Martin's deal had still yet to have been finalised, but it was just a formality. That was going to be all sorted out within a few days of Butler signing on and so that only left Martin Ling who was on the outside looking in.

His situation didn't look like it was going to be resolved in Webb's favour and the former Chelsea full back underlined the reasons why Ling remained an outsider.

"I have said all the way through that it's no good going into a new season with players who are not committed to our single aim - getting the club out of the Third Division. It's absolutely vital to build the right spirit within the camp, having all the players pulling together and you cannot hope to do that if one or two feel their future is elsewhere. Lingy knows exactly how I feel and the next move is up to him."

The West Ham friendly was used as the perfect opportunity to launch the new home shirt for the '90-'91 campaign. The traditional blue remained the main colour for the shirt and socks with yellow shorts being maintained for the sixth successive season. There was, however, a new shirt sponsor as the club had managed to secure an initial twelve month contract with Eastwood based sports firm Hi-Tec having replaced Firholm after their deal with The Blues expired.

Southend Vice-Chairman, John Adams called it "one of the most substantial sponsorship agreements in the lower divisions" and Frank Van Wezel, Chairman of Hi-Tec commented on his own ambition for his sports brand before even likening the deal to similar one's abroad between Bayern Munich & Adidas and PSV Eindhoven & Phillips!

The side selected to face The Hammers welcomed back goalkeeper Paul Sansome and striker Brett Angell who both missed the game at Colchester. Also involved were new signings John Cornwell, Adam Locke & Peter Cawley.

Manager Dave Webb pointed out the different direction the friendlies would now take. "Our pre-season games so far have been all about assessing individuals, but now we must start performing as a unit. We have three big friendly games against Hammers tonight, Ipswich on Tuesday and Spurs the following Monday and it's vital I use those matches to get some idea of the team I want and the way we are going to perform."

Southend started well enough against West Ham and even took a shock lead when Brett Angell opened the scoring after only thirteen minutes with a neat diving header. Although, that advantage was cancelled out when Hammers skipper Julian Dicks crashed home a penalty kick shortly after.

The score stayed level at the interval, but in the second half the visitors started to take control. Kevin Keen, on the right of West Ham's midfield, ran rings around Blues young left back, Christian Hyslop and was beginning to make things happen.

The goals that did inevitably did come were both scored by forward Trevor Morley as Southend went down 3-1 in what had proved a valuable workout for The Shrimpers. There were reasons for the home supporters to go home happy, especially with the new signings on show and despite the loss; Boss Dave Webb wasn't too down about the result. "Overall I was pretty pleased with our performance. The lads worked hard and I think West Ham knew they had been in a game afterwards."

"I know our strengths and weaknesses (and) there are certain positions where we lack a bit of quality and I would like to plug the gaps, but whether we can find the right people is another matter."

There would be another chance for the Roots Hall faithful to see the new look squad in action just two days later when Ipswich Town came into town. Former West ham United manager John Lyall had just taken over at Portman Road and their squad featured the promising young forward Chris Kiwomya as well as former Southend midfielder Glenn Pennyfather, who, unfortunately, was injured for the friendly.

The fixture saw Southend United put in their best performance of pre-season as they turned in a first half performance that left The Blues three goals to the good at the end of the first half.

The central midfield pairing of Dave Martin and Peter Butler set the tone and allowed wide men Steve Tilson on the left and Andy Ansah on the right to create chances.

The first of the goals came on fourteen minutes when some good work by Tilson set up an easy take for Ansah to apply a tidy finish. More was to come for a ruthless Southend when, two minutes later, Martin headed home to make it two-nil from another cross – this time from Ansah.

The Blues completed the scoring when the wingers linked up again for goal number three when Ansah collected Tilson's through ball to lift the ball over the advancing Ipswich goalkeeper, Phil Parkes.

In the second half Ipswich pulled one goal back when the exciting Kiwomya outpaced Cornwell before firing past Paul Sansome, but it wasn't to be enough to prevent Southend getting an impressive win against Second Division opposition.

One admirer was Pennyfather who watched the game from the stands, "I was certainly impressed at the way Blues performed – they made us look decidedly second best, especially in the first half," he said.

"Southend murdered us with real quality crosses. I thought Steve Tilson had an outstanding game on the left side and we were a little lucky to be only three-nil down at half-time and if The Blues continue to play like that then it could be a promotion celebration."

David Webb was also impressed with what he saw. "That was without doubt our most impressive pre-season performance," he declared, but ever the perfectionist Webb added, "We lacked a little bit of professionalism after the break when we tried to chase the game and Ipswich exposed one or two worrying areas, but overall I was delighted with our finishing and the way we worked in midfield."

"Butler seemed to be everywhere and showed why I was keen to get him back into the squad after our little dispute over his contract. He is with us on a week to week basis at the moment, but if he is prepared to battle like that then hopefully it won't be long before we sort out a new deal to keep him at the club."

Butler was indeed very impressive and even more so considering his lack of a proper pre-season. The energy levels he had helped with a quick turnover of possession and that in turn allowed the more creative players to get involved. The fans agreed that a new deal to keep him at the club for as long as possible must have been high on Webb's list of priorities.

All that now remained before the real action began was the home game with Division One side Tottenham. Webb and his Southend side had impressed everyone at Spurs with two very good games in the League Cup the previous season. Spurs went through on away goals over the two legged affair and Spurs manager Terry Venables said after the match "Southend are a lot better than most fourth division sides."

The cup tie from 1989 obviously created a link between the two clubs and since then Venables had snapped up Blues left back Justin Edinburgh for £120,000 and now Webb had managed to get Spurs to come to Roots Hall for a curtain raiser for the start of Southend's season. Tottenham's squad included all of their big guns as Venables included Paul Walsh, Gary Mabbutt, Gudni Bergsson and England's Italia 90 stars, Gary Lineker and the one and only Paul Gascoigne in his starting line up.

Gazza was undoubtedly the star attraction following his exploits in England's World Cup crusade that saw Bobby Robson's team reach the semi-final before going out to West Germany via a penalty shoot-out and there was little doubt that the nation had fallen in love with Gascoigne.

As a result John Adams was expecting a big crowd on the night. "The demand for tickets has been phenomenal. I doubt if a pre-season match has ever attracted such attention. It seems as if everyone wants to be here to salute Gascoigne and Lineker who performed so well in Italy during the summer," said Blues Vice-Chairman.

The manager's thought centred around his team and hoped they would be able to carry on from the good form on display in the previous friendly. "We showed against Ipswich that we are gradually getting things together and it would be nice carry that on tonight," said an optimistic Webb.

"While we want to chalk up a win, my main concern is to see us develop our team play in readiness for the big challenge ahead, starting in Saturday's curtain raiser at Huddersfield."

"I have more or less settled on what I consider is my best line up at the moment and it is up the fringe players to prove they are better if they get on tonight."

There was a crowd of 7,345 in attendance for the game and there was more than a few young ladies amongst them screaming at the mere sight of Gazza at every available opportunity.

Southend started the game a little in awe and Spurs took full advantage with goals from Paul Walsh, Paul Stewart and Vinny Samways all coming with just over thirty minutes on the clock.

This seemed to spring The Blues into life and they started to press Gascoigne who, up until that point, had had things all his own way. As Southend pressed their high profile opponents they started to get more of the ball and, in particular, Ansah began to give Spurs left back Pat Van den Hauwe cause for concern.

The breakthrough eventually came for The Blues when Angell was fouled by Gudni Bergsson in the area for a penalty kick. Midfield enforcer Dave Martin kept his cool to beat Bobby Mimms in the Tottenham goal to reduce the deficit.

In the second half, Southend started well and began to pin Tottenham back with Ansah again at the forefront of Southend's attack and some good goalkeeping from Mimms to deny Ian Benjamin and Steve Tilson kept the score at 3-1.

The game was proving to be an entertaining one for those who came through the turnstiles to watch it. For those in attendance who just simply wanted to see a goal from Gazza was not going to be disappointed either. His goal came from a free kick that seemed to take a deflection off Benjamin's knee for goal number four with only minutes left on the clock and such was the affection for Gascoigne that even his strike was greeted with applause from some of the home fans!

The final score didn't tell the whole story as Southend had given their opponents cause for concern in patches throughout the ninety minutes, but overall the quality of Tottenham had won them the game.

Webb, who stated prior to the game that he knew his starting eleven for Huddersfield, was pleased with what he saw and all thoughts would now turn towards the opening game of the season in just five days' time.

He had worked extremely hard in putting together a squad capable of holding their own in Division Three, but as Webb had stated throughout the summer, he wanted to have a real shot at a second successive promotion.

How good the side was that he had assembled remained to be seen over the course of a forty six game season, but the re-signing of Butler, Clark & Martin together with the addition of Angell and Cornwell certainly created a feeling of belief that this time Southend United would be better equipped to deal with what was a very difficult division.

Throughout pre-season, opposition players had complimented Blues on their performances and spoke highly of Southend's chances for a decent season and that view was echoed by the most famous English footballer at that time. "Good luck to Southend, they've certainly got one or two players who could produce the goods in the season ahead," said the one and only Paul Gascoigne. Fans of The Blues hoped it would very well prove to be the case...David Webb expected it to be.

'Up The Blues!'

August 1990

"Tomorrow is where it all starts and where all the talk and dreams of promotion are put under the microscope."
- David Webb

In the week leading up to the big kick off, the football league tribunal finally convened to come to a decision on the amount that Southend United would have to pay Stockport County for the services of Brett Angell. It was decided that £100,000 was the cost for the young striker and that final figure was closer to the valuation Blues had originally placed on him and someway short of Stockport's.

Angell's pre-season form had been impressive to say the least and at that price it was deemed that if he could carry on in the way he had started life in a blue shirt then it would turn out to be a very good bit of business indeed.

The other transfer that was left in limbo was that of Chris Powell's. He too was waiting to have the cost of his move from Crystal Palace decided by the tribunal and it was due to be announced a week after Angell's. It meant that that David Webb was without what were expected to be his first choice full backs for the first game at Huddersfield.

That was because Dean Austin, the expected first choice right back, was unavailable due to him having a cartilage operation earlier in the summer, but there was now some good news surrounding the former St. Albans defender.

It was confirmed that Austin was back in full training three days before the match at Huddersfield and was right on schedule for a return to match action within two weeks.

That was welcomed news, but for the new campaigns opening fixture young central defender Andy Edwards was to start at right back, with Christian Hyslop lining up on the other side of defence at left back. Both players were only eighteen years old and, even though Webb's hand was forced to a degree, The Blues boss had been satisfied with their displays during pre-season. However, he was aware of the step up once the real thing got under way, "Edwards and Hyslop have performed reasonably well so far, but they know there is likely to be a stiff challenge ahead in the coming weeks," he said.

Webb had decided upon his team prior to the Spurs friendly and, even though midfielder Jason Cook had returned to fitness, it was local boy Steve Tilson who got the nod to play on the left of a four man midfield. The reason for this selection was explained by Blues manager, "I have decided to stick with Tilson with his goalscoring potential just tipping the balance in his favour," explained Webb.

"At the moment we look as if we will mainly rely on Brett Angell and Andy Ansah to get the goals and need someone in midfield who has the ability to hit the net. Tilson certainly falls into that category and that's why I have opted for him at the moment. It's up to him to go out and reward my faith, starting with Huddersfield tomorrow."

It was a huge public backing from Webb to Tilly who had only made twenty-one league starts since joining Southend eighteen months earlier from local Essex side Witham Town.

Tilson's progress at Witham was brought to Webb's attention by former Shrimpers midfielder, Danny Greaves, who was managing the local Essex side at the time. Upon signing his first professional contract he said, "I am not here just to make up the numbers, I want to do well and make a name for myself."

His career started well as Tilly played a huge part in a 3-1 win over league leaders Wolverhampton Wanderers at Roots Hall in March 1989. In that game Tilson scored his first goal for the club he used to support from The North Bank and also put in a man of the match performance to help gain the points.

Big things were expected from then on, but his progress seemed to stagnate as he was in and out of the side for the remainder of that season in which Southend suffered relegation to Division Four. Then, as Webb guided Blues back to Division Three at the first time of asking, Tilson found himself fourth in the pecking order during the season behind Gary Bennett, Martin Ling and Nicky Smith who all occupied the left midfield spot ahead of him.

So, to be handed a start on the opening day of the season on merit was a huge compliment. It was one that supporters hoped Tilson would grab with both hands and that he was finally ready for the rigours for the professional game. Where better to find out the answers than a tough test away at The Terriers?

David Webb was sure the game would be a marker, not only for Tilly, but for his whole team, "Huddersfield have a good pedigree and have been a solid Division Three outfit for two or three seasons now," he pointed out.

"They have brought in one or two players to strengthen their squad in the summer and the game should provide us with a good test and give us a pointer as to how the season is likely to progress."

"It would be nice to get off to a winning start and the lads have shown in pre-season outings they are more than capable of returning with some reward. We have prepared well and the players have all worked hard in pre-season training. Tomorrow is where it all starts and where all the talk and dreams of promotion are put under the microscope."

It was clear that Webby was confident that his team was ready for the challenge that lay in wait at Huddersfield and was prepared to back that up with a positive team selection that he considered capable of getting something out of what was a tough ask on Blues return to Division Three.

Webb stuck with his favoured formation of 442 with wingers Andy Ansah and Steve Tilson giving Southend the width to provide the ammunition for striking partnership of Ian Benjamin & Brett Angell.

The central midfield places went, as expected, to Peter Butler & David Martin and behind them was the back four of Andy Edwards, John Cornwell, Paul Clark and Christian Hyslop. Paul Sansome lined up between the sticks, with Jason Cook and Roy McDonough occupying the bench.

The match was a tight affair with both sides seemingly cancelling each other out and, as often is the case, it took a little bit of magic on thirty-eight minutes to break the deadlock. Unfortunately for The Shrimpers, that bit of magic came from Huddersfield winger Mark Smith who brilliantly turned Cornwell to supply a cross for Town striker Robert Wilson who headed past a helpless Sansome to give the home side a 1-0 lead.

This seemed to lift Blues and they clawed themselves back on level terms within six minutes. The goal was a very well worked one that all stemmed from the good work of Peter Butler.

The busy midfielder collected a pass from Edwards and quickly fed the ball into the feet of Benjamin before advancing past his opponent to receive the return. Butler then carried the ball into the penalty area, committing one of Huddersfield's central defenders to make room for a pull back to the unmarked Brett Angell and the striker made no mistake in making the score at 1-1 on the stroke of half time.

Southend upped their game in the second half and they were getting a lot of joy from the Andy Ansah on the right wing. It was the pace of Ansah that was allowing Blues to get in behind the home side and he was a constant outlet for both Martin and Butler when they had the ball.

On seventy-one minutes, the good work from Ansah led to his side winning a corner after a Steve Tilson header was well blocked by Town's defence.

Tilson himself took the corner which evaded the targeted head of Angell, but it was only half cleared to the corner of the eighteen yard box where the on rushing Andy Edwards drilled the ball low and hard at the near post for a 2-1 lead.

It was now Huddersfield's turn to come at Southend as they desperately searched for an equaliser. To combat Town's possession, Webb ordered Martin to sit deeper to protect the back four. It was the simplest of tactical tweaks, but one that helped Southend see out the game to gain a surprising, yet deserved, 2-1 win over much fancied Huddersfield side.

To come from behind and win away from home showed real character and that word hadn't been associated with Southend in Division Three too often in recent years. It would have been all too easy for The Blues to fold and leave Leeds Road with nothing, but the win signified more than just three points. It meant that David Webb's team could go to places and play without fear - that they were capable of travelling away and winning games of football. That belief counted for a lot and a surprise opening day triumph certainly raised a few eyebrows amongst the other teams in the league.

Surprise was also a feeling that Andy Edwards had after netting the winning goal. "I couldn't believe it when the ball went in," the eighteen year old remarked.

"I've only scored once in two seasons for the reserves and about three times in as many years at youth team level. I usually miss on the few occasions I find myself in a position to have a crack at goal – and from much closer in! So it was great to hit the target this time, especially as it proved the winner."

The manager remained grounded, but was pleased at his team's comeback. "Of course, a few rough edges showed themselves, but that's only to be expected right at the start of a season. But the lads showed such tremendous character in coming back to win at Huddersfield," Webb pointed out.

Now that the campaign had got under way, the games would be coming thick and fast and just three days later it was Aldershot at Roots Hall in the Rumbelows Cup first round, first leg.

Roots Hall stadium was a typical lower league venue that made up for its lack of facilities with character. Southend moved in there at the start of the 1955/56 season with the first game coming against Norwich City on August 20th.

In 1979, the magnificent Liverpool side which included the likes of Ray Clemence, Alan Hansen and Kenny Dalglish came to Essex for an F.A. Cup tie and just over 31,000 squeezed into Roots Hall to witness it.

The capacity at the ground was now considerably less due to the huge South Bank having been vastly reduced due to the sale of the land to property developers who built blocks of flats that now overlooked the playing surface.

The North Bank behind one goal housed Southend's more vociferous supporters and The East Stand, easily recognisable because of the different coloured blocks of seats, was situated behind the dugouts. Opposite The East Stand, was the imaginatively named West Stand which was a terrace and the benefits being that fans could walk to either end of the stand depending on which way the team were attacking.

For Aldershot's visit for the cup tie, there were 2,254 in attendance for a game in which Southend named an unchanged team against the lower league opposition and with that in mind Webb was asked whether his players would be fully focused on the job in hand.

The Southend manager assured fans that wouldn't be a problem, "I don't think I have any need to worry on that score," he said. "The lads know they have to keep on performing to stay in the side. Besides, they are professional enough to know there is no such thing as an easy game."

The first leg of the cup tie wasn't as straight forward as fans would have expected as Aldershot came at Southend and played some nice football. Midfielder David Puckett was particularly one who stood out as The Blues struggled to take control of a game many expected them to dominate.

The opening goal of the game came from The Shots after a very dubious penalty award was given against Steve Tilson for apparently pulling on his opponent in the area after a ball over the top caught out the defence. The penalty was converted and although the decision to award the spot kick was strange, the goal was nothing more than the visitors deserved.

In the second half, it seemed as though Webb had once again worked his magic during the break as his team came out with a lot more purpose and were quickly back on terms.

The equaliser came when Ian Benjamin latched onto a flick on from his strike partner, Brett Angell before feeding the ball through to the on rushing Peter Butler who guided the ball into the net from ten yards.

Southend kept going and the momentum from their equalising goal carried them on to secure the win when Dave Martin headed home from a Butler free kick. The drill that was used was one that would be seen time and time again over the course of the season when Blues had a set-play in the wide areas of the pitch. It involved Butler and Tilson - the latter a left footer, the former favouring his right – and, depending on the flank, one of the two would run over the ball before the other player would put the ball into the area between goalkeeper and defence. When it was a free kick on the right, Tilson would deliver and when it was on the left, it was Butler's turn. It was a training ground routine that had obviously been worked on and Martin was the benefactor on this occasion, opening his account for the season and giving The Shrimpers a 2-1 first leg lead.

The following day there was a departure from the club when Colchester United paid £25,000 for their former striker Mario Walsh. The forward had only been at the club for just over twelve months when Webb paid £5,000 more than the incoming fee. It was a decision that a reluctant Webb felt he had to make, "In many ways I am bitterly disappointed to see Mario go. I had hoped that he would make a big impact here, but he never really settled in," he explained.

"He started off very well last season, but then had a hiccup and could not regain his first team spot. Mario did manage to score fairly regularly in the reserves, but did not seem to produce the goods in partnership with David Crown."

"I tried him alongside our new striker Brett Angell in pre-season games, but they too did not gel and in the end felt it was to his advantage to let him go. Let's hope that a change of environment helps Mario regain his scoring touch."

Webb always spoke of adding to his squad and with the sale of Walsh it meant that there was now a space within it for him to try and do just that. But, if there was no opportunity to bring in the right player it was abundantly clear that the manager had faith in the squad he had assembled.

An opening away day win and a first leg lead in The Rumbelows Cup showed that the belief Webb had showed was not misplaced. However, in September, Blues would be in action on seven occasions throughout the calendar month with tough away games against Stoke City and Cambridge United, as well as home fixtures versus Preston North End and Crewe Alexandra. That calibre of opposition would mean that the faith was about to come under huge scrutiny and it was hoped the management & players would come through it with flying colours.

'Up The Blues!'

Division Three Table August 25th

	TEAM	P	W	D	L	F	A	Pts	GD
1	Leyton Orient	1	1	0	0	3	0	3	3
2	Grimsby Town	1	1	0	0	3	1	3	2
3	Reading	1	1	0	0	3	1	3	2
4	Stoke City	1	1	0	0	3	1	3	2
5	Mansfield Town	1	1	0	0	2	0	3	2
6	Bury	1	1	0	0	2	1	3	1
7	Southend United	1	1	0	0	2	1	3	1
8	Tranmere Rovers	1	1	0	0	2	1	3	1
9	Birmingham City	1	1	0	0	1	0	3	1
10	Bolton Wanderers	1	1	0	0	1	0	3	1
11	Crewe Alexandra	1	0	1	0	1	1	1	0
12	Fulham	1	0	1	0	1	1	1	0
13	Bournemouth	1	0	1	0	0	0	1	0
14	Brentford	1	0	1	0	0	0	1	0
15	Bradford City	1	0	0	1	1	2	0	-1
16	Chester City	1	0	0	1	1	2	0	-1
17	Huddersfield Town	1	0	0	1	1	2	0	-1
18	Cambridge United	1	0	0	1	0	1	0	-1
19	Shrewsbury Town	1	0	0	1	0	1	0	-1
20	Exeter City	1	0	0	1	1	3	0	-2
21	Preston North End	1	0	0	1	1	3	0	-2
22	Rotherham United	1	0	0	1	1	3	0	-2
23	Wigan Athletic	1	0	0	1	0	2	0	-2
24	**Swansea City**	1	0	0	1	0	3	0	-3

'Up The Blues!'

September 1990

"They gave us a real lesson and their finishing was deadly. Southend will surprise a few teams in the months ahead." - Danny O' Shea

September started with some very good news for Southend United regarding the transfer of Chris Powell. The football league tribunal had reached a decision so that the left back could complete his move from Crystal Palace on a free transfer. It was the offer that David Webb had originally tried to capture the services of Powell for when he first made contact earlier in the summer, but The Eagles were holding out for £25,000.

A delighted Webb said, "I feel they (the tribunal) were right to come down in our favour and it's nice to have everything settled and Powell in our squad. Ideally I would have liked Chris to have got a bit of match practice under his belt, but that has not been possible."

It was expected that the left back would make his debut in the first home league match of the season against Crewe Alexandra. He had been training with his new club for a number of weeks, but due to the tribunal's delay in reaching a decision over the fee involved, it meant that he was unable to feature in pre-season and the two competitive games that had been played.

Powell's inclusion in the starting line-up meant that young Christian Hyslop had to make way and although that may have been a tad harsh on him after two solid performances - Webb clearly rated his new full back highly to warrant an immediate start.

Blues were looking to make it three wins out of three over with victory over Crewe and Webb was keen to have his side impose themselves from the first whistle as opposed to waiting until they were a goal behind!

"I want us to adopt a more positive approach against Crewe, more as we did in the second half on Tuesday when we scored twice against Aldershot," Webb declared. "The lads are still finding their feet a little – remember, only six of the current side played together last season. The other five are either new faces or people who came in and out of the side. It will take time to get the blend exactly right and for players to get used to each other."

Webb's demand for a more positive approach was seemingly heeded by the players as they started the game in a very impressive manner which culminated in a goal after just fourteen minutes.

Steve Tilson had found himself on the right wing after his corner was only partially cleared. He cut inside his marker to deliver a deep cross for Brett Angell who headed back across the six yard box for Ian Benjamin to spectacularly scissor kick the ball into the net for 1-0.

Crewe, though, were a good footballing side and carried on passing the ball to feet, patiently trying to play their way back into the game and they weren't to be denied. Their moment came when, on thirty six minutes, an impressive twelve pass move had dragged Blues all out of position before Dave McKearney fed the ball to Andy Sussex, who smashed the ball high into the net from twelve yards.

The first half finished all square and Webb's pep talk during the interval seemed to work its magic again as his side came out and upped their game. The Shrimpers got the ball forwards early and put pressure on the Crewe back four, so much so that a mix up in the area resulted in Jason Smart fouling Angell for a forty-seventh minute penalty.

The spot-kick was the responsibility of Dave Martin and he showed why he was the chosen penalty taker by placing the ball low to the goalkeepers left to restore Southend's lead.

Just eight minutes later The Blues scored again when debutant Chris Powell hit a long ball that Andy Ansah latched onto and the speedy winger squared the ball for Angell to side foot home in front of a jubilant North Bank for goal number three.

With a two goal cushion, Southend eased off a little, but that only gave Crewe more possession and again they got their just rewards for some fine football on seventy four minutes. They broke quickly from defending a corner before Sussex brilliantly laid the ball into the path of Craig Hignett whose tidy finish left Sansome with no chance.

Blues survived a few more anxious moments and managed to see out the remainder of the game for a 3-2 win. It meant back to back wins for Webb's team, but the manager was far from happy and had this to say about the quality of his side's defending, "We worked harder to get goals than we did to prevent them. This game is all about team work and the truth is that we did not defend properly as a unit. The back four did not get the support which they were entitled to expect in certain situations and that is one area of our game which needs to be worked on."

Perhaps in trying to be more positive in going forwards, Southend had neglected their duties at the other end. However, the new strike force had again impressed and it was that duo that had Crewe boss, Dario Gradi, praising them post-match, "They were very aggressive characters – and I don't mean dirty – who made things very difficult for us. Angell was a real handful and always seemed to be in the thick of the action," he said.

Gradi's comments only served to underline Webb's assessment of his young striker, but it was Benjamin's scissor kick that left fans talking the strike up as an early contender for goal of the season. It was also encouraging for the fans to see three goals from their team, just a pity there was fewer than three thousand fans inside Roots Hall to witness the drama.

The debut of Powell was a fairly impressive one, especially when you consider he hadn't played any games during pre-season. Although Webb had criticised the team for conceding two goals at home, he said he was "delighted" with Powell's performance in the win.

Next for The Shrimpers was the second leg of The Rumbelows Cup tie just three days later at Aldershot, Webb was to be able to call upon his other first choice full back as Dean Austin had made his way back to fitness. Webb confirmed that Deano would be getting the minutes he needed to be match sharp.

"It's no reflection on young Edwards who has done a good job, but I feel Dean should help to give us a more solid look. Dean has played in a couple of practice games I fixed up recently for the reserves – against Colchester and Fords – and has come through well although having some slight swelling on his knee afterwards. But I feel the time has now come for us to put him through a tough ninety minutes of real competitive action," he explained.

The Blues 2-1 lead from the first leg of the tie meant that they would have their work cut out to get through to the next round. There was no chance of Southend resting on their laurels and selecting an under strength side for the game. Webb underlined that point the day prior to the match. "If we do that it could be fatal. We must be positive and look upon this as a fresh game and try to keep our early season momentum going" he warned, before making it public what he expected from his team.

"We looked very positive and dangerous going forward against Crewe, but failed to defend as a unit. As attractive and exciting as it must be for the fans we can't expect to win 3-2 every week and must stop being generous to the opposition – I am looking for a clean sheet tonight."

A clean sheet would see The Shrimpers progress, but there was some surprising news on the eve of the game that concerned fans. It was confirmed by The Blues Boss that both Butler & Martin were still playing for the club under week to week contracts after talks to extend their stay broken down. "I am afraid we cannot meet their demands. We have gone as high as we can, but it's not good enough," said a disappointed Webb.

"At the end of the day, unless they lower their sights a little, I suppose they will have to try elsewhere. The ball is definitely in their court. Mind you, I have been impressed with the way they have both been performing despite all the contract problems and the pressure is now on them to keep that up if they hope to attract the attention of other clubs."

"They are signing week to week deals and will still figure in my plans while they show the right commitment and do their stuff on the pitch – it's up to them."

That news came as a blow to many as both players had excelled in the opening three games of the season. It was hoped that things could be resolved as soon as possible, but their dedication to the cause could not be called into question.

Despite their contractual issues, Martin and Butler were selected for the game at Aldershot as Blues carried on their impressive start to the campaign by storming into a 2-0 lead. The goals came first from, full back Dean Austin who scored with a neat finish from inside the box before Brett Angell netted his third in four games for 2-0.

That was the halftime score and a place in round two seemed all but guaranteed, but the clean sheet Webb wanted wasn't given as

Blues conceded two second half goals to give the home side hope of progression themselves.

There was a few shaky moments in the last few moments of the game as Aldershot went for the goal that would have taken them into extra time, but Southend held off for a 2-2 draw on the night, winning 4-3 on aggregate.

After the game, Webb pointed out the main objective had been reached, but still had issues regarding the amount of goals his team were conceding. "We are through to the next round and that is what counts. We had the game sewn up and then let them back into the match. The teams defending is still a concern."

The draw for second round of the competition pitted Southend against Crystal Palace of Division One. It was a mouth-watering draw for many reasons and, aside from Adam Locke and Chris Powell meeting their former teammates, Blues would be testing themselves against some players of real quality. The Eagles boasted a squad that included Ian Wright, Mark Bright, John Salako, Nigel Martyn and Geoff Thomas. The tie was a two legged affair in which Palace would be at home first on September 25th with the return leg being played two weeks later at Roots Hall.

The next league fixture for Southend was away at The Abbey Stadium, home of Cambridge United. Like Southend, Cambridge had just won promotion to Division Three, but they did it via the play offs when a Dion Dublin goal proved enough to beat Chesterfield at Wembley.

In their two league games they had played The U's had won one and lost one. The defeat came at much fancied Birmingham City, but they kicked off their first home game with a win a week later over Fulham. Renowned for their long ball style of play that was preferred by manager John Beck, Cambridge proved tricky opponents in the games between the two the previous year as they took four points from their encounters with The Shrimpers.

The clash was played on a Sunday with a noon kick off and there was an injury doubt over central defender John Cornwell after he picked up a groin strain in the game at Aldershot. Webb was keen for Cornwell to win his fitness battle, but sought comfort from the other defenders in his squad. "I t would be a blow if we were forced to make a change after such a promising start to the season, but luckily we are well served by central defenders at the club and I will have quite a few options if John is forced to cry off."

Those choices he spoke of included Peter Cawley, Spencer Prior and Andy Edwards. The latter of the three would possibly be the favourite to get the nod in his natural position should Webb need to make a decision. "Andy is certainly happier in a more central defensive role," admitted Blues boss.

"He teamed up well with Paul Clark at the end of last season, particularly in our tense promotion clinching game at Peterborough. Another thing in his favour is that he has played in the first team this season out of position at right back and would certainly not lack match sharpness. I shall give the matter a bit of thought and possibly won't make a final decision until before kick-off."

It turned out that it was a decision that didn't have to be made due to Cornwell being passed fit for the game and therefore he took his place alongside Clark at the heart of The Blues defence. Also part of the back four for the first league game of the season was Dean Austin who retained his place after his goalscoring exploits at Aldershot in midweek.

The Shrimpers started well and went into the lead on fifteen minutes through Brett Angell for his fourth strike of the campaign. It came when a Clark free kick on the halfway line was lofted over the Cambridge defence and met by the head of Dave Martin. The midfielder steered his header back across the home side's goal to where Angell had escaped his marker to simply put the ball away from close range.

Cambridge did manage to force their way back into the reckoning with their long ball tactics, but Paul Sansome made a good save down low to prevent Steve Claridge equalising right on half time.

Southend picked up the pace once more at the beginning of the second half and increased their lead on fifty-five minutes. This time the goal was created by Steve Tilson on the left hand side when his cross found its way, via a deflection, to Ian Benjamin who swivelled to fire Blues into a 2-0 lead.

Then, just seven minutes later, it got even better for Southend. Peter Butler played a clever one-two with Benjamin before curling a shot past John Vaughan in the Cambridge goal an unbelievable 3-0 advantage.

The home side looked to have run out of ideas while the Blues simply looked a class above and continued to grow in confidence as the game wore on. Andy Ansah was a threat down the right side and with only seven minutes to go, his cross found its way to Angell for his second of the match and Southend's fourth.

The game was obviously over and the points were heading for Essex, but Cambridge did get a goal that was nothing more than a mere consolation. The goal came from a corner when Mike Cheetham was somehow left unmarked at the back post to make it 4-1.

After the match, Cambridge defender and former Blue Danny O' Shea had nothing but praise for The Shrimpers following the one sided affair. "It's certainly early days yet, but Southend certainly looked a superb, well organised side today," he said.

"I have always thought of Blues as an off the cuff side, but David Webb has produced a good blend who work hard for each other. They gave us a real lesson and their finishing was deadly. Southend will surprise a few teams in the months ahead."

The win left The Shrimpers at the top of the table and with back to back home games coming up against Preston and Shrewsbury, there was a chance for Webb's side to stay in pole position. The manager had set up his team to create chances and he favoured the strikers to do the business in front of goal. "The way we play I always fancy us to score a lot of goals and I don't reckon there will be many teams who will relish facing Angell and co," Webb stated after the game.

It was, without doubt, the best performance of the season so far and, even though it was only three league games old, there was something special about what David Webb's men had just done to Cambridge United.

The defence had looked solid and both Austin and Powell had offered good support form full back. In midfield, Butler continued his outstanding all action display and his partnership with Martin was looking stronger as every game passed. But, as Webb pointed out, it was up front where Southend seemingly had the cutting edge over their opponents at the moment.

Angell and Benjamin had just hit it off from the very first game at Huddersfield and gone on from there. The old, experienced head of Benjamin brought the best out of his young strike partner with his aerial ability and hold up play. Without doubt, it was Angell who was stealing the headlines, but the form of Benjamin was a major factor in the reason behind why the twenty-one year old had hit the ground running.

Benjamin had started his career by moving around three clubs in as many years. Starting at Sheffield United after graduating through their youth team, Benji made only two first team appearances before moving on to West Bromwich Albion and then a brief spell at Meadow Lane, home of Notts County didn't work out for the young forward.

It was at his next club, Peterborough United, where he first felt like he was a member of the first team with eighty first team appearances over two seasons, in which he netted fourteen times.

It was largely thought that Benjamin was somebody's perfect partner. That would be the way to get the best out of the player and when he completed his next move to Northampton Town in 1984, his career really took off.

It was The Cobblers manager, Graham Carr, who partnered Benji with the prolific Richard Hill in 1986 and between them they fired Town to The Fourth Division title with a record breaking ninety-nine points - scoring over a hundred goals in the process. Hill and Benjamin accounted for over fifty of those as they formed one of the most feared strike partnerships in the lower divisions.

Unfortunately for both Benjamin and Northampton, Hill was sold to Watford in the summer of 1987 and as Benjamin's goals dried up, he eventually lost his place in the team. Not wanting to be left sitting on the bench, he moved on to first Cambridge, then followed that up with short spells at Chester City and then Exeter, but the goals wouldn't flow as they had at The Cobblers.

It was while at Exeter City that David Webb enquired about the striker and Benjamin joined the Essex club in March 1990 where he immediately helped Southend win promotion at Peterborough. Now, partnered with Angell, Benji was looking every bit the player who played such a significant role at Northampton. Webb had spotted the potential in the pairing of his first choice front men and the early suggestion was it looked to be a perfect match. At Cambridge, they had run riot over the opposition and fans were rightly encouraged by what they saw.

The next league fixture was a home game versus Preston North End. It was a Friday night fixture and it meant that The Blues had only five days to prepare for the visit of Les Chapman's side after their Sunday best over Cambridge.

The good news to come out of the club a few days prior to that match was that Dave Martin was finally about to put an end to his contract saga and sign on for three more years.

All that remained to be sorted was a few minor details and Martin was expected to sign the new deal over the following day or two. There was obvious relief among the fans who had been delighted with Martin's early season form, but the player himself let out a huge sigh of relief at almost having completed the prolonged negotiations. "Things have dragged on long enough and I just want to get the contract sorted and have a little bit more security for me and my family," said a relieved Martin.

"I was keen to have a longer term than Southend were originally ready to offer because I enjoy playing for the club and would hope to help get them into a higher division during the period of the contract – unless Spurs or Liverpool come in for me in the meantime!"

The midfield enforcer also spoke of the good early season form the team had shown. "It has been a dream start. All the lads are really buzzing and confidence is spreading through the team," Martin said.

"It's obviously early days yet, but the signs are good and I feel the manager has got a very strong squad together which is more than capable of frightening a few teams this season. There is a good blend of youth and experience and hopefully the older heads among us will be able to steady the ship when, as every team does at some stage, we run into a couple of bad results."

When asked about what impact Brett Angell had made to the team, he was quick to praise the £100,000 striker. "It's difficult for anyone to step into and take over from someone like David Crown, but he has done just that. He has linked up well with Ian Benjamin while little Andy Ansah has also performed brilliantly out wide. They are three players who no defence will be happy playing against," Martin explained.

The fact that Martin was now all but signed on for the foreseeable future was more good news to add to the winning start in Division Three. As Webb prepared for the visit of Preston, he voiced his pleasure at finally getting the inspirational midfielder to sign a contract.

'Up The Blues!'

"It will be nice to have David's future sorted out because he has such a lot to offer. He has played well over three hundred games while at Millwall, Wimbledon and Southend and is still comparatively young. David desperately wants to be a winner and hopefully will help take us into a higher grade of football during the period of his contract," Blues manager said.

With thoughts turning towards the season's first Friday night fixture at Roots Hall, Webb was able to name an unchanged team from the one that blitzed a bewildered Cambridge in the previous game.

Preston arrived at Roots Hall with only a solitary point from their opening three league games, but they started the match with a confidence on the ball that belittled that poor record.

With the game just shy of fifteen minutes old, Preston made the most of some neat build up play following on from Ian Benjamin's failure to hold onto the ball. They broke quickly and Graham Shaw's effort was only parried by Paul Sansome before Warren Joyce fired the rebound into the net for a surprise lead.

Southend had their moments in a half where they spent a lot of time chasing the ball. Their closest opportunity came when Brett Angell's header was cleared off the line by Adrian Hughes, but despite Blues endeavour, PNE ended the half with their noses just in front.

It was the second half that Blues came to life and set-plays were to prove vital for David Webb's men.

An equalising goal came about when Benjamin was fouled from behind on the halfway line. Peter Butler took the kick, floated it forwards for the onrushing Dave Martin to head the ball into the net to level the scores. It was a great way for Martin to celebrate the signing of his new contract, scoring his third goal of the season.

Despite Preston's best attempts, The Blues just would not allow them the time and space they had in the first half to impose themselves on the game.

Southend continued to pressurise their opponents and their hard work didn't go unrewarded. On seventy minutes, Peter Butler showed great energy to overlap winger Andy Ansah and delivering a superb cross for Benjamin to loop a header over the keeper to put his side in front for the first time in the match.

With the wind in their sails, Blues continued to press for a third goal, but this time they were punished by Preston when the visitors countered and Chris Powell clumsily fouled Joyce in the area for a clear penalty. John Thomas confidentially strode up to convert the kick, sending Sansome the wrong way with only five minutes left on the clock.

A draw would have been a decent result for The Shrimpers, but this team showed a great desire and will to get all three points by pushing for the late winner. So much so, in fact, that even John Cornwell pushed up the field from defence to try and make something happen - and it wasn't to be in vain.

With the game entering injury time the ball was picked up by Butler who passed it square to Steve Tilson. Tilly, fifteen yards inside North End's half, lifted the ball into the penalty area. His cross was only half cleared by Hughes to where Cornwell had drifted and, after controlling the ball with his thigh, volleyed an unstoppable shot into the net from the edge of the box, sending the North Bank wild.

There was to be no comeback from that for Preston and The Blues won the game 3-2. Southend had shown immense character to get all the points on offer and that win made it maximum points for David Webb's team from the four games played – a feat not achieved since 1980!

The game had everything, but the real talking point was THAT injury time goal from John Cornwell. The goal-scorer confirmed just how much the winning strike meant to him. "That's easily the best goal I've ever scored," beamed Cornwell.

"I made up my mind to have a crack at goal as soon as the ball came out to me. It sat up perfectly and I hit it full on the volley – it was great to see the ball nestling in the back of the net."

Southend had another opportunity for a home victory when Shrewsbury Town rolled into Essex four days later and with the games now coming thick and fast, Webb had a couple of injury concerns ahead of the game.

Captain Paul Clark and forward Ian Benjamin were struggling with hamstring and knee problems respectively. Both hadn't featured in training in the lead up to the Tuesday night fixture, but Webb remained in a positive frame of mind.

"Neither injury looks too serious and both lads are desperate to play. Knowing what tough characters they are, I think they will make it," said a confident Webb, before issuing a challenge for his players to carry on the momentum they had.

"Everyone is buzzing after the start we've made and naturally being able to field more or less a settled team has been a great help. The players have been setting their own standards and can only get better once they develop a greater understanding. But they are only too aware they can't afford to let those standards drop if they are to hold onto their first team places. They need no reminding that there are good players waiting in the wings for a first team chance. Those currently in the side will simply have to keep performing to stay there."

Both Clark and Benjamin recovered from their little knocks in time to be fit for the Shrewsbury match, but after only ten minutes of action, perhaps Clark wished that he hadn't made it. The Blues skipper was defending the near post from a Shrews free kick and in trying to head the ball out for a corner, he only succeeded to head the ball past Sammy to give the visitors an early lead.

Shrewsbury's duo of Dean Spink and Michael Brown were causing Southend a few problems following the opening goal of the game and Sansome had to be at his brilliant best to keep out the former's header to keep the deficit at just the one goal.

As if inspired by their custodian between the sticks, Blues rallied and started to take the game to the visitors. It was a free kick in their own half that got them a way back into the game when John Cornwell's delivery was flicked on by Angell for Steve Tilson to poke the ball under the goalkeeper for the equaliser.

With the home side now in the ascendency, a second goal soon followed on twenty-eight minutes from another set-play. Tilson was the architect this time, his delivery causing mayhem in the Shrews defence and as they hesitated, Andy Ansah tucked the ball away for a 2-1 lead.

Southend had come from behind again and there was a confidence amongst the team that they would not lose it like they had in the previous match. They continued to press forwards at every opportunity and went close to a third goal with decent efforts from both Ansah and Cornwell.

On sixty-eight minutes, that elusive third goal should have come when Tilson ran clear through on goal, but he wasted the opportunity when it looked far easier to score.

It could have been costly when, two minutes from time, a good effort from Paul Wimbleton looked destined for the net until Sammy flew himself to his right to turn the ball away for a corner.

That proved to be the last action of note and the three points belonged once again to Southend. That was win number five out of a possible five and meant it was now officially the club's best ever start to a season since the 1929-1930. Even more important than that though, was that Southend found themselves two points clear at the top of the table after Birmingham City lost their 100% record by drawing with Exeter City.

It was an amazing start for David Webb and his team. To be sitting at the top of the table with maximum points certainly made teams sit up and take notice of them. But, in this competitive division, there were no easy games and a tough trip to Stoke City was next for The Blues in what would be a real test, especially at the intimidating Victoria Ground.

This enormity of the task was underlined by Webb the day before the game, "Stoke are always likely to give you a tough time and I am expecting hardest test so far. They have a first division set up and the whole club is geared for bigger things than the Third (division)," emphasised Blues Chief.

"Even the ground itself can prove a bit over-awing to some players who are used to only playing at mediocre stadiums. But, our lads certainly need not go there with any inferiority complex after the sparkling start they have made. We're on top of the table after some superb displays and I expect Stoke will view our arrival with some apprehension."

Webb was always quick to praise his team in the media, complimenting them on the work they had done in getting off to the great start. It was clever from the manager who rarely gave himself a pat on the back for the work he had been doing, instead taking every opportunity to lift the belief within his squad and with Stoke boasting the likes of Micky Thomas, Tony Ellis, Noel Blake and Wayne Biggins in their side, it was essential that Southend believed in themselves ahead of their biggest test of the season.

The Blues showed plenty of that belief early in their game and after fifteen minutes of action they had registered six corners. However, the corners proved ineffective and the only effort on goal came from Brett Angell who failed to hit the target with a header.

Stoke then started to dominate proceedings from there on and only the acrobatics from Paul Sansome kept Blues goal in tact as he denied Mickey Thomas what seemed a certain goal.

The home side carried on pressing Blues in search of an opening goal and were denied once more when Chris Powell headed Carl Beeston's effort off the line.

On thirty-nine minutes the breakthrough finally came when Paul Ware converted through a crowd of players after Sammy failed to hold Biggins original effort. It was no more than the home side had deserved and, with their tails up, they pushed on for a second goal.

Try as they might, Southend were unable to hold off the attacks and City capitalised on a mistake from Powell for 2-0. The Blues left back's error allowed Stoke to break quickly, stretching Southend's defence and as the ball came into Biggins he showed real quality in killing the ball dead with his first touch, turning and then firing the ball into the corner of the net. That goal seemed to knock the stuffing out of Southend as they looked like a side lacking in confidence for the first time as they trudged off for the interval.

Stoke started the second half as they finished the first and by this point Blues were struggling to get out of their own half. More goals looked inevitable and that proved the case when as Southend just couldn't handle the movement of the home forwards.

It was that movement that made goal number three. Beeston played the ball into the chest of Tony Ellis, who in turn laid it off for the travelling Biggins and the number ten made no mistake with a well taken volley for his second of the game.

Try as they might, Southend couldn't get at their opponents and despite the efforts of Sammy in goal, Stoke scored for the fourth time when the unfortunate John Cornwell headed into his own net after Ellis' cross on sixty-minutes.

That rounded off a dismal afternoon for David Webb's team and after their first defeat of the campaign; the manager wasn't too hard on his players. "We finished up getting a dose of our own medicine. We put together some of our best stuff of the season and virtually played them off the park for thirty-five minutes, but this was one day when we could not turn pressure into goals. We finished up getting a good hiding," was his honest assessment.

After that heavy defeat, perhaps it was a blessing in disguise that Southend had a game they had been looking forward to in the shape of Division One's Crystal Palace in round two of The Rumbelows Cup.

Having lost at Stoke in the manner that they did, the attention was immediately turned to the prospect of playing a team from England's top division and it was hoped that the drubbing received at Victoria Ground would be put to bed in anticipation of a big cup tie.

One player who was looking forward to the trip to South London more than most was Chris Powell who had only officially left The Eagles four weeks earlier. The left back admitted to have been asked by his former teammates about his new club's strengths and weaknesses, but he refused to give anything away. Instead, Powell explained why he felt a shock could have well been on the cards.

"In many ways the pressure is on them because they are expected to win. I know they are a little apprehensive about meeting us and with good reason. In the short time I've been at Roots Hall I know we have several players who could easily play at a much higher level," said the confident full back.

"There's every reason to suppose we can get a result, particularly if we can keep them out for the first twenty minutes or so. I see that as the danger period for us as Palace are the type of side who can really turn it on if they get an early goal."

Powell then joked, "As for tonight's game, it's one I am looking forward to. Naturally I respect Palace a great deal, but my biggest worry is finding enough tickets to satisfy my friends and family who want to watch the game!"

David Webb was less jovial pre-match - instead he made reference to the display at Stoke that left him far from happy. "That (Stoke) was our first defeat of the season so there's no sense in pressing the panic button, but I've let them know in no uncertain terms that I was not happy with what I saw in the second half against Stoke."

"Now I have to see if the message got home. If it hasn't then there is likely to be a change or two for our weekend league match at Mansfield."

It was the same team for the fifth consecutive match, something that Webb clearly felt was important if his team was to get an understanding within the starting eleven. It was hoped that familiarity would help the new players settle and the early suggestions was that it was the case, but away at First Division Palace in the League Cup was to be another test for Webb's new look side.

Southend feared an early goal would be hard to deal with, but that's exactly what happened with the game only three minutes old. Mark Bright was the scorer after he capitalised on a mistake by Cornwell to outpace Austin and fire past Sansome at the near post.

On twenty seven minutes, the home side doubled their lead after another error of judgement from John Cornwell at the heart of the defence. This time it was Bright's strike partner Ian Wright who made the most of the time and space gifted to him for 2-0.

Southend managed to get to halftime only two goals behind, but in truth they had offered very little and at times they just couldn't live with their First Division opponents.

Any hopes that Blues might be able to contain their opponents and perform some kind of damage limitation from the 1500 travelling supporters was quickly put to bed within five minutes of the re-start. It was Cornwell again who was exposed for Palace's third goal as he failed to intercept Alan Pardew's through ball that presented Wright with a shooting opportunity, but even though Sansome parried his effort, Phil Barber was on hand to knock in the rebound for 3-0.

At that point, Webb withdrew Cornwell and brought on midfielder Jason Cook, which meant Dave Martin moved back into defence. Unfortunately, he fared no better as Palace began toying with Southend.

A long clearance from Richard Shaw allowed Wright to out run Martin with relative ease and square the ball for ball for Bright's second, Palace's fourth.

The home side were showing a real ruthless streak now and while there was a question mark about exactly how much some Blues players wanted to be out there, the finishing from Steve Coppell's team showed them no mercy whatsoever.

Goal number five came from Wright's head for his second of the night. The prolific forward completed his hat-trick for number six and then smashed home his fourth following Glyn Hodges free kick to make it goal number seven to ironic cheers from the Southend fans.

Then, as the game drew to a close, Palace scored their eighth and final goal of the night when Bright headed home Wright's centre to cap a miserable and forgetful night for Southend United.

The players cut dejected figures as they trounced off the pitch and after conceding twelve goals in two games and who could blame them? They had been outplayed, outfought and outclassed throughout the ninety minutes and the score line clearly reflected such a gulf in class.

After the match, Blues manager David Webb managed to keep his emotions in check, especially considering what he had just witnessed. Instead of sounding off, he took his share of the blame for the performance – even though he wasn't best pleased with some of his players.

"Too many players, particularly the inexperienced ones, were prepared to accept defeat when they believed there was no way back with just twenty minutes to go. But at the end of the day, I take full responsibility for what happened. Obviously there were glaring deficiencies and it's now up to me to help put them right," Webb said.

As the dust settled over the next few days at Roots Hall, Vice-chairman John Adams spelt out the financial cost of the 8-0 drubbing for the club. "We will probably have to settle for a crowd of between six and seven thousand for the return leg. Had we emerged from Selhurst Park with a realistic chance of winning through to the third round there was every prospect of a sell-out," groaned Adams.

"That's unlikely to happen now and when one takes into consideration the potential loss of programme sales and catering in addition to tickets, we could finish up twenty-five thousand pounds short of what we had hoped for," he added.

Webb would have the chance to put right the recent two displays at Stoke and Palace in the away league fixture at Mansfield Town in the upcoming Saturday, but before then, football once again backed up the old adage that 'it's a funny old game.'

After his side suffered two heavy successive defeats, a story broke in the press that Watford were looking at making an approach for David Webb to become their Director of Football and work with their manager, Colin Lee.

Watford was struggling at the wrong end Division Two and it was common knowledge that Webb was friends with the Chairman at Vicarage Road, but Vic Jobson dismissed the matter out of hand.

"I have had no approach from Watford and am not expecting one, as far as I'm concerned it is merely newspaper talk," said Blues Chairman.

Webb didn't comment on the story, but instead he did heap praise on young defender Spencer Prior's performance in the midweek reserve match against Wokingham. Webb wanted his fringe players to make him stand up and take notice and Prior certainly did that.

"That's the best Spencer has played this season and you can say that he has a good chance of making Saturday's starting line-up," he confirmed, before adding the team was perhaps in need of a change. "I am not the type of manager who makes wholesale changes just for the sake of it, but obviously something has to be done after our recent results."

"The lads who have been brought into the squad showed in a reserve game on Wednesday the brand of fighting spirit we need at the moment. They not only put in one hundred per cent, but showed a lot of quality and deserve promotion into the first team reckoning. Even if they don't all play, their presence should be a warning to the current players in the side that I won't tolerate any more slips in our standards."

"We've been giving sharp lessons at Stoke and Crystal Palace and it's up to the players to show they have learned something and have the character to battle and win back their pride."

Webb was then asked whether the morale and belief that Blues had built on following their good start was now in tatters. "No, the atmosphere in the dressing room is far from depressed," was the swift reply. "Of course the players are disappointed, but there are no big dramas. We've talked about the situation and everyone knows where we've been going wrong and what I want to see to put it right – three points at Mansfield should set us up for the two home games next week against Swansea and Bournemouth when we want to win back the faith and respect of our loyal fans."

Although he didn't say as much, it was quite clear reading between the lines that Prior was going to get the nod ahead of John Cornwell for the trip to Mansfield. Twelve goals conceded in two games was just too great a number to just leave things as they were.

Prior did indeed line up alongside skipper Paul Clark in Webb's only change in the starting eleven, which meant that Chris Powell retained his place despite the good form of Christian Hyslop in the reserves.

There were also changes in the two permitted substitutes with Adam Locke featuring for the first time of the season on the bench

'Up The Blues!'

and the other sub was Cornwell, who managed to stay involved in the thirteen despite his below par performances over the previous two games.

The pitch at Field Mill was heavy under foot and that seemed to benefit the home side more than Southend in the early exchanges, but it wasn't too long before the Essex side took control of the game with Steve Tilson proving a real thorn in Mansfield's side.

It was Tilly who set up both strikers with good chances, but both Brett Angell and Ian Benjamin were denied by Andrew Beasley in the home goal. There was little doubt that Mansfield were the more relieved team at the break to still be in the game with the scores locked at 0-0.

In the second half, The Stags came into the game more and although they had the lion's share of possession, the returning Spencer Prior was in fine form and showed no signs of the rust from the time on the injury table with his broken leg.

Mansfield's best chance came from Graham Leishman who found the only bit of room The Shrimpers allowed their opposition all afternoon, but his shot flashed just past Paul Sansome's goal.

Blues then finally found a breakthrough after Dean Austin's gained his side a corner with only twelve minutes remaining. The kick was taken by Tilson and his in-swinger was met by Benjamin who had come off the near post to send a looping header over Beasley and into the net for a 1-0 win.

The performance was a professional one and one that was very much needed following the recent performances away from Roots Hall. Those were the sentiments echoed by Blues manager after the game. "This was just the dose of medicine we needed," said a happy Dave Webb.

"After conceding twelve goals in the two games against Stoke and Crystal Palace, the lads were feeling a bit low. But this has put a smile back on their faces and I've nothing but praise for the way they bounced back."

"They'd taken a bit of stick for those two defeats, but this latest performance spoke volumes for their character. And to keep a clean sheet for the first time this season was another big bonus."

"That gave me as much satisfaction as the result. It was beginning to play on the players' minds that they had not succeeded in keeping out opposing sides, but now they can approach the visit of Swansea with renewed confidence."

Skipper Paul Clark also spoke of his delight a keeping their opponents out for the first time this season, "Our failure to keep a clean sheet was starting to worry us a bit," he admitted. "It seemed as if every mistake we made was being punished, but we didn't give Mansfield a real sniff and for that everyone deserves credit. We managed to get more bodies behind the ball and that made us a much more solid as a defensive unit."

The three points won at Field Mill meant that Southend had regained the top spot in the division and it as hoped that the confidence would be back to what it was prior to the Palace shambles.

There was still plenty of football left to be played, but to be leading the table with seven games gone suggested The Blues could well surprise a few teams in the division- as they had done so far. Webb had spoken of taking this club into the second tier of English football, but nobody had really believed him and in truth many pundits were not considering that this little team from Essex would be able to last the distance. But The Blues Chief, with his one game at a time approach, thought he knew better.

After Southend had faltered when presented with their biggest challenge to date up at Stoke, a trip of equal magnitude was just around the corner when Southend would travel to the midlands for a clash with many people's tip for the title, Birmingham City. First though, was a midweek home game with Swansea City and, as Webb professed, it was one game at time and all eyes were firmly fixed on the visit of The Swans.

'Up The Blues!'

Division Three league table on 30th September 1990

	P	W	D	L	W	D	L	GD	PTS
1. SOUTHEND UNITED	7	3	0	0	3	0	1	+4	18
2. GRIMSBY TOWN	7	2	1	0	3	0	1	+8	16
3. BIRMINGHAM CITY	7	2	2	0	2	1	0	+5	15
4. TRANMERE ROVERS	7	1	1	1	3	1	0	+8	14
5. READING	7	1	2	0	3	0	1	+6	14
6. EXETER CITY	7	2	0	2	2	1	0	+4	13
7. BURY	7	3	0	0	1	1	2	+2	13
8. BRENTFORD	7	2	1	1	1	2	0	+4	12
9. ORIENT	7	4	0	0	0	0	3	+1	12
10. STOKE CITY	7	2	0	2	1	2	0	+4	11
11. WIGAN ATHLETIC	7	2	1	1	1	0	2	-3	10
12. BOURNEMOUTH	7	1	2	0	1	1	2	+1	9
13. CAMBRIDGE UNITED	7	0	1	2	2	2	0	-1	9
14. CHESTER CITY	7	1	1	2	1	1	1	0	8
15. SWANSEA CITY	7	1	2	1	1	0	2	-4	8
16. PRESTON NORTH END	7	1	0	2	1	2	1	-5	8
17. BRADFORD CITY	7	1	0	2	1	2	1	-3	7
18. HUDDERSFIELD	7	1	0	2	1	1	2	-3	7
19. SHREWSBURY TOWN	7	0	1	2	1	2	1	-1	6
20. BOLTON	7	1	0	2	1	0	3	-7	6
21. ROTHERHAM UNITED	7	1	2	1	0	0	3	-5	5
22. CREWE ALEXANDRA	7	1	1	2	0	0	3	-3	4
23. MANSFIELD TOWN	7	0	1	3	1	0	2	-5	4
24. FULHAM	7	0	1	3	0	2	1	-7	3

October 1990

"That was one of the best goals I've seen at Roots Hall" -David Webb

Swansea City came to Roots Hall on Tuesday 2nd October for a Third Division encounter lying in mid table after a mixed start to the season. Terry Yorath was their manager and he had overseen the club amass eight points from seven league fixtures - the pick of their results being a 1-0 away win at Bradford City. The Swans had a reputation for being hard to break down and Yorath brought his side to Roots Hall having previously picked up a creditable point against Tranmere Rovers.

Southend, however, were in fine form and sitting proudly at the top of the table on eighteen points and there was a real chance of adding to that total with home games versus Swansea and then, three days later on a Friday night, against AFC Bournemouth.

There was a slight injury concern over Peter Butler, arguably The Blues player of the year so far, who was suffering with breathing difficulties. Webb, however, was able to confirm that his midfielder was available to take to the field after an examination revealed there was no sign of a cracked rib as first feared, the x-ray showing up only bruising instead.

This meant that it was an unchanged team for the match and that meant Spencer Prior retained his place in defence and would make his first return to the Roots Hall pitch after eleven months out with a broken leg.

The teenager had played the full ninety minutes in the 1-0 win at Mansfield and his manager was suitably impressed. "Prior grabbed his chance and stays in the team on merit, but so do the rest of those who were on duty at the weekend," Webb confirmed.

"Everyone showed tremendous character and determination in bouncing back after the eight-nil defeat suffered at Crystal Palace

'Up The Blues!'

four days earlier and deserve the opportunity to carry on the good work against Swansea."

With The Shrimpers surprisingly setting the pace in the early stages of the season, Webb kept his feet firmly on the ground and didn't want anyone getting too carried away with the impressive start to the campaign. "It's nice to be setting the pace, but let's face it, the season has only just started and there is a long, long way to go," he said.

There was a crowd of 3,635 in attendance for the Tuesday night game and the home fans in that crowd were treated to a great performance from their team.

With eighteen minutes on the clock, Blues were on their way. Brett Angell rose highest to flick on Paul Sansome's goal kick to his striker partner, Ian Benjamin. Benji then hit a first time pass into the path of the onrushing Andy Ansah who was away from the defence and bearing down on goal. As the winger shaped to shoot he was unceremoniously brought down in the area by Mark Harris for a definite penalty and there was little argument with the red card that followed for Harris' professional foul.

Dave Martin stepped up and coolly sent Lee Bracey the wrong way for an early lead for the home side for his fourth goal of the season.

Southend pushed for a second, but it wasn't forthcoming and as the first half drew to a close it was the visitors who almost nicked a surprise equaliser. Tommy Hutchinson, the football league's oldest outfield player at 43, set up Andy Watson for a scoring opportunity, but he was smartly denied by Sansome to preserve the single goal lead at the break.

At the beginning of the second half, Blues doubled their advantage almost immediately. It stemmed from Benjamin's excellent hold up play which allowed Butler to get in a cross that Angell couldn't convert, but Steve Tilson could with a determined header from only six yards out.

Swansea's ten men now went for broke and pushed for a way back into the game. They got their rewards when, on sixty-five minutes, Southend stepped off the gas for a brief moment and it was Hutchinson again who proved a thorn in Blues side once more. The veteran toyed with Dean Austin before delivering a cross into the area that evaded Paul Clark on its way to Jimmy Gilligan who scored to give the visitors a lifeline.

Webb's reaction was to introduce Adam Locke in the place of Ansah and this proved the impetus The Shrimpers needed to put Swansea to bed. Just eleven minutes after The Swans scored, Martin restored Blues two goal cushion with a header virtually from a yard out after Tilson's right wing corner.

That wasn't to be it, however, and Southend had saved the best for last. With ten minutes remaining Benjamin's smart play sent Butler on his way down the right wing. The busy midfielder's cross was superbly met by Tilson with a first time volley which gave Bracey no chance in goal for the left midfielders second and Blues final goal in an impressive 4-1 win.

Tilson's volley was the icing on the cake and his manager was only too pleased to throw some plaudits his way. "You won't see a better goal than that all season," exclaimed Webb. "It was his (Tilson) best display so far, and not because of the goals he scored. In addition to being a driving force when going forward, Stevie also got through a tremendous amount of work in defensive situations."

There was no doubt that the sending off influenced the game – an angry Yorath said after the match that he felt "the award of a penalty was punishment enough" – but, Southend did a very convincing job on the team that was in front of them and that's all they could do in that situation. Blues had now won seven out of the eight league games played and, with twenty-one points, remained at the summit of Division Three.

Being the side at the top of the table meant that you are there to be shot at and Bournemouth were looking to get their first win on the road having lost three of their first four away games.

They boasted some quality within their squad that made a mockery of their mid-table placing and Dave Martin was well aware who Bournemouth's danger man was. "We have to get in amongst them from the start and cut out any supply to Luther Blissett. His record as a striker over the years speaks for itself and obviously he represents a danger to any defence," he said.

Blissett, 32, was in the twilight of his career having had successful spells at Watford and AC Milan as well as representing England on fourteen occasions. He was undoubtedly their main man, but there was a boost for Blues when influential midfield player Sean

O' Driscoll was ruled out with a groin injury. Even so, Southend knew they would have their work cut out to gain all three points.

"While we are naturally full of confidence, this match will present us with a severe test," explained Webb, before adding, "Bournemouth are packed with players who have experience at a very high level and no-one can ever afford to take them lightly."

Webb, who used to manage Bournemouth, was pleased to declare a clean bill of health for his squad and therefore he was able to name an unchanged starting eleven. However, he opted to include Peter Cawley as one of two substitutes alongside Adam Locke instead of John Cornwell who missed out altogether.

The Shrimpers started the game with a real purpose, going at their opponents like they felt they belonged at the top of the league and were rewarded with a lead as early as the eighth minute.

Forward Brett Angell collected the ball just inside Bournemouth's half and sent Dean Austin on his way down the right hand side. The striker then tremendously made up the ground to get into the area in time to head Austin's cross goal wards and the ball ended up in the net via a deflection off Dave Martin's chest.

The midfielder took delight in claiming the goal, running off in the direction of the East Stand to celebrate his sixth strike of the campaign, milking the applause of players and fans alike.

Blues were now in the ascendency and they really went at a Bournemouth side that seemed unable to get out of their own half. Efforts from Andy Ansah and Angell forced smart stops from Gerry Peyton in the visitor's goal, while Martin almost netted his second with a snapshot that flashed past the post.

Then, with thirty-four minutes on the clock, Bournemouth equalised against the run of play. It originated from a Peyton drop kick that was cleverly flicked on by Blissett which created enough of a gap for Efan Ekoku to roar past Spencer Prior and fire his shot past an exposed Paul Sansome for the leveller.

The score was all square at the break, but Webb was forced into making a change during the interval as Paul Clark was suffering with a hamstring injury. Peter Cawley was the man who came on for the club captain and started the game in a steady and assured manner.

With Cawley & Prior dominating Blissett & Ekoku, it enabled Southend to once more take hold of the game. Butler started to get

Blues going forwards, but even though there was five corners in the opening quarter of an hour, Blues were couldn't find a way past Peyton for a second.

That remained the case until the deadlock was finally broken with thirteen minutes left to play and it was Southend who got the game's decisive third goal. After having his first effort taken off him due to Martin's chest early in the match, this time Angell left no doubt who scored with an intelligent, looping header over Peyton and that nestled into the far corner from a very acute angle. It was Angell's first goal for six games and one clearly pleased him as he repeatedly pumped his fist in celebration.

After the re-start, Bournemouth really went for an equaliser and for Southend it was a real case of all hands on deck as they defended for their lives. The Cherries almost shocked Roots Hall when Gavin Peacock drove a shot just wide and then somehow Blissett failed to connect after a goalmouth scramble with only seconds left on the clock.

That was full time and Southend had deservedly run out 2-1 victors, despite the last minute scare. The win kept Southend on top of the table, which delighted boss Dave Webb. "I've got nothing but praise for the way the lads stuck at it and got the win they deserved," said the happy manager. "You've got to remember Bournemouth were in the Second Division last season and therefore packed with experienced players who had performed at a higher level, but we never stopped trying to carry the game to them and in the end proved the more inventive team."

A relieved Angell spoke after the game about how pleasing it was personally for him to finally net after his barren spell. "After a bit of a lean spell it was great to find the net with what proved the winner. But, having said that, I did not go into the match feeling under any real pressure. Other lads have been sticking the ball away to keep us on the winning trail and that's the most important thing," said the former Stockport man.

The following day, there was some much warranted recognition for the start that Southend had made as David Webb collected the Manager of the Month award for September. During that calendar month, The Shrimpers had won five out of six league games and as a result they climbed to the top of the league. Webb's accolade was richly deserved.

Before the next game, there was a departure from the club when cult hero Roy McDonough was allowed to leave for Essex non-league side Colchester United on a permanent deal.

The big striker had not featured a great deal with the arrival of Brett Angell and the form of Ian Benjamin and didn't really look like he was going to. In truth, the manager was trying to take the club in a different direction and steer away from the battering ram of a target man option that Roy offered; therefore it was felt that the timing was right for all parties for McDonough to move on.

There was a third home fixture on the trot for Southend with the second leg of the League Cup tie that was already over after the 8-0 drubbing that was handed out at Selhurst Park two weeks previous. In the first leg Palace's strike force both scored a hat-trick each and one half of that duo's words must have come as a chilling thought when Ian Wright was quoted as saying: "goals, goals, goals, that's what I love in any competition." Southend had been warned!

There was to be three changes to Blues starting eleven for what was, in all intents and purposes, a game with nothing but pride riding on it. John Cornwell was recalled in place of the suspended Dean Austin at right back and Adam Locke earned his first start in a blue shirt as Andy Ansah was relegated to the bench.

The third change was Peter Cawley in place of Paul Clark who was absent with the hamstring injury that forced him to come off at half time against Bournemouth. It was an on-going issue that the skipper had finally succumbed too. "It's the left hamstring which is causing the problem and the fact that I jump off from that leg hasn't helped. Neither has our early season programme which has demanded playing twice a week, that allows very little time between games for the injury to clear up," groaned Clark.

"I'll probably visit a specialist later this week and I gather there's a possibility that an injection might sort out the trouble. My feeling is that rest might turn out to be the best cure."

Clark, who handed the captain's armband over to Dave Martin, then spoke about Blues being after salvaging some pride against Palace and that how any result would go some way to doing just that. "Our pride took a bit of a battering at Selhurst Park and everyone is anxious to restore it," he said.

"Don't forget that a victory or even a draw would give everyone a further boost for Saturday's important league battle at

Birmingham. In other words, there's everything to play for and while acknowledging what a fine side Palace are, I believe we are capable of getting a good result."

"We were never as bad as our first meeting suggests. Okay, we made some silly mistakes and finished up getting punished for them, but I think Palace will be the first to admit they had one of those nights when all the breaks went their way," reasoned Clark.

When the draw was made, there was an expectant bumper crowd for the game at Roots Hall, but after the first leg it was never going to be the case. Still, a turnout of 5,199 was a decent crowd all things considered.

Southend, clearly determined not to be run around by Wright & Bright for a second time, opted for a more defensive approach to the game and throughout the early exchanges frustrated a Palace side who tried in vain to break down Blues rear-guard.

The home side's attacks were not as frequent as in previous matches at The Hall, but they did manage to get the ball in the net midway through the half, but Brett Angell's effort was ruled out for offside.

It was Palace, however, who did open the scoring for their ninth goal of the tie with five minutes remaining of the first half. It was central defender Eric Young who stabbed home from close range after Dave Martin failed to clear John Salako's corner kick.

The second half started with Palace immediately in the ascendency. They looked to attack at every opportunity and the inevitable second goal came three minutes after the re-start. Salako showed Division One skill to cut inside from the right wing to fire a left footed shot into the far top corner.

The goal was yet another clinical Palace strike in the tie, but Peter Cawley allowed the England winger far too much space to run into and against the quality of the opposition that Blues were up against, mistakes like that would not go unpunished.

It was now a real test of character for The Shrimpers, who were 10-0 behind on aggregate, and to their credit there was a real defiance within the team that they wouldn't be rolled over with the ease in the first leg.

Webb's side started to try and push their opponents back and got some reward midway through the second half with a goal that gave the fans something to celebrate. It originated from Adam Locke's cross that Angell beat Nigel Martyn to and as the ball headed goal wards, Steve Tilson made sure by sliding the ball into an unguarded net from inside the six yard box.

Bizarrely the goal was credited to Angell, even though Tilly looked to have got the final touch and the striker ran off in celebration of his seventh goal of the season.

Blues effort and work rate never dropped throughout the match and, even though Sansome was called into action twice more, the game ended with The Eagles winning 2-1 on the night and 10-1 on aggregate.

In the post-match interview, Palace boss Steve Coppell praised The Shrimpers for their nights work. "If it was hard for us to motivate ourselves, it must have been even harder for Southend following what happened in the first leg. They made a real fight of it and gave us a very tough battle," he said.

While that may have seemed an easy thing to say once your side had triumphed, Dave Webb agreed with his opposite number and was confident his team had got some self-belief back. "This game was all about winning back our pride and the lads succeeded in doing just that," said a satisfied Blues boss, "They gave it everything and deserve every credit for their efforts."

The pride that Webb spoke of was about to be put to a massive test once again with the league trip to Birmingham City that was to be played on the forthcoming Saturday, October 13th.

Like Stoke, Birmingham was a side tipped for the top come May and had yet to taste defeat in the league. In their opening nine fixtures they had drawn five of those and found themselves occupying fifth position, seven points behind David Webb's pace setters.

The Blues boss was, however, wary of the threat City posed. "Their record speaks for itself and the fact they are right up there among the leading bunch does not surprise me at all. I said they would be a threat before the season started and they are proving me a good judge," Webb explained, before building up his own team.

"They have won or saved a few matches by coming from behind so that shows what a resilient outfit they are. Obviously they will be tough opponents, but our form means that we will be making the trip with plenty of confidence. Certainly this is a test the lads are really looking forward to and it's a game which has all the makings of a real cracker which will give great value for money."

The injury to Paul Clark ruled him out of this game and for the next few weeks. This meant that Peter Cawley, who had deputised for the Captain in the last game and a half, would again wear the number seven shirt and line up alongside Spencer Prior at the heart of Southend's back four.

It would be Cawley's first league start for The Shrimpers and that wasn't the slightest concern for his manager. "Cawley came through the cup game (vs. Palace) with flying colours and certainly deserves to stay in," declared Webb. "His was a display which provided further proof that we have a very good squad of players at Roots Hall."

"The competition for places is fierce and that gives me a warm feeling. That's a type of situation which can only be good for the club, although it does make my job that little bit harder, but that's something I'm not going to complain about," smiled Blues Chief.

There were two other decisions that needed Webb's attention and they resulted in recalls for winger Andy Ansah and Dean Austin, who had served his one match suspension. Their inclusion in the starting line-up resulted in both Adam Locke and John Cornwell being relegated to the bench after giving good displays against Palace, but it was this type of competition for places that Webb was after if his side were to remain at the top end of the table.

Throughout the early exchanges it was the home side that were moving the ball around with better effect. In particular, Vince Overson and Dean Peer had Blues midfield partnership of stand in skipper Dave Martin and Peter Butler chasing shadows.

At times, it was all hands on deck for Southend as Prior, Cawley and Chris Powell all blocked goal bound efforts, while keeper Paul Sansome made two important saves himself.

However, it wasn't all one way traffic and for a ten minute spell in the first half, Southend went close with Tilson and Benjamin both seeing their efforts well blocked. Brett Angell also could have scored, but his shot was well saved by the legs Martin Thomas and Butler saw his ambitious attempt crash against the crossbar.

It was an entertaining first half, but the general consensus was that with the game being so open it wouldn't remain goalless for the second forty-five. That was very much the case and it was a very good goal that broke the deadlock on sixty-two minutes.

'Up The Blues!'

The ball had worked its way out towards the left to the brilliant Nigel Gleghorn. The left winger then picked out a superb forty yard defence splitting pass that striker Simon Sturridge instantly brought under control before coolly placing the ball past Sammy for the lead the home side probably deserved.

Things then went from bad to worse for The Shrimpers when Martin saw red for an adjudged elbow on Peer with twelve minutes remaining which left Southend with a real mountain to climb.

Webb's ten men then showed remarkable spirit to force Birmingham back and make them edgy as the clock wound down. It was a case of going for broke with nothing to lose and they managed to get their just rewards with an unlikely equaliser on eight-six minutes.

The visitors, all in yellow, won a corner that caused a goalmouth scramble and, following substitute John Cornwell's effort, the ball fell to little Andy Ansah who span and fired the ball into the roof of the net for the leveller.

Southend's travelling fans danced and sang the wingers name, delighted with the point their team had earned. It was a hard fought game, especially with ten men, but unlike the drubbing at Stoke, The Blues had shown great character and belief to come away from St. Andrews with a share of the spoils. Dave Webb was especially happy with his side's attitude after the final whistle. "At the end of the day, it was a smashing result for us and one which once again underlined the great fighting spirit throughout the team," smiled the happy Blues Chief.

It proved to be a point that meant Blues fell one place in the table to second due to Grimsby Town's superior goal difference, but Andy Ansah remained pleased with his side's hard fought draw and told of his personal satisfaction in scoring after being dropped for the visit of Crystal Palace earlier in the week. "Although I appreciate the boss made a change for tactical reasons, I wasn't happy to find it was me that was left out, but I like to think I've responded in the right way and proved my temperament," explained the rapid winger.

"I rolled up my sleeves and by scoring here, getting us the draw we deserved. Even when we were down to ten men I still had a gut feeling we could get something from the match. We continued to throw men forward and created chances and I'm just grateful I managed to get on the end of one of them."

Ansah, who signed for Southend in March of the previous season, had made an encouraging start to his career with Southend. He had a run of five successive starts and aside from the solitary goal he had to his name during that spell, the winger turned in some very impressive performances during the promotion run in.

Unfortunately for both Ansah and the club, an injury ruled him out for final three games of the 1989/90 season, but with Southend going on to secure promotion regardless, he would be presented with the chance to perform in Division Three after only a total thirteen league starts for both Blues and his previous club, Brentford.

Once the new campaign got under way, it was clear that Webb considered Ansah an important member of his team and after featuring in all of the first ten league games, this was very much the case.

After his performance at St. Andrews, it was a certainty that Ansah would make it eleven league starts for the trip back up north for the October 20th clash with Wigan Athletic. However, there was one surprise that Webb was about spring for that game and it was to be the recall to the first team squad for winger Martin ling.

Ling, who was one of the original four 'contract rebels' from the summer, but since then, three of those players had all agreed deals and were playing week in, week out. Only the wide midfielder still hadn't signed on with the club and was operating on a week to week basis, but after a number of eye-catching displays for the reserves, Webb had no doubts about bringing him in from the cold.

"Lingy is a quality player and his attitude has been tremendous since he re-joined us for training. He has not moaned, been ready to do everything we have asked and really thrown himself into the job of winning his first team place back."

"He has scored in each of our last two reserve games and his mere presence should be enough to keep other players currently in the side on their toes and make sure they don't get complacent," reasoned Webb.

Ling was named as the second substitute along with John Cornwell, the starting eleven remaining the same as the team that played at Birmingham City. It was going to be another hard test for Southend with Wigan's confidence on a high after the 1-0 win over Reading the previous Saturday.

'Up The Blues!'

That win for Athletic left them occupying thirteenth spot in the table, but Webb was aware of the importance of the fixture, as well the back to back home games that would follow. "Wigan is a never an easy place to go for points and they have pulled themselves up after an indifferent start to the season," said Webb.

"After Saturday we meet Exeter and Bury at home and all three games will be really hard and help prove whether we've got what it takes for our push for Division Two. Exeter proves last term in winning the Fourth Division championship and they are strong and well organised while Bury are one of my dark horses for promotion."

"If we show the same battling qualities as we did in that great draw at Birmingham last weekend then we should have nothing to fear. I keep telling the players that they have set standards for themselves and must make sure they maintain them."

"If we can come through this week with three good results then you can really reckon we are developing into a likely promotion force," he concluded.

The 'promotion force' Webb was hoping to see on display from his players was never on show at Springfield Park. In fact it was the total opposite as Blues defending returned to that similar showing at Stoke and Crystal Palace.

It took only six minutes for Wigan to take the lead when a free header from a corner made its way through to the unmarked Don Page who slid the ball into the net as Southend stood still and watched.

It was a case of déjà vu eight minutes later when the home side won another corner on the right hand side. The resulting kick was met by the head of Spencer Prior, but the ball came straight back into the area and after Peter Cawley failed to deal with it, Phil Daley drove the ball into the net for a quick-fire 2-0 lead.

After that, The Shrimpers managed to stem the flow of Wigan's attack for the remainder of the half, but without putting a dent in the home sides defence in the process.

That changed though two minutes after the re-start though when the Tilson and Butler free-kick set up Cawley who atoned for his first half error by out jumping his marker and heading into the net to give Southend a lifeline.

The Blues pushed hard for an equaliser and went close with both Butler and Tilson both being denied by goalkeeper Nigel Adkins, before Ian Benjamin saw a headed chance flash just past the post.

Then it was Wigan's turn to attack and a third goal was soon coming. The goal itself came from the penalty spot that was neatly converted by Bryan Griffiths, but it was needlessly conceded when Cawley was all over Page as the ball was played into the box.

There then followed a period of poor football in which both sides were guilty of being unable to hold onto the ball before a fourth goal came for The Latics. The goal was again a result of poor defending in allowing a cross to come in from the right win that Paul Sansome misjudged and Griffiths was presented with the simplest of tasks for his second goal of the game.

Webb immediately introduced both Ling and Cornwell in place of Ansah and Martin, but the damage had already been done. It was a hard defeat for Southend to take and brought them back down to earth with a bump after gaining ten points in the previous four fixtures. Webb was furious with his side and couldn't hide that very fact after the final whistle. "Our defending was diabolical – at least three of their goals were the direct result of woeful work by our back four and goalkeeper," he fumed.

"The one consolation is that we have not lost much ground (on Grimsby) and with two home games to come we have a great chance to get the promotion bandwagon back on the road."

In the days that followed the Wigan defeat, Webb turned his attentions away from his preparations for the Tuesday night visit of Exeter City to reward one half of his strike force with a contract extension.

It was Ian Benjamin who received the recognition for his excellent start to the season with the offer of an extra year from the club having only signed from Exeter just seven months earlier. There was no question from Blues manager as to whether the experienced number ten warranted the new deal. "Benji has been a revelation this season. He adds so much to our forward play and has hit some vital goals as well," Webb explained.

"I felt it was right to reward him for all he has done and his contract keeps him at Roots Hall at least until the end of next season."

The contract extension was welcomed by fans who, like the management team, knew how vital Benjamin had proved to be as an individual, but more importantly for the team – and in particular Brett Angell.

There was another chance to see the front two in action against Exeter who were coming to Roots Hall having only won four games out of a possible eleven and only taken two points from the last fifteen.

However, The Grecians had proved a thorn in Southend's side the previous season which saw both clubs gain promotion from Division Four by beating The Blues 2-1 both home and away, so there was a score to settle as far as Southend United were concerned.

David Webb was still without Paul Clark for the game, but there were a few raised eyebrows when the team remained the same as the one that had lost heavily at Wigan. The manager had resisted the temptation to hand starts to the likes of John Cornwell, Andy Edwards, Adam Locke and Martin Ling and as a result showed brave loyalty to the same eleven from the nightmare at Springfield Road.

It didn't take long for Southend to show that it was the right call by Webb as they flew out of the block to take a sixth minute lead. The goal came from the unlikeliest of sources too when Chris Powell found himself unmarked on the apex of the penalty area after Andy Ansah's mishit cross evaded a crowded area.

Powell's first touch was to get it under control and the second was a left footed strike that went across the diving Kevin Miller and into the far corner of the net. The young full backs first goal for the club was also his first as a professional and his delighted smile appeared across his face lit up Roots Hall.

They say you're at your most vulnerable after having just scored a goal and this proved the case as Exeter struck back immediately after the re-start. Attacking straight from the referee's whistle, The Grecians won a free kick that was taken quickly by Danny Bailey and then converted by central defender Shaun Taylor who was somehow unmarked at the far post.

Blues then took control of nearly all the rest of the first half. They had the majority of the possession and it was largely played in the visitors half of the pitch. Ansah, whose pace was causing Exeter's left back Richard Dryden all sorts of problems, went close on more than one occasion, but none of his efforts tested Miller.

Both Brett Angell and Steve Tilson also had opportunities to score, but they failed to get the shot off before being closed down by a hard working Grecian defence.

Then, after all Southend's possession, it was Exeter who came closest to getting the games third goal right on the stroke of half time. First, Peter Cawley made a superb last ditch tackle to deny Steve Neville a clear path towards Paul Sansome's goal and then Powell managed to bravely beat Bailey to a loose ball, heading it to safety only a yard from the goal line.

The second half was a fairly even affair with both sides having their keeper to thank for some tidy work between the sticks. One piece of goalkeeping from Sammy received enthusiastic applause from the home fans as he dived well to his right to keep out an effort from former Blues loanee, Mark Cooper.

Shortly after that though, Roots Hall erupted for what proved to be the match winner for the home side. A lofted ball forwards from Powell was instantly controlled by Ian Benjamin twenty yards from goal. The Southend number ten, who had the attentions of Taylor right behind him, looked for support to the left, right and then left again before deciding to go it alone and curl the most perfectly placed shot into the corner of the net past a helpless Kevin Miller.

It was a goal that was worthy of winning any game at any level and Benji's excellently executed winner had his manager in no doubts about the quality of the strike. "That was one of the best goals I've seen at Roots Hall - and there's been one or two extra special ones this season," declared Webb, before he pointed out the areas needed for improvement, despite the 2-1 win.

"What concerns me is the easier chances we are failing to tuck away. We saw enough of the ball to have wrapped up the points early on, but in the end finished up making heavy weather of it. We can't always rely on spectacular goals like the one Benji scored to collect the points."

It was a fair point and one that needed to be taken notice of because there were enough opportunities for Blues to beat Exeter out of sight over the ninety minutes. Instead, Southend could have easily drawn or lost the game had it not been for one moment of pure genius from Benjamin – who had celebrated his contract extension in style.

However, the match winner, who very much a team player on the pitch, certainly didn't change from that mantra off it either when asked about his goal. "What pleased me most was it gave us three points. As long as Southend keep winning I'm not really bothered who is scoring the goals," explained Benjamin.

Further good news came after the final whistle when the 2-2 draw Grimsby could only manage against Orient. That result meant that the victory put The Shrimpers back on top of the league with a terrific return of twenty eight points from twelve games and they also made it six wins out of six at fortress Roots Hall.

There was no doubt about it, David Webb was carrying out his belief that Southend could make it back to back promotions and with Bury the visitors to Essex four days later, Blues were heavy favourites to make it win number seven.

The possibility of Paul Clark returning for that fixture took a blow when the Skipper was forced off near the end of the reserve match versus Orient. After the match Kevin Lock, Blues assistant manager said; "He (Clark) did fairly well but was substituted near the end when he reported feeling a slight twinge. It's nothing to worry about, but he needs more treatment and I think he'll have to wait a bit longer before he can think in terms of a first team comeback."

The match itself proved a good exercise as they ran out 3-1 winners with goals coming from Martin Ling, Peter Daley and youngster Adrian West all scoring. But, it was the performance of Adam Locke that caught the eye of the watching Dave Webb with a very impressive display and one that put him firmly in contention for the visit of Bury.

One player who featured against Exeter who would now miss out due to his red card at Birmingham was vice-Captain Dave Martin. The midfield enforcer was to sit out the first of his three game ban and was to be replaced by John Cornwell, himself now becoming somewhat of a utility player for Blues.

The manager had no reservations about Cornwell's ability to play in the midfield after having been signed primarily as a centre back. "I have no qualms about putting Cornwell in midfield, although he is pretty versatile, he has probably played there more times in his career than anywhere else," explained Webb.

"If he does a good solid job then I will certainly stick by him – it's all up to John. It's no use me demanding honesty from the players if I don't do the same and it would be dishonest to leave him out if he has performed well simply because Martin is available again."

"The players here now there is competition for places and they are stupid enough to get themselves banned then they must expect to battle to win their place back. No-one can be allowed to take their first team place for granted."

Webb's stern words were clearly not meant just for Dave Martin, but also to the rest of the squad. He had wanted to build a team that could challenge for promotion and to be able to do that he needed to be able to call upon able replacements should he need them. So far into the campaign Webb had been able to do that with the likes of Andy Edwards, Christian Hyslop and Peter Cawley all coming into the side and fitting in without destabilising the rhythm and momentum that had been generated up to this point.

Webb, though, never underestimated the opposition and wasn't about to start with Bury's visit on Saturday 27th October. "They are a strong, experienced side but our home form has been tremendous and it will be they who come here with a little trepidation," said Blues boss.

Although Webb's verdict of Bury's mentality about visiting Roots Hall may well have been correct, they themselves had shown good pedigree over the previous five matches having only lost the once.

But, the Southend Chief was demanding his side approach the game in the right matter from the first minute to the last in order to get the right result. "I would like to see us tighten up at the back and concentrate for ninety minutes instead of putting ourselves under pressure by giving sloppy goals away. If we do that and continue to show the same fire and flair up front then I am sure our fans will be celebrating another Roots Hall win."

The enforced change of Cornwell coming in for the banned Martin was Webb's only alteration to the side that defeated Exeter. With both first choice and vice-Captain unavailable for The Shrimpers, the aforementioned Cornwell was surprisingly given the nod to take over the armband duties for the afternoon. Adam Locke earned a spot on the subs' bench alongside young defender, Andy Edwards.

It looked like being an afternoon of normal service after Blues went into a sixteenth minute lead with Brett Angell managing to steer a volley into the net from close range after Dean Austin's long throw had somehow found its way to the young striker.

That goal though, only seemed to inspire Bury in upping the game and they did just that. Southend began to struggle all over the park and the inevitable equaliser came only nine minutes later when Phil Parkinson scored while Blues back line didn't respond to Bury's neat approach play.

The away side continued to pin Blues back and it was the performance of a strong defensive back line, particularly Spencer Prior that managed to keep Bury at bay.

On the occasions that Bury did manage to get past Prior and co. they found Sansome in inspired form and a superb full length save to tip the ball over the bar was the pick of the bunch.

With the scores somehow still all square at half time, Blues came out to right the wrongs of a poor first half. They started to outwork and outplay Bury and went close on numerous occasions themselves through efforts from Ian Benjamin and Peter Butler soon after the re-start.

The home fans didn't have long to wait for the Southend to take the lead. After some fine work from Andy Ansah and Benjamin on the right wing, the ball was worked across the face of the goal to where Steve Tilson was waiting to simply side foot the ball home at the far post for 2-1.

On sixty-five minutes Blues had the perfect opportunity to further the lead when Ian Benjamin was adjudged to have been fouled in the area, but in the absence of regular taker Martin, Angell saw his effort well saved by Gary Kelly to keep the deficit at only one.

Southend, heeding their manager's pre-match words, kept control of the remainder of the match and went close to adding to their lead, but Kelly was in fine form and the final score line finished at 2-1 to The Shrimpers.

It was very much a game of two halves, but nevertheless the all-important three points meant Blues 100% home record was upheld and that meant that Southend continued to sit at the summit of Division Three.

After the game, Tilly spoke of his surprise at seeing his effort go in past a keeper in great form. "Andy Ansah and In Benjamin worked it in from the right, but I over ran it and the ball was just behind me, but somehow I got my foot back and hooked it in," said the relieved midfielder.

"It was great to see the ball in the net because up until then we had struggled and looked to be hard pressed to claim one point let alone three. The goal sparked us off and in the end we could have had three or four," added Tilson.

It was true that performance hadn't been great to begin with and even though another three points were in the bag, manager Dave Webb was once again frustrated at his team's inability to take dominate the opposition for the duration of the game.

"This is the tenth game we have won by the odd goal this season and again was a match we should have claimed with a few more to spare," he claimed, before speaking of the Angell's penalty miss. "I blame myself for the penalty miss with regular spot-kick specialist David Martin out suspended I didn't really designate anyone for the job. I should have given it to Peter Cawley because no-one in the club strikes a better dead ball than him and although the keeper made a good save to keep out Brett's effort, I don't think Cawley would have given him a sniff of the ball."

Prior to the afternoon's proceedings, Webby picked up the manager of the month award for September and admitted the hard earned victory was a good way to start his weekend. "It all came right in the end and it was nice to celebrate my award with another three points – it was the icing on the cake," he smiled.

The win left Southend at the top of Division Two as October drew to a close and this was despite Grimsby's impressive win over third placed Stoke City. Blues led The Mariners by a single point, but there was then a further six point gap to Stoke City.

It had been a marvellous and unexpected start to the season for Dave Webb and his squad. But, as The Shrimpers sat at the top of the tree after thirteen games, there was now a slow, but steady increase in the belief that Webb had transmitted to his players from the beginning and it was now reaching the terraces. The fans had started to dare to dream that promotion was a possibility – and as supporters of Southend United, that was a dangerous – and unusual - thing to do.

'Up The Blues!'

Division Three table up to October 27th 1990

	TEAM	Pl	W	D	L	W	D	L	Pts	GD
1	Southend United	13	7	0	0	3	1	2	31	7
2	Grimsby Town	13	5	2	0	4	1	1	30	13
3	Stoke City	13	3	1	2	4	2	1	24	6
4	Tranmere Rovers	12	3	2	2	3	2	0	22	12
5	Brentford	13	3	1	2	3	3	1	22	3
6	Cambridge United	13	2	2	3	3	3	0	20	5
7	Birmingham City	13	2	4	0	2	4	1	20	2
8	Wigan Athletic	13	4	1	1	2	1	4	20	0
9	Bury	13	4	1	1	1	3	3	19	0
10	Leyton Orient	13	5	0	1	1	1	5	19	0
11	Reading	13	2	3	2	3	0	3	18	3
12	Chester City	13	2	1	3	3	2	2	18	2
13	Bradford City	13	3	0	4	2	2	2	17	-2
14	Huddersfield Town	13	3	1	3	2	1	3	17	-2
15	Preston North End	13	2	3	2	2	2	2	17	-4
16	Exeter City	13	2	2	2	2	1	4	15	0
17	**Swansea City**	13	2	3	1	2	0	5	15	-6
18	Bolton Wanderers	13	2	2	3	2	1	3	15	-6
19	Bournemouth	12	2	3	0	1	2	4	14	1
20	Fulham	13	3	2	2	0	3	3	14	-3
21	Shrewsbury Town	13	1	2	4	1	2	3	10	-4
22	Crewe Alexandra	13	1	2	4	1	1	4	9	-7
23	Mansfield Town	13	0	1	5	2	2	3	9	-8
24	Rotherham United	13	2	2	2	0	1	6	9	-12

November 1990

"You can use all the superlatives you like and it won't mirror the achievements of our players" - David Webb

Setting the pace at the top of the table meant that Southend were now there to be shot at by every other team in the league. They had earned their place at the summit of Division Three, but that now presented Blues with the added pressure of teams looking to make a statement by beating David Webb's team.

That was to be the case when Southend travelled to Griffin Park, home of Brentford Football Club, on Sunday November 4th – a game which had the unusual kick off time of 11.30a.m. The Bees had enjoyed a very good start to the season themselves having accumulated twenty-two points from thirteen games, a total which left them in fifth position.

Brentford manager Phil Holder had players within his squad that deserved instant respect and would give Blues cause for concern. Midfielders Keith Jones and Neil Smillie were very creative operators, whereas strikers Gary Blissett and Marcus Gayle were a dangerous proposition for any team in the division.

One player in The Shrimpers ranks who was keen to get one over his former club was winger Andy Ansah. The move from West London to Essex came eight months prior to this encounter, but it wasn't a move that left Ansah with any regret.

"It was the best move I could have made career wise and I don't regret joining Blues for a minute. (Scoring) One goal (against them) would be great, two even better, but I don't really care who scores as long as we pick up three more vital points," said Ansah, before casting question marks over The Bees defence.

"I think we can do it, especially if the Brentford defence collapses as it did the last time I saw them when they lost three-nil at home to Cambridge."

'Up The Blues!'

Asked if he felt there was anything to prove to the home side and their fans, Ansah's response was short and to the point. "I don't think I need to prove myself to the Brentford fans or management – being in a side at the top of the table does the talking for me!"

The side chosen by David Webb was the same as the one that had beaten Bury 2-1, but for the trip to Griffin Park, Ian Benjamin was handed the captaincy instead of John Cornwell in the absence of Paul Clark and Dave Martin.

Unfortunately, the official team sheet that confirmed this and Southend's starting line-up was late in reaching the referee after The Blues team coach had fallen foul to the unpredictable London traffic. Even Webb's dramatic attempts to make the deadline by jumping into first team physio's Alan Raw's wife's car proved futile due to the heavily congested roads that got the better of Shrimpers boss and his team.

There wasn't even time for a warm up prior to the game and with only twenty minutes remaining until the match was to start, Blues were forced into a desperate rush to get changed and get out onto the pitch in time for the morning kick off.

It was hardly the ideal preparation for a professional club to adopt and the performance was one that had Southend looking exactly like a side that had been stuck in traffic as opposed to a side who were leading Division Three.

Their passing was lacking the sort of fluency that had taken them to the top of the table and the understanding just wasn't there for large parts of the game. However, there was one department that Blues did match their opponents in and that was their work rate.

The game proved scrappy and that was probably down to the effort and closing down coming from Webb's boys in blue. They managed to stifle Brentford and restrict them to as few chances as they had managed to create for themselves in the opening half hour.

Then, against the run of play, Southend managed to put together two passes that presented Brett Angell with the opportunity to set Andy Ansah free on the right wing. The former Bee forced his way into the area and fire a cross-cum-shot across the face of the goal where stand in skipper Ian Benjamin was on hand to slide the ball into the roof of the net in what proved to be the last action of a very forgettable first half.

'Up The Blues!'

As the second half got under way it was clear that the home side were not going to allow their visitors to frustrate them any longer. Straight away Paul Sansome once again underlined his agility between the sticks by somehow managing to turn away Simon Ratcliffe's long range effort. Minutes later Sammy was at it again, this time denying the same player at close range.

Brentford kept coming at Southend hard and looking for an equaliser, but The Shrimpers were standing firm with Spencer Prior relishing his aerial battle with Marcus Gayle and as time passed, the young defender was getting the better of his opponent more often than not.

The Bees then caught a lucky break when Ansah received his marching orders after he was booked for his second mistimed tackle with only twelve minutes remaining. This only served to inspire Blues to hang on as Brentford failed to penetrate the Essex sides defence, much to the disappointment of the majority of the 8,021 crowd.

It was a hard fought and perhaps undeserved three points for Southend, but Webb refused to put the result down as a fortuitous one in the post-match interview. "Some people are saying we were lucky today, but I felt we got our reward for a real battling display and made our own luck. Our lads chased and fought for everything - they did themselves and the club proud," underlined Blues boss before giving his take on Ansah's red card. "Let's just say that I felt there were far worse things going on out there from both sides that went unpunished. But Andy's dismissal only seemed to make us dredge up more spirit and resilience...it might have done us a favour in the end!"

Paul Sansome was the obvious choice for Southend's man of the match after several fine saves and the former Millwall stopper was pleased with the result which also meant he had kept only his second clean sheet of the season. "It was not a classic match, but you will have a lot of those in a season when the points go to the more committed and that summed us up today. We defended superbly well and it was nice for me that anything the lads in front of me missed, I held onto."

It was time once again for David Webb's attentions to switch from the league to a cup competition with the visit of Aldershot in The Leyland Daf Trophy preliminary round just over forty-eight hours later on Tuesday November 6th.

The remit was clear as far as The Shrimpers Chief was concerned; to simply go as far as they could in the tournament. "This is our big chance to get to a Wembley final, which is the dream of every club and player and nothing must be allowed to side-track us from that goal," explained Webb.

The opponents, who had made the same trip in round one of The Rumbelows Cup back in August, had more pressing worries about their future with serious monetary concerns that had left their very existence in serious jeopardy.

However, Southend were determined to go about the job in hand in a professional way with Webb promising that Aldershot's problems wouldn't hinder his side's preparations. This was underlined when he revealed that the team chosen for the game was going to be unchanged from the one that had been victorious over Brentford two days previous.

"I have decided to stick with what I believe is our best side. The more they play together the better understanding they will develop," reasoned Webb.

"We will need to be at our sharpest to ensure that Aldershot don't bring us down. They will come here with absolutely nothing to lose and we must keep our concentration and not go out thinking we only have to turn up to win – that would be fatal. We adopted a professional approach in our last encounters (the Rumbelows Cup ties) and must make sure we do the same again."

There was a disappointingly low crowd of only 1,281 inside Roots Hall for what was, in all reality, a minor cup competition that fell a distant second in Southend's fans priorities at that time in the season. However, those that did make the effort to support their team were treated to an unbelievable evening's football with record equalling victory for Blues.

The goal drama started as early as the sixth minute when midfielder Steve Tilson ran unchallenged to collect a pass from Peter Cawley before cutting in from the left to fire a rare right footed shot past Jon Sheffield in the visitors goal.

The Shrimpers were playing with a real confidence and seemed able to create chances at will. This was displayed when the second goal of the game came eight minutes after the opener. Again, it was Blues number six Steve Tilson, who doubled the advantage with a well guided header following Andy Ansah's trickery on the right wing.

More was to come for David Webb's table toppers, this time it was the turn of ace marksman Brett Angell. Tilson's corner kick was flicked on by John Cornwell to the waiting striker whose one touch and volley into the net in front of The North Bank made the score 3-0 with only twenty-five minutes on the clock.

Southend added a fourth seven minutes later when Aldershot's high back line could only watch as Angell capitalised on the advancing Sheffield's miss-kick to have the easiest of tasks for his second goal of the game.

With the home fans already in dreamland, Angell then managed to complete a very decisive first half hat-trick for a 5-0 lead at the break. This time, it came from the striker's head after Ansah linked up very well with Ian Benjamin before crossing for the £100,000 man to convert with relative ease.

Southend would have been forgiven for taking the foot of the gas in the second half. The tie was already won, but with Webb's words of maintaining a "professional approach" ringing in their ears, Blues went about endorsing exactly that.

On fifty-five minutes they got goal number six when Tilson's second attempt at a delivery from the right was superbly headed home by Spencer Prior for the defenders first goal at Roots Hall since August 1989.

Goals number seven, eight and nine all came in a ten minute spell midway through the second half from Ansah, Angell - his fourth of the night - and Benjamin as Webb's side were now not only in pursuit of double figures, but a club record as well!

The chants of "we want ten...we want ten..." from The Blue Army did not go unnoticed by the players and they only seemed too happy to please as that unimaginable figure was reached. Peter Butler broke from midfield and drove a shot goalwards that proved too hot for Sheffield to handle. Benjamin was quickly on hand to keep the ball alive before laying it back for Tilson to complete his first senior hat-trick with a simple tap in, making the score Southend 10 Aldershot 0.

It was fairy-tale football from Blues and there was under ten minutes remaining until a new club record was surely about to be set by the rampant home side. The current record up to that point was the two 10-1 victories over Golders Green in 1934 and, thirty-four years later over Brentwood. Both results came in The F.A. Cup and now, in 1990, Roots Hall was poised to celebrate a record breaking score line, but there was to be yet one more goal – and it was one that prevented that record from being broken.

It was great testament to Aldershot that they pushed forwards at 10-0 down and scored a cracker of a consolation goal. It was Dale Banton who worked his way in from the left past Dean Austin and curled a peach of a shot that flew past a diving Paul Sansome and into the corner of the net. The strike was met with ironic applause from The North Bank who had witnessed an absolutely magical night at The Hall and despite the all-time record win not being surpassed, the 10-1 score line now had three occupants in Blues eighty-four year history.

A bewildered Aldershot manager, Len Walker, called the match, "the most embarrassing moment of my football career," before adding "I don't think I ever got beat by double figures when I played in the Cubs!"

His opposite number, however, was overjoyed at the score line and performance, but in typical fashion, he insisted his players would keep their feet firmly on the ground. "What can you say about a display like that? You can use all the superlatives you like and it won't mirror the achievement of our players," said a delighted Webb.

"I want them to celebrate tonight's win because results like this only come once in a lifetime. But, I can assure you it will be business as usual when they report back for training on Thursday and start preparing for the Fulham game. There won't be time for a heads in the clouds attitude, I'll see to that!"

It appeared that Webb's words were already being heeded by his players as four goal hero, Brett Angell, echoed the manager's sentiments - himself having half an eye on Fulham's league visit four days later. "The lads were simply magnificent tonight, but we are all professional enough to know that we must keep our feet firmly on the ground and not get carried away by this result – the Fulham game is one we must focus all our attention on. Results like this are great for morale, but we must not let it side-track us from our sole objective and that's promotion from Division Three."

Of course, the league was obviously Blues number one concern, but the scale of victory over Aldershot did not go unnoticed within the football circles. Even amongst Southend supporters, it was yet more evidence to back up Webb's belief in his players and it was a belief that was now growing game by game within fans own minds.

The concerns over the departing David Crown prior to the season starting had well and truly gone as a result of the prolific Brett Angell who now had twelve goals to his name in all competitions. His partnership with Ian Benjamin had clicked instantly and the young striker was clearly enjoying his time with his new club.

However, it wasn't just Angell who was amongst the goals for The Shrimpers. They had scored a total of forty-three goals in all competitions. Of that tally twelve belonged to Angell, Benjamin had seven, Dave Martin had rattled home six, Steve Tilson had scored five and Andy Ansah had a respectable return of three. That's thirty-three goals accounted for by five different players and that was an extremely impressive statistic.

The ability to score from all over the pitch was clearly serving Webb's side very well. There was a distinct pattern to the style of play that presented many players with the opportunity to score goals and it often started from Paul Sansome. Both Sammy's drop, and goal kicks, was being used as a means to get the ball into the final third of the pitch very quickly where Angell and Benjamin would battle to win the headers. From there the likes of Butler, Tilson and Ansah would get in close, look to win the second ball and then play from there.

By no means, though, did this make Southend primarily a long ball team. There was an obvious strength in the striker's aerial ability, so why not use it? Some of the goals scored after they had won their headers were simply breath-taking with the movement off the ball, as well as the football being played, a joy to watch.

Blues were opening teams up and, at times, scoring at will and while that was making them a real force going forwards, only the two clean sheets at the other end was a slight cause for concern.

Both those shut outs had come away from home, which in itself was an amazing stat given that Southend still had a 100% home record in the league. It was that form at Roots Hall that had more than helped propel them into pole position three months into the season and it was a record that faced another stern test with the visit of Fulham on the back of the record equalling 10-1 win.

Prior to the game, manager Dave Webb reiterated the importance of his team not losing focus on Fulham's impending visit.

He also expressed his joy that his leader scorer, Brett Angell, was in tune with Webb's own way of thinking.

"I was pleased to read comments from Brett in the Echo after the game when he rightly said that the team was not to get too side-tracked from the main job of winning promotion to Division Two. That's just what I have been impressing on the players – if they go out with their heads still in the clouds then Fulham could bring them down to earth with an almighty bump," explained Webb, who then added, "but I am sure we have the players here who won't allow a one off result like Aldershot go to their heads. We have worked hard to where we are in the league and the lads are in no mood to start throwing it away now."

The 10-1 triumph had once again raised the bar for Southend and Webb was keen to see the impetus of having scored a glutton of goals at Roots Hall set them up for the forthcoming match. "I want to see a continuation of that tomorrow when we should endeavour to keep Fulham under pressure from the word go. We have exciting players in the side who look good going forward and it's up to us to our authority on the game early on," he said.

There was food for thought for Webb over his team selection with the return to the squad of Dave Martin, fresh from his three game suspension for his red card at Birmingham. Martin's replacement, John Cornwell had performed well for the previous three games, but Webb wasn't keen on confirming a decision either way.

"I won't make up my mind until late, but David knows he had no divine right to a first team place," Webb pointed out. "It was his own fault that he got sent off and Cornwell has done well since coming into the side, improving with every match," he added.

Fulham, who had been widely tipped as promotion challengers, had suffered a very indifferent start to their season. Having yet to win away from Craven Cottage, they found themselves lying fifth from bottom, but they still would pose a threat because of the quality they had in their squad. Manager Alan Dicks, a former Shrimper who played eighty games for Blues in the early 1960's, was now under a bit of pressure to turn things around for his club, starting with the trip to Essex.

When matchday arrived, it came as no surprise that it was John Cornwell who held onto the number four shirt to retain his place in the eleven that remained unchanged from the one that demolished

Aldershot. There was a change amongst the substitutes and that was Martin being preferred to defender Andy Edwards.

The game started well for the home side and after nine minutes of action, Webb's decision to stick with Cornwell paid dividends when the utility man's close range strike flashed past one time Southend keeper, Jim Stannard for a 1-0 lead.

If the 5,808 people (the largest crowd of the season) in attendance expected Blues to push on and perform in the same manner as they did four days earlier, they were very much mistaken. Fulham, belittling their league position, played some lovely football and kept Southend pinned in their half for the vast majority of the first forty-five minutes.

In fact, if it wasn't for the two wonderful saves from Paul Sansome to twice deny Gary Brazil, the west London side would have gone into the interval with a lead, rather than being one behind.

As the second half began, Blues come out with a little more purpose and should have doubled their advantage when Brett Angell was through on goal, but he delayed his shot just long enough for Justin Skinner to make the tackle.

Fulham then began taking the game to Southend once more and got their rewards when, on fifty-three minutes, Brazil collected Angell's poor headed clearance to finally get the better of Sammy from eighteen yards.

The away team, now with their tails up, kept Blues pinned back and Sansome was once again called into action with a great full length save, this time thwarting Gordon Davies.

As the half wore on, it seemed inevitable that there would be a winning goal and it looked like it would be Fulham who got it. Dicks' side were finding it alarmingly easy to cut through the middle of Southend's defence. Webb reacted to counter this by bringing on Dave Martin for Steve Tilson to play as a third centre back in an attempt to shore things up. Martin's introduction did indeed stem the Fulham attacks and with no more action of note, the game finished level.

That tactical change by Webb said all that was needed to know about the mind-set of Blues manager and the way the game was going at that time. Fulham racked up an impressive corner count of ten to Southend's five and there was there was no point underplaying

Paul Sansome's role in the 1-1 draw – without him Fulham would have left with all the points, instead of just one.

Jim Stannard dealt out the praise for his opposite number after the final whistle. "Sammy was simply brilliant - Southend can thank him for their point. That's the best we have played all season and I felt we did enough to win the game, but Sansome stopped everything," rued the Fulham goalkeeper.

It couldn't really be argued that The Shrimpers were fortunate to earn a draw and in the post-match press conference, Dave Webb certainly didn't try to. "Fulham set us a lot of problems and our general display was far below the high standards we have set this term. They put us under the sort of pressure we normally exert on other teams and in the end I was happy to settle for a draw," was his honest assessment.

With the 100% home record now gone, Webb was keen to take a positive from the match and perhaps lower the expectancy level that had now been attached to his team. "This result might have done us a favour in the long run because it might help convince one or two people that there is still a long way to go before we can start talking about promotion. But I am sure the lads will have learned a lesson and will be even more determined to put it right."

It was true that there was a slight air of disappointment at having drawn with Fulham, but overall the club and everyone surrounding it was over the moon with the start Southend had made. It was the sort of start that was never, ever expected – even in the fans wildest dreams - but Webb was proving to be a class act and the hope was that the form showed could be maintained all the way through until May. But, even for the most optimistic Shrimper, there was a deep lying belief that things wouldn't stay this rosy for that long – after all this was Southend United!

The 1-1 draw versus Fulham left Blues still sitting at the top of the table with a single point lead over second placed Grimsby Town and there was now an eight point gap between SUFC and third placed Stoke City. The table would remain that way for a fortnight as the attention now switched from league to The F.A. Cup and Southend faced a tricky away trip to Brisbane Road, home of fellow Division Three side Leyton Orient.

In the week leading up to the first round tie, Blues second string won 3-1 away at Slough Town. The performance of winger

Martin Ling stood out as Webb considered Lingy or Adam Locke for a place in the first team squad for the short trip to east London.

That wasn't the only consideration for Webb because captain Paul Clark was once again fit enough to be considered for a recall after a hamstring injury forced him to spend over a month on the sidelines. Clark managed to complete the ninety minutes at Slough and he put in a performance that confirmed his injury worries were well and truly behind him.

"He did exceptionally well – well enough to come into consideration for the Orient clash," was Webb's verdict.

With the manager keeping his cards close to his chest over the two obvious decisions he had to make, he was pleased that the trio of Dean Austin, Steve Tilson and Peter Butler all recovered from their slight knocks suffered against Fulham in time to be considered for Orient. That news, of course, was welcomed by Webb, but he pointed out that a fit squad didn't always make his job an easier.

"That's a situation I'm not going to complain about," he said. "Every manager would rather be confronted with the problems of who to leave out as opposed to wondering if he can raise a decent enough team. At the end of the day it means that I will be unpopular with those players who don't make the line-up. But that's part of the job and one has to accept that it's impossible to please everyone."

"My job is to pick the best possible team for any given game. I can appreciate the disappointment felt by those who may not get the nod, but they know only too well that I will not hesitate to give them their chance if others fail to come up to expectations."

It also emerged in the lead up to The F.A. Cup match that The Blues Chief was on the lookout for new faces to add to his squad, despite the marvellous start the club had made to the campaign.

"Naturally I'm delighted by the magnificent efforts of the players during the first three months of the season to get us to the top of the table," he said, "this is the time to try and consolidate, not sit back with a smug smile of satisfaction."

"For, while the players here have proved they are capable of competing with the best in the division, I am only too aware of the pitfalls ahead. Things like loss of form, a bad run of injuries and a crop of suspensions can play havoc with your plans and one has to be prepared to meet and overcome those sorts of problems."

The reasoning behind Webb's quest to strengthen an already competitive squad still, could not be argued with. His constant desire to improve and keep on improving also let the current batch of players know that there could be no resting on their laurels in the belief that they have achieved anything just yet. The message the manager was sending out was clear – the standards had now been set and falling below them would not be tolerated.

Over recent seasons The F.A. Cup had not been kind to Southend as their record of progressing past the first round only once in the previous eight years proved. In the 1989 – 1990 season the first round draw saw David Webb and his team travel to non-league Aylesbury, nicknamed The Ducks.

Blues were top of Division Four at the time of the tie and heavy favourites against their non-league counterparts who were 5/1 with the bookies to beat Southend. Webb had underlined the importance of the game to Aylesbury and warned his team against any thought that they would just simply have to turn up to progress into round two.

So, it came as a massive shock and disappointment for Blues boss when he saw his team crash out to an eightieth minute Glen Donegal header that sent the non-leaguers through to the next round and The Shrimpers out with their tails firmly between their legs. The verdict from Webby was that Southend had "let themselves down" and that they had gone about the job in the most "unprofessional manner."

Speaking about the Aylesbury defeat twelve months earlier, Webb recalled how his side were in a no win situation. "Going to Aylesbury was a trip into the unknown and we became victims of a giant killing after what was a flat and totally uninspiring performance. We were on a hiding to nothing, especially as we were away from home, but full marks to Aylesbury who lifted their game on the day and deserved to win," he remembered before turning his attentions back to the job in hand in East London.

"This time we know what we are up against and I am looking forward to what should be a cracking cup tie. Orient have, like ourselves, made a very good start to the season and are currently fourth in the table which gives a measure of the task we face."

"We must overcome Orient (to progress) – a side I rate as one of the best in the Third Division. It won't be easy and we must go out with the same attitude we showed at Brentford in our last away game. Hopefully we shall also be backed by a big and noisy following from Southend – anyone who was at the Brentford and Cambridge matches will know what a lift that can give to the team."

The Southend manager also took the unusual step of revealing his team on the day before the game, resisting the obvious temptation to recall David Martin and a fit again Paul Clark to the starting eleven. "I did toy with the idea of making a change or two, but in the end opted to stick by the lads who have won three games and drawn one of the last four games," confirmed Webb.

"They deserve another chance to play together, but must know that they cannot afford to relax with such quality players as Clark and Martin waiting in the wings. Adam Locke, too, has looked good in the reserves and is itching to get his big chance in the first team. I think he could prove a very good player indeed and once he forces his way into the side will be very hard to displace."

The weather on the day of the match was typical for the month of November – cold, dull and wet. The game itself replicated those miserable conditions as the two teams cancelled each other out for the most part of a poor first half.

There was hardly a chance of note from either team and only an Ian Benjamin header that was ruled out for offside was the only time Blues travelling fans had anything to cheer.

Despite the lacklustre performance throughout the opening half, Webb's main concern was the injury to John Cornwell who had damaged his ankle ligaments on the half hour mark. Dave Martin was introduced to the action in his place, but it was a tough break for Cornwell who had turned in some impressive performances over the past few games during Martin's absence through suspension.

The second half started brighter, particularly for the away side. Southend managed to get the ball in Orient's final third and carve out three decent chances. First, Benjamin saw his shot well saved by Paul Heald to win a corner. Minutes later Dean Austin, up from full back, tried to score with an ambitious effort that went just wide and, on sixty-five minutes, Steve Tilson's header just crept the wrong side of the post when perhaps it was easier to score.

But, as often is the case in football, it was Orient who got the opening goal after surviving some pressure from their opponents. There was sixty-seven minutes gone when Steve Castle capitalised on

'Up The Blues!'

Peter Cawley's missed opportunity to clear his lines and rifle home the ball for an undeserved 1-0 lead.

That goal sparked the start of a crazy seventeen minute spell that saw a further four goals with the first of which came in the form of an equaliser for Blues just two minutes after going behind.

Brett Angell was the scorer of that goal after Heald could only parry Tilson's shot straight back into Blues number eleven's path and he managed to prod the ball home right in front of Southend's travelling supporters. That gave an almighty lift to those in the away terrace and chants of 'One Brett Angell...there's only one Brett Aaaannngggelllll..." drowned out the home fans.

Those cheers and chants were soon cancelled out as Orient unbelievably went straight up the other end and instantly went back in front. Straight from the kick off, striker Kevin Nugent outworked Spencer Prior to allow Danny Carter to deliver a deep cross towards Greg Berry. Berry, inexplicably unmarked, headed the ball back across goal to where Nugent had made a storming run into the area and he powerfully headed the ball home.

A further five minutes later, the home fans had more reason to celebrate. Again the defending from Southend was poor, failing to react to a quickly taken free-kick and Berry's low centre was side footed past Sansome by Castle for Orient's third goal in ten minutes.

Blues did battle on and even though Adam Locke, who was on as a replacement for the concussed Cawley, did instigate Angell's second goal of the game – Southend were unable to score a third that would have forced a replay.

Apart from the down side of yet another exit at the first hurdle in The F.A. Cup, the defending for all three goals infuriated David Webb. "We defended poorly. We were sloppy and Orient must have thought it was their birthday the number of gifts we gave them. It's very disappointing to come here, score two goals against a side which has only conceded five in the league at home all season and still lose," he said.

Goalkeeper Paul Sansome, who hadn't really been troubled up until the sixty-seventh minute, echoed the managers take on the below par defending. "We seem to have spells in a game when we go to sleep, lose concentration at the back and get punished," was Sammy's view, before he added, "having pulled it back to one – one, we should have just tried to consolidate, but we didn't and paid the penalty."

Webb was obviously an angry man and set about eradicating these continuous defensive errors that had seen his team keep only two clean sheets in all competitions. He had received an approach from Exeter City for centre back Peter Cawley a few weeks prior to the Orient game, but turned it down. Now he was ready to listen to what Devon club had to say as he looked to tighten up his back four.

The offer for Cawley was to take him on a free transfer and Webb explained his reasoning for letting his player talk to Exeter's manager Terry Cooper. "Exeter came in some while ago, but our injury situation was such that I could not entertain letting him go. But things have improved recently and I told Exeter that they could talk to the lad."

"I would expect him to go there providing the personal terms come up to what he wants, it's down to Cawley now."

The return to full fitness of Paul Clark was clearly a major part in allowing Cawley the opportunity to leave. As well as Clark, there were sufficient options for Webb to choose from with youngsters Spencer Prior and Andy Edwards able to perform in that position. There was also John Cornwell and Dave Martin who could play at the back so there was no cause for immediate concern that Cawley's departure had left Blues light in terms of options for centre back.

It was back to the league for Southend in the attempt to get back to winning ways with a trip to Reading. The Berkshire club had so far had a fairly average start to the season with a return of twenty-one points from the fifteen games played. However, like The Shrimpers, they had been eliminated from the F.A. Cup in round one – Essex non-league outfit Colchester United beating them 2-1 at Layer Road.

Reading, though, boasted Trevor Senior, Mick Gooding and Michael Gilkes in their squad and Southend would have to be prepared for another hard game – something that did not escape boss, David Webb.

"Reading were knocked out of the cup at Colchester last weekend and I should think they will come out with all guns blazing in an attempt to wipe out the memory of that defeat. We won't underestimate Reading, who on their day can be very dangerous opposition," he pointed out.

As far as team selection was concerned there were some enforced changes that had to be made. Peter Cawley's decision to accept the move to Exeter meant that he would obviously have to be replaced in the heart of The Shrimpers back four.

The transfer brought an end to the central defender's four month spell at Roots Hall during which he had made a total of nine starts for the club in four competitions. The decision to allow the player to leave suggested that Webb thought there were better options available, not only at the club at that time, but in terms of potential targets too. The defence was seemingly an area that remained a work in progress as far as personnel were concerned.

Cawley's replacement was to be Paul Cark, who had further shown manager that he had now recovered from his hamstring injury by featuring in the reserves 3-1 win over Cambridge in a midweek fixture.

This was welcoming news for Webb and he was very pleased to have his Captain back for the trip to Reading. "Clarky is my type of player – someone who doesn't know how to give less than a hundred per cent and refuses to accept the word defeat. I am sure he will help bring stability to the back four which is basically young and inexperienced," he enthused and then added, "Paul has now recovered from his injury and showed on Wednesday in the reserves against Cambridge that he is raring to go."

Another position that had to be filled was on the right side of midfield due to the suspension of Andy Ansah. Webb confirmed that the number nine shirt would be worn by Adam Locke who, not only impressed in a cameo performance at Orient, but also in the reserve match against Cambridge.

Southend's man in charge felt that the player he signed from Crystal Palace in the summer was ready for the step up. "I am sure Adam Locke won't let the team down on his league debut," confidently said.

"Adam has tremendous ability and providing he keeps his head (he) could make a big impression. He is a good all-rounder – superb in the tackle and with the ability to take players on. He also has tremendous vision and tight control. I know he prefers to play a more central role rather than having to go wide, but he has enough natural ability to fill that spot"

Webb also felt that once Locke was playing in the team, he wouldn't give up his position without an almighty fight. "Adam has improved by leaps and bounds and is desperate to get his league chance. I don't think he will be prepared to give it up once he is in possession."

The third change that forced the boss' was due to the ankle ligament injury John Cornwell suffered at Orient. The injury would mean the versatile Cornwell would face several weeks on the sidelines and that allowed David Martin to come back into the starting line-up. The two substitutes named for the game at Elm Park was Martin Ling and Christian Hyslop.

Southend started the match like a team wanting to show the rest of the league that they were deservedly in top spot– they really looked like they had a point to prove. Peter Butler, seemingly buoyed by having the returning Martin alongside him, set the tempo that never really let Reading into the game.

If it was Butler providing the drive for The Blues, then it was quality coming from the flanks that began cutting Reading open. Steve Tilson was proving effective on the left, but Adam Locke on the opposite wing was having an absolute field day. Reading's Michael Gilkes just couldn't live with the winger's skill and creativity.

That became increasingly evident as the half went on and on thirty-nine minutes Locke's quick feet won a free kick on the right hand side. Tilson took the kick and his brilliant inswinger was met by the head of midfielder Martin who powerfully guided the ball into the back of the net.

It was the midfielder's seventh goal of the season and one that gave The Shrimpers a solitary goal lead despite their superiority warranting more in the opening forty-five minutes.

The second half proved different for one main reason – Southend started to convert the chances that they fashioned.

Just after the hour mark The Blues - playing in all yellow – doubled their advantage and the scorer was once again Dave Martin. It was Tilson who instigated the move from the right wing after his corner had been half cleared. His accurate left foot then picked out Brett Angell and the forward had enough time to tee up Martin who fired in a left footed shot that was too hot for Steve Francis in the home side's goal.

A third goal followed just six minutes later and yet again it was created on the right wing. Dave Martin won the ball well which allowed Locke to take over and deliver a superb deep cross that evaded everyone bar Steve Tilson who had the easiest task of knocking the ball over the goal line in front the jubilant travelling fans.

Those who had made the trip to Reading were witnessing a top performance by their team and, at 3-0 up, didn't even mind the getting a soaking in the open air terrace in the cold November rain.

The confidence that a three goal cushion gives a team allowed Southend were able to play some 'ole' football by switching the play, keeping possession and creating further chances, so it was hardly a surprise when a fourth goal came along for Blues.

It came on seventy-one minutes with Locke once again being the architect from the right wing. His cross was perfect for Angell to get his name on the score sheet after the striker had the time to control the ball, steady himself and finish well. Angell celebrated right in front of the Southend fans, arms aloft and revelling in the adulation from the blue army behind the goal.

And Southend just kept on coming forward, always looking to add to their afternoon's goal tally. Angell perhaps should have done better, but was unable to direct his effort the right side of the post and his strike partner Ian Benjamin also saw an effort miss the target.

The game then slowed down as The Shrimpers began taking their foot off the gas a little. Too Reading's credit, though, they then tried to take advantage and after winning a corner with five minutes left to play, they pulled back a goal. The corner brought a smart save out of Paul Sansome, but Steve Moran was on hand to scramble the ball over the line.

Almost instantly after their first, the home side then grabbed a second after Southend's back line were caught napping. It was a long ball over the top that gave Trevor Senior something to chase. The striker beat both Clark and Prior to the ball and bared down on Sammy's goal before toe poking the ball to the side of him to make it 2-4.

All of a sudden the home crowd were cheering on their team as they chased the unlikeliest of comebacks. In contrast, the away fans were now biting their nails and praying for the final whistle. That was even more the case when Blues defence went missing again and

Moran found himself inexplicably clean through, but fortunately he could only drag his shot wide of the post.

That was the last action of a pulsating match and after Southend having been in complete control for all but the last five minutes of the game, Reading had almost completed the most undeserved of comebacks.

The Essex side were simply that good for the majority of the game, but defensive lapses had yet again showed reason for concern for David Webb. "We lost concentration at the end of the game and conceded two goals, that's a failing I don't want to see too often. We must learn to become a real mean machine at the back and make the opposition earn anything they get instead of giving it to them on a plate," was his honest assessment.

However, there were plenty of positives to take from the 4-2 victory that left The Shrimpers four points clear of Grimsby Town after they suffered a 1-0 reverse at home to Bolton Wanderers.

One such positive was the performance of winger Adam Locke, who enjoyed his first league start for Southend. That opportunity for Locke only came about due to Andy Ansah's suspension, but he turned in a man of the match performance that suggested he had given Webb a headache when picking his next eleven.

The twenty year old Locke was optimistic that his display on the right flank would be enough to retain his place in the team. "Andy (Ansah) will be available again next weekend and obviously it's up to the manager who he picks, but hopefully I did enough to stay in the side," he said.

Locke's first start almost never happened as he revealed that he suffered an injury scare in the midweek reserve fixture against Cambridge. "I had a fitness test before the kick-off, but it would have had to have been a really bad injury to keep me out – that's how desperate I was to grab my chance."

There was little doubt that Locke had grabbed his chance with a very impressive display and he had certainly given Webby food for thought when his attention turned towards the away trip to Rotherham the following Saturday.

But, it wasn't just Locke that shone in Reading's nightmare at Elm Park. The return of Dave Martin and Paul Clark added more steel throughout the spine of the team, while Steve Tilson on the left continued to get better as the weeks went by. The pairing of Brett Angell and Ian Benjamin continued to cause defences many problems, partly because they could both adapt their game to any situation. They worked hard, were physical, they were team players and were both deadly in front of goal – as the twenty-two goal return between them showed.

Having kept a high level of performance going throughout the early part of the season, many wondered how David Webb's side would bounce back after yet another early F.A. Cup. Add to that fact that there had been key players missing at Reading which resulted in necessary changes to the team, the trip to Berkshire was when Southend were tipped to possibly slip up.

Nothing, as it turned out, could have been further from the truth. The win at Reading was arguably the best away performance of the campaign and quickly dispelled any notions that Southend were not up to lasting the pace of a forty-six game season.

Never mind the small squad and the injuries and suspensions that it had suffered. Never mind there were bigger clubs in the division and forget about the questions that arose regarding the team spirit after that Cup defeat. The season was now sixteen games old and as it was about to enter the month of December, Southend United were still sitting pretty at the top Barclays League Division Three table.

Division Three Table up to November 24th 1990

	TEAM	Pl	W	D	L	F	A	Pts	GD
1	Southend United	16	12	2	2	33	23	38	10
2	Grimsby Town	16	10	4	2	27	14	34	13
3	Stoke City	16	8	4	4	23	16	28	7
4	Leyton Orient	16	9	1	6	22	19	28	3
5	Tranmere Rovers	16	7	4	5	28	20	25	8
6	Cambridge United	16	6	6	4	26	21	24	5
7	Bournemouth	16	6	6	4	22	17	24	5
8	Bury	16	6	6	4	24	21	24	3
9	Brentford	16	6	6	4	20	18	24	2
10	Birmingham City	16	5	9	2	18	16	24	2
11	Huddersfield Town	16	7	3	6	21	20	24	1
12	Bradford City	16	7	3	6	19	18	24	1
13	Bolton Wanderers	16	7	3	6	19	20	24	-1
14	Wigan Athletic	16	7	2	7	24	26	23	-2
15	Reading	16	6	3	7	26	26	21	0
16	**Swansea City**	16	5	4	7	15	22	19	-7
17	Chester City	16	5	3	8	18	20	18	-2
18	Preston North End	16	4	6	6	16	22	18	-6
19	Exeter City	16	4	5	7	16	17	17	-1
20	Fulham	16	3	6	7	18	23	15	-5
21	Shrewsbury Town	16	3	4	9	24	30	13	-6
22	Crewe Alexandra	16	3	4	9	21	27	13	-6
23	Mansfield Town	16	3	4	9	17	25	13	-8
24	Rotherham United	16	2	4	10	18	34	10	-16

December 1990

""We set really high standards against Grimsby and would have beaten any side in the division on that performance" – David Webb

There is an old adage in football that the Christmas month of a season will be a bigger indicator than any other as to whereabouts a team will finish. Whether it's pushing for promotion, battling to climb out of relegation danger or even seeking comfort in mid-table anonymity, the congested fixture list around Christmas can make or break a team's campaign.

David Webb's team's schedule for the festive period centred around back to back home games against Bolton Wanderers on Boxing Day and two days later versus Bradford City. These games were preceded by a trip to Chester City on the 22nd and that was to be the start of three important games in only six days.

Before attentions could turn towards that trio of fixtures, Southend faced a huge test with the visit of promotion rivals, Grimsby Town. The Mariners were due to come to Essex on December 15th and with a comfortable points cushion on the third placed side, it was going to be a mouth-watering clash between the league's top two regardless of the results in the one league fixture they each faced before they met.

As fans and the media talked up the showdown between first and second, there was two fixtures that had to be played before Webb and his players could allow themselves to turn their attentions to Grimsby.

Due to Blues early exit from The F.A. Cup, they had a spare weekend and took up the option of fulfilling their outstanding Leyland Daf group game away at Reading, who had also been dumped out of England's premier cup competition at first hurdle. Before that though, Southend made the trip up to Yorkshire for an away league fixture at Rotherham United.

'Up The Blues!'

Rotherham's season had been a disappointment to their fans with a paltry return of just ten points from their sixteen games played. That left them rooted to the bottom of the division and having only won a quarter of their eight home games. With this in mind, a visit from the league leaders was not a welcome thought.

As ever was the case, Blues man in charge would make sure his players didn't take the opposition for granted and ensure that they would approach the game in the right manner.

"Anyone who takes victory for granted in football is a fool. If you go into a match too cocksure then there's nothing more certain that you will fall flat on your face," Webb pointed out. "My message to the players will be to forget Rotherham's current troubles and treat them as if they are a top of the table side. They will be trying to knock us off our perch and we will need to be at our best to get the right reward," he added.

Webb then suggested that the confidence in his camp should be riding high. "The way we took Reading apart last Saturday must send us into action in confident mood and I want to see a repeat of that forward power plus a tightening up at the back. We lost concentration towards the end of the game and conceded two goals – that's a failing I don't want to see too often. We must learn to become a real mean machine at the back and make the opposition earn anything they get instead of giving it to them on a plate."

It was more than a concern for Southend that they had still had only managed a mere two clean sheets all season – not a particularly good return for a side leading the pack. How Blues had conceded some of their goals was very disappointing. It wasn't so much that there had been stand out poor individual displays, or that there had been a glut of glaring mistakes, but there was a problem in that part of their game and it was one that Webb was looking to solve, starting with the match at Rotherham.

The team for the top versus bottom encounter would have an enforced change from the victory at Reading the previous Saturday. The stand out player in that game was Adam Locke who more than impressed in deputising for the suspended Andy Ansah, but Locke would be absent due to him suffering with a calf strain.

The obvious choice to come in for Locke was Ansah, available once again having completed his one match ban. However, the speedy winger was also ruled out Webb's plans after suffering a thigh injury in training during the build-up to the weekend.

The attention then turned towards Martin Ling who was still a peripheral figure at the club and had yet to force his way into the match day squad, but unfortunately for all concerned, he too succumbed to injury and an Achilles problem therefore ruled him out.

This left Webb with little alternative but to look to Paul Smith, a central midfielder by trade, but a player that the manager felt could fill in on the right hand side of midfield. "I am sure Paul Smith won't let us down. He has produced some powerful displays in the reserves and now it's up to him to grab his first team chance."

"I have stressed to all the players that we have a squad system here and if anyone comes in because of injury or suspension and does well then he stays in the side. You must be honest with your players or you get no loyalty or honesty in return."

It was traits such as those that Webb demanded and the respect he had with his players was a key component in the team's magnificent start to the season. Trips to teams at the bottom of the league was always a cause for concern, so an honest performance would have to be required to leave Yorkshire with the three points on offer.

Smith lined up on the right of the favoured four man midfield, Steve Tilson started on the opposite flank with Dave Martin and Peter Butler taking up their usual positions in the centre.

Smith's selection meant that Southend would have less pace and skill on the right than when either Andy Ansah or Adam Locke featured. But, by including a centre midfield player in that role Blues looked a bit more solid as Smith didn't venture out wide like a natural winger, instead holding a starting position of ten yards further in.

In hindsight, a less attack minded midfield benefited the team in this away fixture as Rotherham made The Shrimpers battle for every minute of the ninety played.

The home side had an early shout for a penalty turned down after the ball appeared to strike Spencer Prior's right arm following a corner. Blues ignored the calls for a spot kick and countered with Chris Powell finding himself in a rare advanced position. The left back lifted the ball forwards towards Smith whose flick header released Brett Angell and, although the forward did everything right as he lifted the ball over the onrushing Billy Mercer, he saw his effort miraculously hooked off the line by Gerry Forrest.

Angell and his colleagues remonstrated with the referee in the belief that it had crossed the line, but the lineman on the near side was adamant Forrest's right leg got to the ball just in time and the score stayed level.

The game began to descend into a physical battle that the home side hoped would turn the tide in their favour. Fighting for their lives at the bottom of the league they hoped they would be able to out muscle and out work the side at the very top of the table.

They didn't reckon on the fact that Southend would be able to meet their opponents head on in the physical battle that ensued. Martin, Butler and Paul Clark relished the hard work they had to put in to get the right result for the club. The tackles, too, were being made with full force from the boys in blue.

The effort from all eleven players on the pitch started to pay dividends as The Shrimpers managed to carve out two half chances that both fell to Peter Butler who was unable to hit the target on both occasions, leaving the game goalless at half time.

The second half started and with Rotherham losing out on the physical aspect of the game and in all honesty, they didn't have a lot else to offer. This was Blues opportunity to impose themselves on the home side as they began to put more and more pressure on their hosts.

They won several corners that amounted to little, but without doubt, the tidiest passage of play all afternoon resulted in the only goal of the game.

Southend kept the ball moving from one side of the pitch to the other, leaving the home side chasing shadows. The ball reached Dean Austin on the right who rolled the ball into Butler. The Blues number eight turned neatly before knocking it forwards to Angell who was closed down quickly, but luckily the ball ran kindly for Ian Benjamin whose shot took a wicked deflection off Nicky Law that wrong footed a helpless Mercer in goal.

Rotherham never really offered up much after that goal and although they kept working, there was a lack of quality from them that allowed Southend to return to Essex with the full three points.

The Yorkshire team, much as Webb predicted, proved a test for his players, albeit in a different form. Never having really troubled

Paul Sansome, the manager was pleased with his side's application and the 1-0 win. "Rotherham may be bottom of the table, but this game highlighted the fact that there is no such thing as an easy game," reasoned Webb.

"Because of our position there's bound to be additional pressure on us as opposing sides strive to knock us off our perch. The attitude and character of the lads has to be right to withstand it – as it was in this game. There was no sign of complacency. Everyone gave his all in what was a real battling performance."

It was a very good result for the club and one which maintained their four point lead over Grimsby Town who were also victorious over Mansfield. The 1-0 win was a sign of the team's character and belief that they had, but should it have been a 2-0 result instead? Well, according to Ian Benjamin it definitely should have been. The forward who netted his eighth goal of the campaign was in no doubt as to whether Brett Angell's effort crossed the line.

"It wasn't even a close thing. I was coming in on the angle and I'm certain the ball was a good foot over the line before it was cleared. Thankfully it didn't matter in the end and we finished up getting the victory we deserved from what was a fine team performance."

The victories for both of Division Three's top two sides set up a mouth-watering clash when they were to meet at Roots Hall in two weeks' time. It was a game that was expected to welcome a big crowd and although the buzz around town was in full effect, the game was still a while away and Blues had to first concentrate on the trip to Reading in The Leyland Daf Cup on 7th December.

There was some good news to come for Dave Webb in the days before the club's second visit to Elm Park in thirteen days. The news was regarding his two right wingers who had missed the fixture at Rotherham through injury.

First, Webb revealed that Andy Ansah had made a miraculous recovery from his thigh injury that he fell victim to in training had now been given the all clear. "We had virtually ruled Andy out of our plans for a couple of week, but he has made remarkable strides. That's great news because it helps to hot up the competition for places at a vital stage of the season," said his delighted manager.

It was unlikely, however, that Ansah would be risked for The Leyland Daf tie and that was partly down to the full recovery of the squad's other right sided wide man, Adam Locke. And the former

Palace player was keen on getting his place back in the first team straight away. "I have been struggling to overcome a calf injury and then went down with flu which gave me no chance of making the line-up at Rotherham on Saturday. Then, to rub it in, I crashed my car in the Dartford tunnel on the way to training," bemoaned Locke and his rotten luck, before confirming he was ready to return. "I am still feeling my injury, (but) hopefully I can put it all behind me now and concentrate all my efforts on winning my first team place back."

The Friday night game at Reading was only a day away when it was confirmed by the club that reserve midfielder Peter Daley was allowed to leave the club and join Essex non-league side Chelmsford City. Daley was the second player to leave Roots Hall in a matter of weeks after Peter Cawley joined Exeter City towards the end of November.

With a relatively small squad getting even smaller, Webb appeased fans fears by reiterating his desire to introduce some new blood in the upcoming weeks to replace the two that had left for pastures new.

"I am definitely looking for new faces and have my eye on one or two players," said Blues boss. "We have let two men go in recent weeks and need to replace them."

"We are pretty thin on the ground, injuries and the young players being needed for an F.A. Youth Cup tie meant that Coach Kevin Lock and I had to be included in the reserves this week!"

"I also feel that this is the time in the season to bring in one or two players to help spice things up and keep everyone on their toes. The lads currently in the side have done tremendously well, but it only needs an injury to a key player and it all can change."

Webb was then asked about his team selection for the next day's cup tie at Reading and after the 10-1 romp over Aldershot in the other group game in the completion, it was a game that Blues could lose 7-0 and still qualify.

"It's important that we keep things ticking over and try to maintain our form. I could have brought in one or two of our young reserves, but with no match before next Saturday's big game with rivals Grimsby, the first teamers might have got a little stale," he reasoned.

"Anyway, we want to go out at Reading prove that our 4-2 win there a couple of weeks ago was no fluke. It's vital that you keep up the winning habit and that's what we will be trying to do."

The managers desire to keep that momentum going did indeed, as expected, mean that it was the strongest side possible that travelled to Elm Park on a wet Friday night.

There was only one change to the starting eleven and that was the inclusion of Adam Locke. Locke's return to full fitness had earned him the expected recall in place of Paul Smith who dropped to the bench. It was a signal of Webb's intent that he wanted success in this tournament and the team he chose certainly reflected that.

The overall performance was a thoroughly professional one that gave their manager exactly what he was looking for in proving that their success thirteen days earlier was no accident.

However, before The Shrimpers began to convert their chances into goals, it was the home side that struck first with a freak goal from midfielder Mick Gooding. Reading won a free-kick on the left hand side of which Gooding took. His curling delivery evaded players from both sides, as it was allowed to bounce and leave a hesitant Paul Sansome only able to watch as the ball end up into the far corner of the net.

It was a disappointing goal to concede, but one that Southend cancelled out five minutes later with eighteen on the clock.

Locke, carrying on from thirteen days earlier, worked his magic and won a corner after teasing left back Michael Gilkes – oh how the Reading full back must have been sick of the sight of his tormentor!

Steve Tilson came across to take the kick and his cross brought out a smart save by Steve Francis who denied Spencer Prior's bullet header. The ball was only cleared as far as Tilly whose inswinger this time found the near post run of Ian Benjamin and The Blues number ten intelligently stole a march on his marker before managing to guide the ball into the roof of the net for the equaliser.

Southend then continued to press for a second goal and perhaps should have had one when Benjamin failed to score after good work from Locke once again. That wasn't to be though and the scores were level at the interval.

After half time, Reading couldn't get out of their half as Blues continued to dominate the game. In particular, much the same as in the league encounter, both Tilson and Locke were being allowed too much time and space in the wide areas and the home side were soon to be punished for this.

Goal number two was inevitable and it duly came on sixty-four minutes when yet another attack from the flanks brought success. It was down the left hand side that the goal was created after Chris Powell had overlapped Tilson to deliver a pinpoint cross that was met by Peter Butler to give his side a belated, but well deserved lead.

The pitch conditions seemingly began to sap some of the energy out of the home players, but not so those legs of a confident away side. Locke was still full of running with only minutes left to play, twisting one way and another before crossing for the head of Benjamin who scored with great ease for a two goal cushion.

A fourth goal followed with almost the last kick of the game. Again, Locke was involved as he came in from the right flank to play a neat one-two with Benji. He spotted the run of Tilson and perfectly played the ball into his path. Tilly, not having to break stride, sent over a deep cross for Brett Angell who had time to control, set and convert Southend's fourth goal of the game.

The 4-1 win not only saw the progression to the next round of The Leyland Daf Cup, but it also served as a great morale boost to the team prior to Grimsby's visit. It was a fantastic result and to better the 4-2 result in the league against Reading pleased the boss, David Webb, who called it, "the best performance form our boys this season," before offering his post-match thoughts.

"We absolutely slaughtered Reading who, quite frankly, were delighted to get off so lightly. The only possible criticism could be that we were not ruthless enough. I lost count of the number of times we were through with only the keeper to beat and missed. But, it would be churlish to moan too much after winning 4-1 away from home."

"It was the best possible way to prepare for Saturday's Third Division match of the day against Grimsby. If we can reproduce anything like that sort of form then we need fear no-one," he concluded.

It was high praise indeed, but whether Webb really believed it was the best display so far or whether he was pumping up his players with Grimsby in mind, the attacking aspect of his sides play was, at times, simply breathtaking. Whatever his motives were, with confidence amongst the squad at a high, it was a perfect time to turn their attentions towards the top of the table clash eight days later.

In 1990 there was a football show that aired on Saturday lunchtimes on ITV. The show previewed the day's football and was hosted by former Liverpool forward Ian St. John and Chelsea, Tottenham and England legend, Jimmy Greaves.

Southend, who often played on a Friday night, received some air time and gained favourable backing from Greaves, whose son, Danny, was the youth team coach at Roots Hall at that time.

Greaves senior, who was a member of the 1966 World Cup winning squad, was based in Essex and through his son, kept in close contact with the club - sometimes even attending home games. He was considered a jovial figure within the game and his football catchphrase of 'it's a funny old game' made him very popular in the media circles.

As well as the hit TV show, Saint and Greavesie, Jimmy also had a weekly column in local newspaper, The Evening Echo. In the week leading up to the crunch game at Southend, he took the time out to praise the achievements of The Blues in the aforementioned column, backing The Shrimpers for promotion in his lead piece.

These were the thoughts of Jimmy Greaves in his article printed on Tuesday December 11th:

"Some of the most enjoyable and entertaining football I have witnessed this season has been down in the Third Division far away from the television eye. I take a close interest in the fortunes of Southend United, a club with a big heart to match the size of their ambition.

In their eighty-four year existence they have never been above Third Division status and now everybody connected with the club is holding their breath because the distinct possibility of promotion is beginning to loom as large as the seaside town's famous pier.

Southend's match this Saturday against Grimsby Town at Roots Hall could prove one of the most vital in the club's history. Grimsby are Southend's nearest challengers at the top of the Third Division.

A win for United would widen their lead to seven points and then the promised land of the Second Division would begin to look within shooting range.

I will be kicked by the club's enthusiastic Chairman, Vic Jobson, and their wise, unflappable manager, Dave Webb, for even breathing the word promotion. They are only too aware that the club has broken too many promises in the past for anything to be taken for granted and they are studiously ensuring that the players taken each game as it comes. But if they can clear the Grimsby barrier even they will have to start admitting that promotion is a distinct possibility.

Weather permitting, try to search out a game in the Third or Fourth Division this weekend. I think you will be surprised with the standard and delighted with the entertainment. A day trip to Southend, for instance, should be rewarded with a cracker of a match."

With that glowing endorsement from Jimmy Greaves himself, a large crowd was expected to turn up and get behind their local team. With the big game fast approaching, Vice-Chairman John Adams, was predicting over 7,000 supporters through the turnstiles at Roots Hall.

"This is the division's match of the day – first against second – and the game that most football people in south Essex want to see. I always felt that people in Southend would respond if the team maintained their superb form and that's exactly what is happening," crowed Adams, before adding, "Providing the weather does not take a dramatic turn for the worse in this area then I reckon we will have more than seven thousand at the big match."

It wasn't just the home fans that were expected to turn out in force either. It was anticipated that Grimsby's away contingent would reach around the impressive figure of 1000 which would only serve to add to the atmosphere within the ground.

The average attendance for league fixtures at Roots Hall in the eight games they had played had been 4461, so the anticipated crowd of over 7000 for the match would lend credence to the belief that if Southend United were winning football matches and doing well then they would see the increase of supporters through the turnstiles. Could the advanced numbers and the scale of the match create some nervousness amongst the players? David Webb certainly didn't think that would be the case twenty-four hours before the kick-off.

"They (Grimsby) must be the ones coming here a little apprehensive at meeting a side with such a magnificent unbeaten home league record and which has only lost one of its last eight games," Blues boss pointed out. "Of course we are expecting a tough game, but the atmosphere among the players is very relaxed, they are quietly confident."

"It has all the makings of a great match and one which everyone at Roots Hall is looking forward to. It's the biggest game in Division Three and great for us and our fans to be involved in something like that at this stage of the season. The attitude of the players has been tremendous in recent weeks and I have seen them almost visibly seem to start believing in themselves. We have had knock backs like going a goal behind at Reading last week, but always look capable of bouncing back and that's just the type of spirit every team needs."

The squad for the game was again without the injured Andy Ansah and John Cornwell and therefore it was widely expected that Webb would name an unchanged side to the one that beat Reading eight days earlier. That would mean that Adam Locke would make his first home start in the league on the right of midfield - a position that Webb admitted he didn't primarily expect the ex-Palace player to play in.

"I didn't originally sign Adam with a view to playing him wide because he has played most of his games in a central midfield role, but he had done superbly well in the matches he has played there. Adam is a brilliant crosser of the ball and should provide plenty of ammunition for Brett Angell and Ian Benjamin. He also finishes well when he gets in goalscoring positions," he explained.

"In fact, that has been the whole team's strength this season. I doubt if many clubs can boast goals from all but two of their current outfield players while four of them are in the division's leading goalscoring charts. That's in stark contrast to recent seasons at Southend when the burden tended to fall on one individual, i.e. Richard Cadette or David Crown, but now the opposition doesn't know where the shots are coming from next."

On the day of the game as kick off fast approached it was clear that there was going to be considerably more than the seven thousand through the turnstiles that had been anticipated. In fact, the official attendance was 8,126 – almost four thousand more than the average crowd at Roots Hall throughout the season. Everybody, it seemed, had their eyes on the match – even Father Christmas managed to take a break from his busiest time of the year to be in Essex and on the pitch prior to kick off!

'Up The Blues!'

The huge, expectant number of fans did not cause any anxiety amongst the players as was first feared. Instead, just as Webb predicted, they rose to the task with a supreme belief that their manager had spoken of twenty four hours earlier.

From the very first whistle, Blues harassed their opponents and that was none more evident as when Dave Martin clattered into John Cockerill inside the first few seconds. The tempo was set as the front six chased, pressed, worked and forced Grimsby into many mistakes before then getting at the team four points below them in the league.

After four minutes, Southend got early success from taking to their opponents. After winning the ball back in the middle of the pitch, it was played wide to Adam Locke on the right wing. Locke's quick feet took him past Kevin Jobling with apparent ease and the bamboozled left back was forced to bring him down for a free kick.

It was the familiar sight of Steve Tilson and Peter Butler who stood over the ball as Dave Martin, Spencer Prior, Brett Angell and Ian Benjamin all took up their positions in Grimsby's penalty area.

Tilson's left foot swung it over towards Martin, but he was beaten to the ball by the head of Andy Tillson. The danger wasn't yet over though as Butler was first to pick up the loose ball. In possession and facing his own goal, Butler rolled the ball back towards Tilson who struck the ball with his left foot from fully thirty yards into the top corner and past a helpless Steve Sherwood for the lead.

A packed Roots Hall went wild with delight, as did the players who all surrounded the goalscorer of what was an absolutely outstanding strike. The technique Tilson showed was perfect and to score such an amazing goal in such a big game was what dreams were made of for this local lad.

Despite going one up early on, Blues didn't take their foot off the pedal. Grimsby had a reputation of playing some good football, but was never given the opportunity by a dominant home side. All the away side could muster was long balls forwards which was comfortably dealt with by Prior and Paul Clark at centre back.

Such was the one sided affair in the first half that it seemed inevitable that a second goal would eventually come. It did, but fans had to wait until there was forty-four minutes on the clock to raise the roof once more.

This time it was a goal made by Tilson's trusty left foot after the wide midfielder delivered a low free kick in from the right that was met by the diving head of a brave Dave Martin for a well-deserved 2-0 lead at the break.

Grimsby's pride had been dented in the first half and come out for the second with a lot more purpose right from the re-start. Forcing a corner, Dave Gilbert's resulting cross came in and almost caused embarrassment for Angell as he could only watch Paul Sansome tip his misplaced header over the bar.

Buoyed by this, Grimsby carried on looking for a way back into the match and on fifty-five minutes Cockerill brought out a fine save from Sammy who underlined his reputation as one of the best keepers in the division.

From that point on, Southend resisted all Grimsby's efforts to pull a goal back with some superb defending from all ten players in front of Sansome's goal. Particularly both Chris Powell and Dean Austin were excellent in preventing any crossed coming into the area in what was proving to be the best display from the back four all season.

The midfield, too, somehow never tired and put unbelievable amounts of effort tom keep working for the full ninety minutes.

The Shrimpers could, and should, have added to their tally, but Brett Angell uncharacteristically missed the target from close range before going even closer with a header that hit the bar.

As the final whistle sounded some fans who were rightly overjoyed with the performance and delighted with the result some fans rushed onto the pitch to celebrate with the players at full time while those that remained in the stands gave the team a deserved standing ovation.

The significance of the result and the seven point lead Blues now had at the top of the table was not lost on the players either. They applauded the bumper crowd for their support as well as congratulating each other on a job very well done.

Skipper Paul Clark spoke of the team spirit that was running through the camp after the 2-0 victory. "Everyone is keen and enthusiastic and they all want the ball which makes it so much easier. We are playing as a unit and make life so difficult for the opposition," he explained.

"Confidence is so high at the moment that we go out expecting to win games and that early goal today really sparked us off and Grimsby were never given a chance to settle. They only had two real goal attempts all afternoon and that's when Paul Sansome showed what a fine keeper he is by coming to the rescue with a couple of great stops."

A jubilant David Webb was pleased with his side and the match he witnessed, "It was like a cup tie out there and our lads were simply superb. They fully deserved victory because of their ninety minutes of non-stop effort – the work rate was phenomenal."

"It was a tremendous game, a great advert for Third Division football and remember, that was a win against the best team we've faced this season and it took two quality goals to see them off. But that's the sort of performance the boys will need to reproduce from now until the end of the season because teams will raise their game and be determined to try and knock us off our perch."

The result over Grimsby was a culmination of the season's work up until that point -such was their dominance of their opponents. The seven point lead at the top of the table was a very encouraging and comforting cushion, but league titles are not won in December. There was still plenty of work to be done and in the days that followed the win over Grimsby, Webb was well aware that a benchmark had been set and it was extremely important that it didn't now slip for the trip to north to face Chester City in their next game on the 22nd December.

"We set really high standards against Grimsby and would have beaten any side in the division on that performance, but it's vital that we guard against complacency. Football has a horrible knack of kicking you in the teeth if you get too cocky," said Blues chief.

It was abundantly clear that Webb wouldn't allow for his players to think they could just turn up and win against teams just because the league table saw them sitting top after eighteen games. His players were in great form and very confident, none more so than one half of the engine room in Blues midfield, Dave Martin.

Unfortunately, though, after picking up another booking versus Grimsby, he was now due to face his second suspension of the season. The amount of games that he would miss due to his accumulation of yellow cards had yet to be confirmed, although two was suspected to be the likely outcome. It was anticipated that the ban would start with the New Year's Day away fixture at Tranmere Rovers. Webb spoke of his disappointment at Martin's impending absence, "It's obviously a big blow to both David and the club because he is having a superb season."

"Not only is he doing a Trojan job in the defensive midfield role, but has also got forward and scored nine goals already. David will miss at least one game and we shall have to wait and see if he gets a heavier punishment."

Martin had indeed been one of the reasons for the incredible first half of the season. His partnership with Peter Butler was very strong and not too many opposing teams were able outwork and physically dominate the pair in the middle of the park - and that's not to overlook their football abilities because they were showing that they could play too.

During Martin's previous suspension for the red card he received at Birmingham, he was ably replaced by John Cornwell. The versatile Cornwell had not been near the first team since his ankle ligament injury he suffered in the 3-2 defeat at Orient in The F.A. Cup, but as Martin's ban loomed there was some good news surrounding Cornwell and his injury.

The former Swindon man had resumed first team training in the week after the win over Grimsby and Webb was hopeful he would not suffer any adverse reactions and start to push for a first team recall.

The game away at Chester City three days before Christmas would obviously come too soon for Cornwell, but it was better news concerning Andy Ansah who had recovered from his thigh muscle injury to declare himself available for first team action once more.

Many thought the trip north would be a comfortable win for the league leaders as Chester had been struggling in the league and found themselves lying sixth from bottom in the table. Add to the fact that they had failed to score in their last five league encounters, it was easy to see why an away win was a popular pick on the pools coupon.

They were playing their home games at Macclesfield Town's Moss Road ground due to their former Sealand Road home being sold for re-development earlier in the year. At the time, Macclesfield was a non-league club and David Webb wasn't exactly expecting a Wembley type surface upon his team's arrival.

"The surroundings at Macclesfield are, I understand, pretty poor, but we must forget all that and go out and do a professional job. If we play to our usual standard then Chester should prove no problem, but we certainly won't underestimate them. Chester have some experienced players who, on their day, are capable of beating anyone in the division and our position at the top gives them extra incentive," he said.

Despite Andy Ansah's welcome return to full fitness, manager David Webb resisted the temptation to give him a start in place of Adam Locke as the team predictably remained unchanged from the one that beat Grimsby. Ansah had to make do with a place on the bench alongside teenage defender Andy Edwards.

It was a very muddy and uneven surface that greeted Southend upon arrival at Macclesfield Town's Moss Road stadium. It led to the conclusion that this was to be a game that was going to be a battle and from kick off Southend's back four were very impressive as they blocked, headed and kicked everything that came their way.

Unfortunately, at the other end of the pitch they weren't creating a great deal themselves. Adam Locke, who had provided Blues creative spark of late, was getting very little joy from Chester left back, Martin Lane and as the game began to resemble an untidy battle in the midfield, forwards Brett Angell and Ian Benjamin was having to come deeper than usual to try and get involved.

There was a good chance for the Essex team on thirty two minutes when the first decent passage of play saw Peter Butler pick up the loose ball and play in the forward running Steve Tilson. An unopposed Tilly cut in from the left and as home keeper and as Billy Stewart looked to narrow the angle, The Blues midfielder smashed his shot onto the crossbar from twelve yards out. It was a chance that Tilson should have converted, but perhaps the pitch was on his mind as he set up to shoot and his decision to go for power didn't come off this time.

In the second half Southend looked to impose their superiority on Chester, but when half chances fell to Benjamin and Angell, they failed to connect with the ball properly. This kick started the home side to try and create a few chances of their own, but when they did manage to shoot on goal, they found Paul Sansome in good form.

The game as though both teams would have to settle for a point apiece when an innocuous free kick was awarded to Chester just yards inside the Southend half with two minutes left to play.

The resulting free kick was half dealt with by Spencer Prior and as The Shrimpers immediately pushed up for offside, Graham Abel lifted the ball back into the area where Keith Bertschin had made a late run. A quick look at the linesman from both teams confirmed that he was onside and his chip over Sansome was met by Carl Dale who withstood the pressure from Clark to nod the ball into the net from only a yard out.

The lateness of the goal meant there was no chance for The Blues to come back after that. Chester had managed to turn the form book on its head and get a surprise win, gaining a massive three points in their fight for survival.

It was a huge comedown for Southend United after defeating their closest challengers seven days earlier, but in truth, there wasn't really that spark that had seen Blues score thirty-six league goals in the eighteen league games that they had previously played.

Webb said afterwards that unused substitute, Andy Ansah, was an obvious consideration to try to unlock the Chester defence and it was a decision that he regretted not making at full time.

"I did think about putting Andy on, but then felt it might be unsafe to disrupt things as I couldn't see us failing to get at least a point. In the end we lost it to a sloppy goal and I might just as well as made a change. I learned from that bit of indecision and will be more positive if I find myself in that situation again," he vowed.

Watching from the stands was former Southend forward Gary Bennett, now of Chester City. Bennett made fifty appearances while at Roots Hall over his sixteen month stay at the club and was surprisingly positive towards his former team after the game at Moss Road.

"Southend certainly look good enough to go up. They were a little unfortunate today - the result could so easily have gone their way. I must admit I had doubts when I saw they had set such a hot pace early in the season, but after seeing them in action I reckon they will get into Division Two. Sometimes a little knock back like they suffered today can give them the jolt every side sometimes needs during a season. They have the quality players who can quickly make amends for this shock," was his post-match assessment.

The chance to make amends would come, like all fixtures over Christmas, very quickly, as they had back to back home games in the space of two days. The first of these two matches was on Boxing Day and then two days later when Bradford City came to town for a Friday night kick off.

With this in mind, and perhaps the defeat at Chester still occupying his thoughts, Webb confirmed that the squad would have to report for training on Christmas Day in preparation for the upcoming games.

"I am not a party pooper and appreciate that the players want to be at home with their families, as I do myself, but we must remember that we are professionals and have an important game against Bolton. It's important to try and look on Christmas Day as if it was a normal day before a match so that the lads do not get out of their usual routine," reasoned The Blues manager.

"It's obviously hard for pro footballers as this time of the year, but they know that if they have too much to eat and drink they will be letting themselves, the team and supporters down. I am sure that no-one wants to put all that at risk simply by having an extra beer or two or too much Christmas pud."

"There will be plenty of time for celebration if, please God, we achieve our ultimate ambition and get promotion and three points against Bolton could give that a huge boost."

Webb then spoke of what how the loss in their previous game might have brought expectations down and how he looked to turn that into a positive. "That result will have given one or two people a sharp reminder that there is still a long way to go before promotion honours are claimed," he said.

"Everyone knows we did not perform up to our usual high standard at Chester and will go out double determined to put it right. The atmosphere on Saturday was as if we had just lost The F.A. Cup – the players have got into the winning habit and don't like to lose. That must be a good thing and let's hope Bolton catch the backlash."

If Bolton were to feel any backlash then the performance would have to be improved greatly as they were coming to Essex as a side in fine form. Wanderers were lying in fourth spot in the league after putting together a very impressive run of form that saw them earn twenty-three points from a possible twenty-seven. They also hadn't suffered a defeat since the beginning of October when Stoke beat them 1-0 at Burnden Park.

While Southend were losing at Chester, second placed Grimsby bounced back from their miserable trip to Roots Hall with a thumping 5-0 win at home to Bournemouth. That meant that Blues lead had been cut to four points, so the importance of getting three points over Bolton could not be overstated.

The only change to the thirteen involved on Boxing Day was the inclusion of Martin Ling who was named on the bench with Andy Edwards the player missing out. That presented the perfect opportunity for the starting eleven to make amends for the disappointment at Chester by winning against Bolton.

There was a bumper Christmas crowd of 7,539 inside the ground for the festive fixture that was a noon kick off. It was testament to Southend that the majority of those fans were now becoming expectant of getting another three points in the quest for promotion, rather than fearing the worst.

It was a wet and very windy Boxing Day and those conditions certainly made life difficult for both teams over the course of ninety minutes. It was hard for either side to get the ball on the deck and play, but there were occasions when both Blues and Bolton looked the every inch the sides that the table suggested they were.

Midway through the first half, as the ball bobbled around the centre circle, Dean Austin came across from full back to win the ball strongly with a hard slide tackle on Mark Winstanley. The loose ball fell invitingly for Peter Butler to take it on and he held onto it long enough for Austin to superbly make his way up the right wing. Butler then passed the ball into the right back's path allowing the full back the opportunity to cross to the far post where Steve Tilson was unable to really test David Felgate in the Wanderers goal.

There was a further chance for the home side with five minutes left of the first half and it was one that should have been taken. Good combination work from Brett Angell, Ian Benjamin and Butler put Adam Locke in the clear, but the shot from Locke was dragged wide of the goal when he should have done better.

In the second half, with the wind getting stronger, Southend did carry on looking for a goal and got their rewards in the sixty-eighth minute.

Paul Clark took a free-kick on the halfway line and sent the ball high into the box towards Dave Martin. The midfielder rose well, flicking the ball towards Angell whose header found the unmarked Tilson and he finished in style, showing superb technique in executing a right foot volley into the top corner.

Bolton, who had yet to test Paul Sansome, were still matching Blues work rate and commitment, but found the weather conditions slightly harder to deal with than their hosts. The game was now turning into an awful spectacle, but it was still 1-0 to Southend and that was good enough for the home side and their fans.

However, for the second time in two games, The Shrimpers conceded a late equaliser and this time it denied Blues all three points. It was with five minutes left on the clock that saw Bolton snatch the leveller that spoilt the Christmas spirit for the large crowd watching on.

The goal that came was a very poor one to concede for any side at any level and it simply should not have happened.

It started when Felgate drop kicked the ball high into the air and it was carried by the wind so much that the huge bounce lifted the ball over Paul Clark and Prior, who quickly turned to avert the danger.

Unfortunately, under no immediate pressure, Prior attempted a back pass to his keeper, but totally mishit the ball. That was all the invitation Tony Phillskirk needed to beat Sammy to the ball and square it to substitute Scott Green who had the easiest of tasks to roll the ball into an empty net for a share of the spoils.

Speaking after the match, Bolton boss Phil Neal aired his delight at the result, "This was a big test for us today following our ten match unbeaten run in the league and we are pleased with a point. It was a tremendous battle and I felt a draw was just about the right result," he said.

Neal's opposite number had contrasting emotions after seeing his side lead up until the eighty-fifth minute. "I am bitterly disappointed because we had the better chances and then got punished for one silly slip up," moaned Webb. "Unfortunately we are making a habit of conceding bad goals late on and that's something we must work on to improve concentration But, overall the lads performed superbly in very difficult conditions and I don't see any trouble in lifting them for Friday's vital clash with Bradford. We just need to go out with the same positive attitude and perhaps lady luck will smile on us for a change...it's about time we were gifted a soft goal – everyone we get seems to be a blinder!"

The scorer of that "blinder" also spoke of the disappointment at the outcome of a match they seemed to have won, but for that error at the end. "The lads are all sick because we know we threw away three points today, the game was there for the taking and we blew it," said a dejected Tilson. "That's the second match running that we've conceded late killer goals. We must make sure we are not so generous against Bradford on Friday night," he concluded.

The only good news that was taken from that day was that Grimsby had suffered a shock 2-0 loss away at Reading. That meant that Blues had increased their lead by a further point and the cushion was now five over their nearest rivals. After second placed Grimsby there was a gap of eleven points between Southend in first and Brentford in third. It was still a very healthy lead from the automatic promotion spots down to the play off positions and that made it even more perplexing with the crowds muted reaction to the draw with Bolton.

With their side leading the way in Division Three, frustration can creep into fans minds as a chance to further cement that top spot isn't taken. It's not a slight on the player's performance, but by leading the way in Division Three there comes an adding expectancy from the terraces.

The ride up to that point had everyone connected with Southend United dreaming of the impossible – a history making season that, ultimately, would see promotion to unchartered territories and that meant Second Division football. The attendances had been up for the last two games and that hadn't gone unnoticed by vice-chairman, John Adams, who pointed out the value of a good turn out on match days.

"We had just over eight thousand for the Grimsby match and another seven thousand five hundred on Boxing Day for the visit of Bolton and that type of support gave the players a tremendous lift. Now everybody is hoping the fans will continue to flock to Roots Hall. We know it is asking a lot for people to find cash to turn up for a second home game in three days, especially after the expense of Christmas," Adams said.

"We would love them to make the effort to provide the sort of atmosphere which has given the lads such a huge tonic in the last couple of games. They, more than anyone, feel sick they failed to reward supporters with victory on Boxing Day, but that only made them more determined to turn in a super show tonight."

The team that entertained The Bantams remained unchanged, so it was the perfect opportunity to put behind the disappointment of the Bolton game. Bradford was having a mediocre season as they lay in thirteenth position in the table, but having been unbeaten in their last six away games they would look to push Southend all the way.

The visitors certainly started with the belief of a side that could cause an upset at Roots Hall as they pushed high up the pitch in numbers that meant that the opening few minutes were played in Blues own half.

The Shrimpers, though, were league leaders for a reason and their very first attack produced the opening goal with only six minutes on the clock.

Peter Butler covered the ground well to collect a pass from right back, Dean Austin. Under pressure, Butler moved the ball quickly to Dave Martin in the centre circle who held off a challenge before splitting the Bradford defence with a pass made to measure for Steve Tilson. Tilly then took it inside the desperate defender to set himself up for a smart left foot finish that nestled into the corner of the net.

Bradford responded to going a goal behind well and some neat football produced a shooting chance for Steve Torpey, but the striker's effort failed to trouble Paul Sansome in front of The South Bank.

Southend then started to up their game and were beginning to take over in a match that looked as though they might struggle with early on.

The football on display from the home side was a pleasure to watch and how they didn't add to Tilson's goal was a mystery. Twice Adam Locke had the perfect opportunity to double the lead, but on both occasions the winger somehow managed to clear The North Bank with his efforts.

Locke wasn't the only culprit in regards to missing chances, Brett Angell and Peter Butler both should have done better with efforts that were saved by Bantams keeper, Paul Tomlinson.

The score remained 1-0 to Southend at the interval and the buzz around Roots Hall among the 6,767 fans was that a welcome three points was surely on the way for their team. They had created

'Up The Blues!'

enough chances to be two or three goals further in front and, as far as they were concerned, those goals would soon be coming in the second half.

A second goal in the match did come soon after the re-start, but it was scored by Bradford midfielder Paul Jewell on fifty minutes.

It was a free kick to the visitors that didn't appear to cause concern for Blues, but the high ball into the penalty area wasn't dealt with on two occasions by Martin and then Tilson. This allowed Lee Duxbury to cross to from the right wing, where Austin failed to direct his headed clearance anywhere other than straight at Jewell who placed his shot beyond the outstretched Sansome for 1-1.

Roots Hall fell into a stunned silence at the unlikely equaliser as the fans and players rued the missed first half chances that they now hoped wouldn't prove too costly.

David Webb watched on for just under another ten minutes until he replaced the out of sorts Locke with Andy Ansah. Unfortunately, that did little to quell the Bradford resurgence as they started to create good chances that forced Sammy into action with decent stops from Duxbury and then Torpey to keep the scores all square.

The Southend back four were now working extremely hard to repel all their opponent's advances. In particular, Chris Powell at left back, was performing heroics as the home side struggled to get back into the game.

But, they did manage to turn tide back in their favour once again and with time running out for Blues, they pressed hard for a winner.

Dave Martin twice went close with two efforts that almost put his side back in front, his first effort skimmed the bar and the second was saved by Tomlinson with a fine stop to deny Southend's number four his ninth goal of the season.

Ansah also went close and nearly won the match when he looked set to capitalise on a poor back pass, but Tomlinson again was on hand to deny the league leaders and earn his side a deserved point.

It was considered a good point for the visitors, but it was looked upon as two points dropped by Southend. Webb, however, was upbeat at the final whistle after seeing his side create numerous chances to win the game.

"There are one or two areas in the team which are giving me cause for concern at the moment, but we can't be that bad if we are dominating teams and just not getting the rub of the green in front of goal," he said.

"Against both Bolton and Bradford we played some of our best football of the season and could easily have won by three or four goals. Nobody would be talking about a crisis then."

There was a few concerns emanating from the supporters after a return of only two points from a possible nine over Christmas, but there was still plenty to be happy about as 1990 drew to a close.

The day after Blues 1-1 draw with Bradford, Grimsby Town suffered a second successive loss when they went down 1-0 at Cambridge United. This left The Shrimpers six point clear of The Mariners in second place and still an impressive eleven points ahead of Brentford in third.

The league made for very good reading at the end of the year and, despite the last two home results, Southend were in a very strong position in the table. To be in and around the top ten with half an eye on the play offs would have been considered a very good situation to be in, so to be six clear and leading the way was fairy tale stuff for the club.

If the month of December had provided a strong indicator as to where Southend's season was heading, then the suggestion was crystal clear, Blues had their sights firmly locked in towards promotion to Division Two. Webb had always believed that, as now did his players and that belief was spreading. The club's hierarchy was becoming subscribers too and the bookmakers had already jumped on board. Now, were even the fans even daring to dream that history was in possibly in the making?

'Up The Blues!'

Division Three Table December 31st 1990

	TEAM	Pl	F	A	W	D	L	F	A	Pts	GD
1	Southend United	21	15	14	14	4	3	38	26	46	12
2	Grimsby Town	21	11	11	12	4	5	34	19	40	15
3	Brentford	21	19	14	9	8	4	29	23	35	6
4	Leyton Orient	20	9	17	11	2	7	28	24	35	4
5	Bolton Wanderers	21	15	14	10	5	6	28	25	35	3
6	Cambridge United	21	15	10	9	7	5	36	28	34	8
7	Bury	20	12	15	9	6	5	33	26	33	7
8	Stoke City	21	10	12	9	6	6	29	24	33	5
9	Reading	21	12	12	9	4	8	32	30	31	2
10	Tranmere Rovers	21	15	15	8	6	7	32	26	30	6
11	Bournemouth	21	5	14	7	9	5	25	24	30	1
12	Bradford City	21	12	10	8	5	8	24	25	29	-1
13	**Swansea City**	21	10	19	8	5	8	26	28	29	-2
14	Huddersfield Town	20	9	13	8	4	8	25	26	28	-1
15	Wigan Athletic	21	11	19	8	3	10	31	34	27	-3
16	Birmingham City	21	10	13	6	9	6	21	25	27	-4
17	Preston North End	21	14	19	6	7	8	25	31	25	-6
18	Exeter City	21	12	19	6	6	9	24	26	24	-2
19	Chester City	21	11	15	6	4	11	21	27	22	-6
20	Fulham	21	8	15	4	8	9	23	27	20	-4
21	Crewe Alexandra	21	19	21	4	7	10	33	39	19	-6
22	Shrewsbury Town	20	21	24	4	6	10	33	38	18	-5
23	Mansfield Town	21	13	17	4	6	11	20	30	18	-10
24	Rotherham United	21	7	25	3	5	13	22	41	14	-19

January 1991

"It's bitterly disappointing to lose when we had enough chances to win the game three times over." – David Webb

As 1990 was given a fond farewell, 1991 was warmly welcomed and it was hoped that it would be as prosperous for Southend United as the previous twelve months had been.

It was straight down to business for The Shrimpers who faced a tough trip to Tranmere Rovers on New Year's Day. Tranmere had promotion aspirations too having amassed thirty points up to that point and that left them only five points adrift from third place.

It was another big test for The Blues and after two successive home draws, manager David Webb understood the value of three points. "We will go to Tranmere looking for victory. The two slip ups at home make it even more imperative that we get back on the winning trail," he said.

"I am convinced we are the type of side which is better going forward. We've proved that we are not much good at sitting on a lead – just four clean sheets all season shows that. I don't want us to lose sight of what has got us into our current position, playing attractive football and creating chances."

"Obviously we must start turning those chances into goals again, but there is nothing wrong here that a good win won't put right," Webb reckoned, before calling for a good start to the New Year. "We come unstuck at Chester recently and I reckon Tranmere will give us a sterner test than that. We will need to recapture some of the sparkle we showed at places like Cambridge and Reading if we hope to go into 1991 on the right note."

Before the New Year's action kicked off at Prenton Park, it had emerged that there was some positive news surrounding the long term futures of five first team players. Right back Dean Austin, midfielders Adam Locke, Steve Tilson and Peter Butler plus winger

Andy Ansah had all agreed new deals with Southend that would keep them at Roots Hall for the foreseeable future.

Webb spoke of his delight at seeing all five sign the new deals on offer. "They are all young players, very much the future of this club."

"I am very pleased that they want to pledge themselves to Southend United and believe that we are going places. They have all shown the right attitude both on and off the pitch and will hopefully play a major role in this season's promotion drive."

Indeed, all five had all played important roles in the first half of the season and were all deserving of their new deals. The performances of Tilson, Ansah, Locke and Austin had impressed with their form and they had all adjusted to Division Three football without any problem whatsoever.

Perhaps, though, it was the displays of Peter Butler that had really caught the eye. An outcast back in August after contractual disputes, Butler had since bought into Webb's vision and gone on to turn in a string of man of the match performances that had not gone unnoticed from the club's powers that be. He was rightly given a new deal and it was widely thought that if Blues was to make their promotion dream a reality, then Butler would be a key figure in achieving that.

For the match against Tranmere there was a decision to be made as to who would partner Butler in the middle of the park due to regular starter Dave Martin serving the first of his two match suspension for an accumulation of yellow cards.

After his red card at Birmingham earlier in the season, Martin was replaced by John Cornwell, but he was still recovering from ankle ligament damage that was sustained at Orient in November.

That left Webb with limited options and so he opted to give young Paul Smith his second start of the season. Smith's only other appearance in the starting eleven was during the win at Rotherham where he played on the right of midfield. Now he had the chance to show what he was capable of in his more natural position alongside Butler in the centre.

Smith for Martin was the first of two changes from the team that drew with Bradford over Christmas with the second alteration being tactical with Andy Ansah earning a recall at the expense of Adam Locke.

Blues came out for kick off and applauded the travelling fans that had made the long trip to The Wirrall. The players looked calm and ready for the job in hand, so what was about to follow was a freak football occurrence that sometimes defies all logic.

The home side kicked off and two passes later had bypassed Southend's defence to play in striker Ian Muir who had a free run at Paul Sansome in goal. Muir was a clinical finisher and displayed such skills as he easily beat Sammy to put Tranmere ahead after only eight seconds!

It was a ridiculous goal to concede and one that should have easily been avoided had both Butler and Smith not been drawn straight to the ball from kick off. The result of the eagerness of the two central midfielders meant that Paul Clark was drawn out of position and that was all the space that Muir required to find himself through on goal.

Southend responded in a positive fashion, forcing the play in Tranmere's half and David Webb's team got their rewards as soon as the tenth minute. A corner was won after some neat build up play involving Andy Ansah and Dean Austin on the right flank. Steve Tilson made his way over from the left to take the kick on a sodden Prenton Park pitch kick. His near post delivery was perfect for Brett Angell to out jump his marker and head home the leveller right in front of the away fans.

Buoyed by this, Blues continued to take the game to their hosts and should have taken the lead six minutes after they got back on level terms. Ian Benjamin had somehow managed to find some space in a crowded penalty area, but the experienced forward saw his effort well saved by Eric Nixon in the Rovers goal. It was a good stop by Nixon, but a frustrated Benji was well aware he should have put his side in front.

Now it was Tranmere's turn to take control of the game and, in particular, Neil McNab was starting to dominate a Southend midfield that was missing David Martin greatly.

Unlike The Shrimpers, Rovers made the most of their chances and reclaimed the lead with twenty-six minutes on the clock. The goal came thanks to the good work of right winger Johnny Morrissey, who got behind Chris Powell to deliver a cross that was only half cleared by Austin. The loose ball was collected and then pulled back across goal by Jim Steele for Muir to expertly finish for his second goal of the match.

There was no question that Tranmere was fired up for the visit of the league leaders. They carried on getting at Blues and the back four, who were offered very little protection from the midfield as they struggled with the pace and movement of their opponents. Yet they somehow Rovers couldn't add to the two goal tally and the game reached halftime with Southend 2-1 behind.

In the second half and against the run of play, The Shrimpers twice went close through Austin's long range shot that sailed just over the bar and a Tilson free-kick that brought another smart stop from Nixon.

It was to be the last real effort from the away side before Tranmere put the game out of reach on the hour mark.

The ferocity and pressure Rovers created suggested that they would increase their lead at some point and so it proved to be the case. Hard work from Tranmere's forwards had prevented Blues from clearing their lines properly, gifting McNab the ball. He showed great vision to pick out Steele whose awareness set up Morrissey to smash a third goal past the helpless Sansome from twenty-five yards.

Even with a 3-1 lead, the home side continued to push for more goals and if was not for Sammy in goal then the defeat could have been considerably heavier. On the solitary occasion that Sansome was beaten, the post came to his rescue following full back Dave Higgins long range effort that deserved a goal.

It was arguably the worst performance of the season up until that point – even taking into consideration how well Tranmere played. There were far too many poor performances from the players and the amount of chances and possession Rovers had was a cause for concern.

The news that Grimsby had beaten Fulham 3-0 at Blundell Park added to the disappointment of the defeat for Blues as it meant that their cushion at the top of the table was cut to three points.

The meant that since the impressive 2-0 win over Grimsby on December 15th, Southend had only gained two points from a possible twelve. It was a poor run at a crucial time of the season and one that manager David Webb hoped would end sooner rather than later.

"We have certainly lost our way a bit recently and I want us to get back to how we were playing before the Chester game which started our poor run," he said before pinpointing reasons as to why the felt the form had suffered, "We tended to sit back more and catch people on the break. At the moment everyone is flying forward and tending to get in each other's way. We need to be much more patient and controlled," explained Webb.

He then revealed that his on-going search for new faces was possibly about to pay off with a deal in the offing for a central defender on the cards. "I have spoken to one top club about a player and intend to follow that up this week. Hopefully we will get a positive response."

"As well as the lads have done over the first half of the season, I believe there is a need for a fresh face or two. The competition for places in some departments is not as great as it should be and one or two new arrivals could give everybody a gee-up."

The chances of Webb managing to agree a deal for a player to come into the club before the next fixture was increased by the fact that there was no game for Southend for a week due to defeat in The F.A. Cup at the hands of Orient. Ironically they were due to meet The O's at home that weekend, but their progress in the competition meant that the fixture would have to be re-scheduled for later on in the season.

As a result, the next time they were in action was at Roots Hall on Tuesday January 8th when Maidstone United came to town in the first knockout round of The Leyland Daf Cup.

Unlike Blues, Grimsby Town were not afforded a weekend off as their league clash at home to Bury was still able to go ahead due to both sides having been eliminated from the cup.

It presented The Mariners with a perfect chance of pulling level with Southend, but in what came as a very welcome surprise to Blues fans and players alike, Bury's 1-0 win at Blundell Park maintained Southend's three point lead at the top of the table.

The break in the schedule presented the club with the perfect opportunity to sort out a new contract for David Webb as reward for the fantastic progress the team had made. It would see Webb stay at Southend United for a further twelve months and that would take him up until the summer of 1992. It was very welcoming and pleasing news for the supporters that it had all been sorted out so his commitment to the project was there for all to see. Webb, too, expressed his delight at his new deal and the importance of tying himself to the club for a further year.

"After (recently) persuading players to sign new contracts tying them to the club, I felt it was only right I should do the same. I know we have had a hiccup or two recently, but despite gaining just a couple of points from our last four games we are still top of the table and have every chance of staging Second Division soccer next season."

"Now that I have put pen to paper, all I want to do is channel my efforts into making that dream a reality. I think our results and progress over the last few months show that the club is geared for bigger and better things. That is why I decided to sign a new contract."

"We are all faced with a tremendous challenge here and it is one every individual is looking forward to. And together I am convinced we will succeed and can look to an exciting future."

With Webb's future now sorted, he wasted no time in getting to back to the task of strengthening his squad and he was delighted to announce that he had successfully negotiated a deal for Arsenal's highly rated central defender, Pat Scully. The 20 year-old was a Republic of Ireland under 21 international and had signed for The Shrimpers on an initial one month loan deal.

Webb had been watching Scully – who had yet to figure in the first team at Highbury - in action for Arsenal reserves and liked what he had seen. "The lad certainly impressed me and I feel he could become a big asset to us in the months ahead," he declared.

"He is a big, strong old fashioned type of defender who, although short of league experience, has won Irish under 21 honours and figured in the full international squad. I am sure he will do well during his time at Roots Hall and we have the option to buy him at the end of his months spell."

The Southend manager went on to explain the reasons behind his pursuit of a central defender. "Since letting Peter Cawley go I have been worried about our lack of defensive cover. Apart from Paul Clark and Spencer Prior we only have young Andy Edwards, who got a bad whack in training last week which needed stitches in his shin. We are now coming into a vital stage of the season and it would be a crime if we slipped up simply through lack of cover for players in key positions," explained Webb.

Scully, unavailable for the Leyland Daf Cup tie due to having played for Northampton in the competition during another loan spell earlier in the season, gave his thoughts about the move to the club. "It's a good move for me. Playing league football is certainly better than turning out for Arsenal reserves," he said, then added what his personal aims were during the initial month at Roots Hall. "Southend are obviously a good side, their position in the Third Division table tells you that and hopefully I can help them stay there or draw further ahead during my time here. What happens after that we'll have to see."

It was also confirmed by Webb that he had failed in his attempts to bring in experienced front man Paul Goddard of Millwall. The former West Ham striker had been granted a free transfer by The Lions and Webb had met with Goddard to discuss a possible deal. Unfortunately the wage demands of the player were too high, much to Webb's disappointment.

On the day of the Maidstone game, Webb faced one or two decisions over who would feature that evening. New signing Pat Scully was ineligible and he was still without Dave Martin and John Cornwell, who were suspended and injured respectively. So, the main question was to what he would do in the midfield after Paul Smith's disappointing showing at Tranmere and who would get the nod to partner Peter Butler in the engine room.

The manager opted to reshuffle his pack somewhat and Ian Benjamin was asked to play a slightly deeper role alongside Butler in the middle of midfield with winger Andy Ansah partnering as Brett Angell partner up top.

The space vacated by Ansah on the wing was filled by the forgotten man of Roots Hall, Martin Ling. The one time contract rebel had hardly figured all season and Webb was ready to hand Ling a chance versus Maidstone.

"We will be trying something a little different. With (Dave) Martin out suspended and Cornwell still not match fit following his long layoff through injury, we don't have a naturally defensive midfield player."

"I tried young Paul Smith in there at Tranmere, but the job did not really suit his style and so I have decided to switch things around a bit. It's a golden chance for Ling who has shown the right attitude since coming back into the fold. He has worked hard in training and done everything asked of him. He deserves his chance and it's up to him to now go out and make it impossible for me to drop him. A player of his quality firing on all cylinders could be vital in the coming months," reasoned Blues boss.

Ling for Smith in the starting line-up was the only change from the side that lost at Tranmere and even though it wasn't a competition that compared with promotion, Webb was taking it seriously.

Fourth Division Maidstone United had just replaced manager Keith Peacock with former Northampton boss Graham Carr and that raised a slight concern for Southend's chief.

"No doubt all there players will be out to make a quick impact on the new boss – mind you, every team we face at the moment seems to be eager to raise their game and try to knock us off our high perch," Webb explained.

"That's one of the big problems you face when you are at the top of the table – you are there to be shot at, but the game gives our lads a chance to get back into winning ways after recent hiccups."

Weather conditions for the Tuesday night match making it extremely difficult for both teams and so it was game for rolling your sleeves up and getting the job done.

That was the case for The Shrimpers back four who were giving their all to keep the visitors at bay early on and when they had been beaten, Maidstone found Paul Sansome in typically good form.

At the other end, Southend were looking back to their menacing best as they were carving out chances that should have given them the lead.

Andy Ansah should have done better when Benjamin set him through on goal and Dean Austin's long range effort was well saved by Mark Beeney in the opposition goal.

The one player who's game was seemingly unaffected by the heavy pitch was Steve Tilson. The midfielder carried on his run of good form with a display that left his opponents in tatters as he ran at them at every opportunity.

This proved to be the route to Blues opening goal of the game after Chris Powell's clever play freed Tilly on the left and his low cross caused defender Gary Cooper to inadvertently put the ball past his own keeper.

In the second half Blues continued to work hard in trying to break down a determined Maidstone United side that had set out their stall to desperately keep the score down to a single goal.

It was midway through the half when Brett Angell went close after doing everything but score from Ansah's cross as his well placed shot was superbly cleared off the line by full back Jessie Roast.

It was beginning to look like the own goal would be all that was required to progress to the next round, but with a quarter of an hour remaining the tie was put to bed with a neat finish from Angell.

The chance stemmed from the accurate cross of the lively Ansah, who had enjoyed a rare foray in a striking role. This time Angell made no mistake with a clinical finish at the near post for his eighteenth strike of the campaign and, more importantly, the final goal in a 2-0 win which meant progress to the next round.

The relieved striker spoke after the game about his double joy of getting back to scoring goals and seeing the team return to winning ways. "We needed that victory after the hiccups over Christmas and New Year. I am sure now that will give us the lift we were looking for to get back on the winning road again – hopefully up at Crewe (next) Saturday."

"We were always in control tonight although it was a real battle in those very difficult conditions and I was delighted to get the all important second goal which killed Maidstone off. That's the tenth goal I've scored in cup competitions this season and I desperately want to start banging them in again in the Third Division."

It was hoped that the confidence Angell felt after his eighteenth strike in all competitions would reap the rewards for the club. He had shown his predatory instinct by being in the right position at the right time and took his goal like any good goalscorer should.

Overall, it was night where the result was the important thing after four games without a win and so it was even more pleasing that it came about when Webb had to approach the game in a different manner with injuries and suspensions beginning to take their toll.

Forward Ian Benjamin had turned in a decent performance in midfield. His professionalism and versatility earned him praise from his boss after the match. "This was a night for battlers and nobody does more in that direction then Benji," raved Webb. "Of course we missed his ability to hold the ball and prise openings up front, but I felt he did a great job in the middle of the park – just the calming influence we were looking for."

Having got back to winning ways, Blues were able to prepare for the trip to Crewe Alexandra over the next few days in an upbeat mood, firmly looking forward to getting their league form back on track. That was, however, before rumours started to circle about Leicester City and their possible pursuit of four members of Southend's first team.

The manager of Division Two side Leicester was former Luton and Tottenham boss, David Pleat. Pleat had made the trip to Roots Hall himself in the 2-0 win over Maidstone to check out potential new signings that were on display in the blue of Southend. Although it was purely speculation, it was thought that Pleat had his eye on defender Spencer Prior, midfielders Steve Tilson and Peter Butler as well as striker Brett Angell.

When asked exactly what the situation was regarding the rumours, David Webb confirmed that Pleat was keen on some players, but that was as far as it had gone. "I think he is watching three or four of our players. From a conversation he had with one of our directors on Tuesday it seems as though he likes the way we play and enthused over several of our lads."

"We are talking purely hypothetical at the moment because neither Pleat or anyone else has come in with a bid for our players. I have always maintained that we are out to build a side for the future here and not break it up by unloading."

"That's the reason I have signed players like Tilson, Butler and Austin on longer term contracts recently and have also offered Prior a new deal which he has so far rejected. My main intention is to strengthen our squad – bringing Arsenal defender Pat Scully here on loan this week is the first step in that direction," Webb reassured concerned supporters.

Prior's contract offer, and the subsequent rejection of that offer, was news to the fans. It was anticipated that the club would talk with the young defender again and was another good sign that these players were in the forefront of the clubs mind when thinking towards the years ahead.

For the Crewe match there was good news surrounding team selection with David Martin free from suspension and in line for an immediate recall to the side. There was no doubt that Martin had been sorely missed at Tranmere and his availability would mean that Ian Benjamin could return to his more natural position as striker.

Also available for the visit to Gresty Road was loan signing Pat Scully who was to make his debut for The Shrimpers at the expense of

Prior in the centre of defence. Webb confirmed that he had spoken with the teenage defender who understood the situation.

"Spencer knows my reasons and I would rather not go into them in the press. I suppose he can consider himself a little unfortunate, but it's up to him to show the right attitude and battle to get his place back. It's a test of character for the lad. Scully will know that Prior is breathing down his neck and it all helps to improve the competition for places."

It was imperative that Blues got back to winning ways in the league sooner rather than later and, as ever, David Webb was respectful of the challenge Crewe possessed. "The lads seem to have got the spring back into their step, but we will need to be at our best if we hope to get any reward tomorrow. Crewe showed what a good and dangerous footballing side they are when they came to Roots Hall earlier in the season and were a shade unlucky to lose three-two in what was a very tight me."

There was more good news too with the return to full training for both injury victims John Cornwell and Adam Locke, although neither would be considered for action for Crewe, but it was hoped their return would soon to be on the cards. That returning duo would certainly add to the pool of players at Webb's disposal, but the Southend manager also admitted that Pat Scully wasn't to be his only signing as he was actively looking to strengthen other areas of the team.

The return of Dave Martin to the starting eleven meant that Benji could move back alongside Brett Angell in attack and Andy Ansah was then able to switch back out to the right wing. Martin Ling was the man who missed out despite starting against Maidstone and he had to make do with a place on the bench along with the man Scully replaced, Spencer Prior.

The impressive display Crewe put on in the reverse fixture at Roots Hall back in September had not been the standard bearer on their season that they had hoped as they found themselves lying fourth from bottom. They had only nineteen points from the twenty-two games they had played and, perhaps more alarmingly, they had only won one at Gresty Road all season. It was hoped that this particular statistic would give Blues a great chance to get all the points on offer.

'Up The Blues!'

It was an opportunity that proved not to be wasted on David Webb's players as they immediately took control of a match that they never really looked like losing.

A key component in the game for Southend was that they were able to involve both full backs in their attacks from very early on; such was their self-belief and dominance of the football match.

It paid dividends as early as the seventeenth minute when left back Chris Powell carried the ball inside his opponent with relative ease and then fed Benjamin who intelligently released Angell. The number eleven tried to work an opening for a shot, but he was well closed down by the defence. The ball then ran loose and fell to Andy Ansah, who saw his snap-shot parried by goalkeeper Dean Greygoose before the lively Angell beat two defenders to the ball to have the simple task of putting it into an empty net for a 1-0 lead.

Blues continued to attack Crewe as they searched for a second goal and they went close to achieving that when both Ansah and Tilson fired inches wide of Greygoose's goal.

Typically Crewe kept trying to play and from a well worked corner kick they almost pulled it back level when Dale Jasper flashed a header that went just wide of the goal, much to the relief of Paul Sansome.

In the second half it was pretty much more of the same for the visitors. They were controlling proceedings comfortably and only the heroics of Greygoose between the sticks kept the score at 1-0. But, as so often is the case, the game was almost levelled with what would have been the unlikeliest of equalisers.

It was a long free-kick forwards that found the head of Andy Sussex in a crowded penalty box and from the flick on, Craig Hignett managed to head the ball over the diving Sansome, onto the crossbar and back into the grateful arms of Blues number one.

Southend then went straight on the attack to try and put the game to bed and they completed the job when there was only eight minutes left to play. Again the architect was Powell whose impressive work down the left in advanced positions had been hugely effective all game.

One on one, Powell beat his man with a neat trick that gave him enough time and space to deliver a peach of a cross that was met by the head of Angell who could do little else but score - such was the quality of the cross.

The game ended 0-2 in Blues favour and, in truth, it could have been more. Aside from two Crewe attempts on goal, Southend dominated all over the pitch and were well worth what was had turned out to be a long awaited league win.

There were several individual performances that stood out throughout the team on what was a fine display, but the brace from Brett Angell that took his season tally to twenty goals was the man who got much of the headlines.

Crewe boss, Dario Gradi, couldn't help but sing The Shrimpers praises after the final whistle. "Southend are the best team we've met in the league this season. They are strong and well organised in every department and if they can maintain this sort of performance then promotion should be a formality," he said before casting an envious eye over The Shrimpers top scorer. "Brett Angell looked a different class to anything we've got in front of goal," he groaned.

The twenty goal man continued to impress with his all round performance and not just for his goals, but the striker was quick to praise his teammates for a job well done. "It's obviously nice for me personally to bang in a couple of goals, but this was a great team performance, everyone played their part in getting a result we desperately after a couple of recent slip ups," emphasised Angell.

Not only was it Blues first win since Grimsby, it was also their first league clean sheet since then too. This was another pleasing facet in the win against Crewe and one in which saw new signing Pat Scully fit into the team with no trouble at all. The on loan Arsenal defender looked solid alongside Paul Clark in central defence and was pleased with both the result and performance.

"It's not always easy settling into a new team when you don't really know the lads around you or how they play, but they made it easy for me and I was impressed not only the way they battled, but also with some of the good football they played...we got the result we thoroughly deserved."

The delight at winning all three points at Gresty Road was made even sweeter when the results of promotion rivals were confirmed. Second placed Grimsby Town had lost 2-0 at Wigan; Brentford could only draw 0-0 at home to Mansfield and Bolton scraped a 1-1 home draw versus Bradford City.

Those results gave Southend a six point lead from Grimsby, but there was a big mover into the top three that made the most of

'Up The Blues!'

the draws Brentford and Bolton managed -and that was Cambridge United.

Under John Beck, The U's had put together an impressive run of five wins and a draw in their previous six matches that had seen them progress up the table to third place after beating Fulham by a single goal at The Abbey Stadium.

Unconcerned and very satisfied with the win over Crewe, manager David Webb hoped it would kick start a run for his side. "I always felt we were good enough to come through that recent little dodgy spell - we can on now to build on this very useful and important result," he said.

The goalscoring exploits of Brett Angell goals had already got him in the press regarding speculation over rumoured interest from Leicester City. Now, in the days following his brace at Crewe, there was more press talk over a bid that had supposedly been made by Scottish Premier Division side, Dunfermline.

The story had appeared in two Sunday papers and both had mentioned the figure of £300,000 having been offered for the player, but Webb was quick to rebuff any notion that that was the case.

"As far as I'm concerned these stories are utter rubbish," declared Blues boss. "I just don't know where some of these papers get their information from – they are about as accurate as the tooth fairy."

"I can honestly say that I have not spoken to any Scottish club about Angell or anyone else. I suppose that any player that has scored as many goals as Brett is bound to encourage speculation, but there have been no enquiries from Scotland or anywhere else."

In fact, rather than let any of the playing squad leave Roots Hall, Webb was still looking to add to his playing staff. The loan signing of Pat Scully hadn't quenched his desire to bring in a new face or two and, prior to the home clash with the January 19th clash with Huddersfield Town, Southend's manager confirmed that the club had been unsuccessful in their attempt to sign Walsall forward, Stuart Rimmer.

"I am always looking to strengthen the squad and have been given the chance to spend some money. I felt it necessary to try and improve one area of the team and decided to try and tempt Walsall to let Rimmer go, but they felt my offer was below their valuation," Webb revealed.

'Up The Blues!'

Although he stopped short of revealing the amount offered, it was believed to be in the region of £150,000 for the 25 year old striker who had since been valued at £500,000 by his manager Kenny Hibbitt.

Rimmer had come to prominence with sixty-seven goals in one hundred and fourteen Chester City appearances from 1985 – 1988. Unsuccessful spells at Watford and Notts County followed and then led to a switch to Division Four side Walsall where Rimmer had rediscovered his goalscoring boots. Having had one bid turned down, Webb was not going back for the player as the two clubs were miles apart over the transfer fee. However, that wasn't to be the end of his pursuit for another forward and he explained why he felt that was an area that needed reinforcements.

"It may seem strange to some of our fans that we are the top scorers in Division Three and have four players in the leading marksmen charts – Brett Angell with twenty, Steve Tilson on eleven and Ian Benjamin and David Martin who have hit ten – and yet still want to bring someone else in," Webb admitted.

"The simple explanation is that I feel we need a player who can add a bit of variety to our forward play. We tend to be a bit stereotyped and have nobody who looks capable of getting a goal out of nothing."

"There is no-one in the squad who gives me any alternatives. No-one who can get the ball with their back to goal and make something happen or who will make a thirty yard run and put defenders under pressure. Most of our goals have come through team play, relying on people to prise openings before landing the killer blow."

With Rimmer now seemingly out of the equation, Webb confirmed that there was "one or two" other options available to him and he would be following those players up with an enquiry about the possibility of a deal being done.

The Southend boss refused to comment on the identity of the two forwards, but it was strongly rumoured that former Blue, Richard Cadette was one and Aldershot's David Puckett was the other.

Webb was right, it was deemed quite strange by Blues fans that he was actively seeking to add to his forward line, especially when the current one had netted thirty goals between them. Add to that the rest of the goals that had spread around the team it seemed fairly obvious to supporters that perhaps the defence needed addressing due to their seeming inability to keep a clean sheet.

Brett Angell had arrived from Stockport with little expectancy, but the striker had shown great ability in the air, he worked hard, scored all types of goals and was getting better and better as the season progressed. And, for someone so young – still only 21 – he was speaking with great maturity and assurance that belittled his years.

Ian Benjamin, was a different type of player, but had no trouble finding the net almost as frequently as Angell. Benji was much more experienced than his partner and that was evident in the way he played the game. His awareness of others around him was perhaps his strongest asset, but that would be an injustice to the other aspects to his game. The hold up play was exceptional for the third tier. Benji was also strong in the air and could play one touch when needed. He, too, scored a vast array of goals and was a role model and influence to many of the younger players in the squad.

While it was Angell who received many of the plaudits for his goals, Benjamin's contribution to the team hadn't gone unnoticed to many fans and it could be argued that he was one of the first names on Webb's team sheet.

Individually, both Angell and Benjamin were very good, but in as a partnership they were even better. They complimented each other so well and that's what made it seem a little odd that Webb sought another striker to add to the two he had. A back up would have been understandable, but £150,000 offer for Stuart Rimmer hardly suggested he would have been third choice. The offer was £50,000 more than what the club paid Stockport for Angell's services in the summer, but there was no doubting the manager's judgement – after all, he had done superbly well so far and he had the fans fully behind whatever decisions he made.

While Webb was busy looking to add to his forward line, there was also the task of preparing his side for the visit of Huddersfield Town who Southend had already beaten in the first game of the season at Leeds Road.

The previous week's win at Crewe had reignited the talk of promotion being on the cards amongst the fans. It was something that Webb was keen to play down, preferring instead to take each game as it comes.

"It's vital that everybody at the club keeps their feet firmly on the ground. It's fatal to start looking too far ahead. I know it's an old cliché, but it's important to just take very game as it comes. Huddersfield are a fine example of what I mean. They are a side currently in the bottom half of the table, but with the potential to give you a shock if you go out with your head in the clouds and not concentrating on the job in hand."

"I am a bit surprised to see Huddersfield as low as they are because when we played them on the opening day I felt they would be strong promotion material despite our two-one win up there."

There were no new injury concerns for Webb to contend with and that meant there would be no changes to the side that won and performed so well at Crewe.

So, after an impressive debut for the club, Pat Scully would now have the opportunity to make his first appearance for the club at Roots Hall as he lined up next to Paul Clark in the middle of defence.

Scully's debut had pleased the manager who was quick to praise the on loan Arsenal defender. "Pat slotted into what was a fine all round team performance at Crewe. I was delighted with his display especially when you consider he had very little time to settle into his new surroundings or meet his teammates. He is a cool customer – someone you can rely on in a pressure situation. At the moment Pat is with us for a month and we shall reassess things at the end of that period," said an impressed Webb.

Another vital cog in Blues return to winning ways was without doubt the fact that Dave Martin was free from suspension to resume his key partnership with Peter Butler. Martin had been nothing short of superb for Southend over the first half of the season, a fact that was not lost on his manager.

"David returned at Crewe and showed the qualities which we badly miss when he is out of the side. He gives us a much better balance and his presence allows Butler and Tilson to get forward more which gives us an additional cutting edge."

With the team having performed so well at Gresty Road, it virtually picked itself. All that remained was for Webb to players who would take up the places on the bench. Spencer Prior remained as one of the two, but Martin Ling lost his place to Adam Locke who was fit enough to be a substitute after another seven days training and rehabilitation.

'Up The Blues!'

The hope amongst the majority of the 5,509 crowd was that Southend would be able to build on the previous week's crucial win. Unfortunately, they were to endure an extremely frustrating afternoon as they missed several chances to win the game.

The game started very open and both teams had their chances to score. For the home, side they found Steve Hardwick hard to beat in Huddersfield's goal as he prevented both Andy Ansah and Ian Benjamin from getting their names on the scoresheet.

At the other end the visitors saw two efforts hit the woodwork, first from Robert Wilson and then striker Iwan Roberts followed suit. Paul Sansome could only watch on both occasions as he was well beaten and was thankful to see the frame of the goal come to his rescue.

There was to be a goal in the first half though, but it wasn't to the home fans liking as Huddersfield took the lead in such simple fashion.

It was a long kick forwards from Hardwick that was controlled by Roberts before he laid it off for midfielder Chris Marsden who played Phil Stant through to the right of the penalty area. Making the most of the space granted to him, Stant was able to pick out the onrushing Mark Smith who calmly put the ball past a fully stretched Sansome.

In the second half, Blues were clearly fired up after what must have been a dressing down from Webb. They took the game to a Huddersfield team that had decided to spend the remainder of the game camped in their own half.

The chances inevitably came for The Shrimpers, but they were unable to equalise as Dave Martin missed two good opportunities and Ansah saw his effort hit the bar from only six yards out.

On sixty-four minutes, Webb made the decision to bring on Adam Locke for top scorer Angell. It was a substitution that raised more than the odd eyebrow amongst the fans as Locke lined up on the right wing with Ansah moving up front.

Blues kept plugging away as time was running out and with seven minutes left to play, Peter Butler found Steve Tilson with an inch perfect pass that sent Tilly through on goal with only the keeper to beat. As Roots Hall drew anticipated breath, Tilson's touch proved too heavy and Hardwick was able to bravely dive down and get two hands on the ball.

'Up The Blues!'

That was the last opportunity of the match for Southend and when the final whistle sounded it signalled not only the end of the ninety minutes, but also the end of Blues unbeaten home record.

The chances that had not been converted had clearly cost the team and the notion of a new striker arriving suddenly didn't seem so alien to fans.

A frustrated Webb rued his team's inability to get on the scoresheet after the match. "It's bitterly disappointing to lose when we had enough chances to win the game three times over," he said.

"We lacked composure in front of goal and failed to punish Huddersfield for some glaring defensive mistakes, yet we make one error and the opposition cash in – it's annoying to say the least."

The manager's frustration was understandable and he was in quite clear in how he felt his players could convert the chances that were being created. "It's back to the training pitch. We are creating plenty of chances and must not start panicking. I am sure we will soon be back to what we have proved so good at this season – taking as well as making chances."

The defeat cut Blues lead to just three points as Grimsby had trounced Preston 4-1 to close the gap. There were also wins for the form side Cambridge United - whose impressive 3-0 away victory over Birmingham didn't go unnoticed – and Bolton Wanderers who leapfrogged Brentford into fourth spot following their 1-0 win over Shrewsbury.

Things were certainly tightening up at the top end of Division Three and there was now only seven points separating the top four. The pressure was on Southend to keep getting positive results and stay ahead of the chasing pack, but even more important was that they remained in the automatic promotion places.

The following weekend's fixture away at Preston North End was to be the last one in January. It was always going to be a tough away trip, but after PNE's drubbing at Grimsby they would obviously be looking for a better performance against the league leaders.

The other factor that would make the trip north even harder was the fact that Preston played their football on an artificial pitch which would mean the players would have to contend with a highly unpredictable bounce as well as play against a team who were used to all the little problems that an artificial surface could throw up.

However, Blues assistant manager wasn't so keen on raising this as an issue for the players and confirmed the possibility of preparing on a similar pitch during the week. "We are concentrating all our work this week on playing on that type of surface either at our normal training ground in Gloucester Park (Basildon) or over at Grays leisure centre. Mind you, the lads should be pretty used to it anyway because we always play on the artificial pitch in Basildon once a week."

There was another departure from the club during the week leading up to Preston when Martin Ling was allowed to join Mansfield Town on a month's loan. Ling, who had hardly featured for Southend had become a peripheral figure who, in reality, was only ever considered by Webb when options were limited.

The form of Andy Ansah and Adam Locke had obviously restricted Ling's involvement, but fans couldn't help but think that his stance over a new contract during pre-season had left him on the outside from the beginning. He had been unable to dislodge the aforementioned duo whereas Webb saw the trio of Clark, Martin & Butler as integral figures in his plans and it never felt like the manager considered Ling in the same light. He was happy to see the likes of Ansah and Locke flourish in the wide positions in his team while Ling was sitting in the stands looking on.

When asked about the departure, Webb clearly bore no grudges over the player and was diplomatic in his response to Ling's exclusion from the first team for the majority of the season. "Martin has not really shown the form we have come to expect from him this season and the switch to Mansfield could well be just the shot in the arm he needs to resurrect his career," he said.

"We are well served by players who can operate wide right – a position which I feel best suits Martin – with Ansah and Locke both ahead of him when it comes to first team selection and I felt it was only fair to give him the chance to move on."

"It's not really in the lads best interests to hang around here playing in the reserves when he can have the chance of league action. We will certainly want a fee for Martin if he eventually goes there on a more permanent basis, but in the meantime he leaves with our best wishes."

With Ling departing, albeit only for a month initially, there was an increased possibility of a new face arriving sooner rather than later.

Webb still fancied another forward and reiterated his desire to add to that area of the team a couple of days before the trip to Preston.

"The players here must be aware that I am looking around in an effort to bolster the squad with a front player as top priority. I have virtually ruled out hopes of getting Stuart Rimmer after Walsall slapped an unrealistic price tag on him, but I have several other irons in the fire," announced The Blues manager.

"I shall be pursuing one or two possible avenues next week and it's up to the men currently in the side to make sure the axe doesn't fall on them if and when we sign someone."

"We have been creating plenty of chances in all our recent matches, but the reason why we have only won one of the last six games is because we haven't been putting them away. Hopefully that will change as we will get back to the deadly finishing we showed earlier in the season - the lads have certainly looked sharp in training this week and it's up to them to do it on match day."

There was a fresh injury concern for Webb to consider with influential midfielder Peter Butler struggling with a knee injury that threatened to get the better of him for the forthcoming game.

It was an obvious concern for the boss and he was worried about how much the plastic pitches had affected Butler's complaint. "(He) has been plagued by a knee problem for several weeks now, but training on artificial surfaces this week to prepare for the Preston trip has aggravated matters. Peter had to pull out of training yesterday for treatment and will also be on the physio table today. He is a brave, gutsy character who will play through pain and hopefully will give the thumbs up because we need his all action style."

That suggested Butler might struggle through the pain to feature against Preston, but should he not make it there was other players to call upon. The favourite to take his place was the fit again John Cornwell who was now just lacking the match practice after a lengthy spell on the sidelines.

Another possibility was to play Adam Locke in a more central role, a position in which Webb had primarily signed him to play in, but his performances on the wing and the form of Butler and Dave Martin had meant that Locke hadn't had a look in in the centre of midfield.

Webb confirmed that he would give Butler every opportunity to prove himself and despite Preston occupying nineteenth position in the table, Blues Chief's main concern was how much of a factor the artificial pitch would prove to be.

"Obviously it's an advantage to them playing on that surface as they are used to it week in and week out," Webb stressed before backing his boys "but, although I personally don't like those pitches we have to go up there and adopt a positive approach. I am confident we have the players here with the ability to adapt."

As expected, Butler took a chance and opted to play through the pain and line up in the heart of Blues midfield. However, there was one change to the team that suffered a first home defeat of the season to Huddersfield and that was the inclusion of Adam Locke at the expense of right winger Andy Ansah, who was relegated to the bench alongside John Cornwell.

Southend started the game well and didn't seem to be affected by the plastic pitch as they tried to get the ball forwards and play in their counterparts half.

There was an early shout for a penalty for The Shrimpers that was ignored when Mike Flynn looked as though he'd fouled Dean Austin as the full back made his way towards goal. The appeals from the players fell on deaf ears as referee, William Burns, waved them away.

As the game progressed, the home side predictably began to take control of the game, putting their experience and familiarity of the artificial surface to good use.

Some of the Southend players were beginning to show signs they were struggling with the pitch, particularly when turning on it and this become evident with Preston taking the lead after twenty minutes.

Striker Brian Mooney ran at Paul Clark and had Blues skipper in all sorts of trouble as he easily turned his man to get a shot away that was only parried by Sansome straight into the path of Gary Swann who couldn't miss for the game's opening goal.

There was a couple of half chances that Southend failed to make the most of in reply to going a goal behind, but it was clear that there was a massive difference in the way both teams were coping with the pitch.

Despite not being as comfortable with the plastic, Blues fashioned the best chance of the game when Ian Benjamin found Locke with an intelligent square pass that left the wide man with an open goal. It was the easiest of tasks to score, but somehow all Locke could manage was to send the ball wide of the unguarded net, much to everyone's disbelief.

After the break Preston continued to work the ball well and had the visitors chasing shadows as Blues continued to work hard, but failed to get any real time on the football.

Inevitably, a second goal came and it was no surprise that Preston doubled their lead. The goal came on fifty-six minutes and no small part was played by Mr Burns who harshly adjudged Clark to have fouled Warren Joyce on the edge of the area.

It was a decision that baffled the captain and his team mates, but there were no question marks over the resulting free-kick which Jeff Wrightson brilliantly curled around the wall and past Sansome's token dive for a two-nil lead.

Southend upped their game and through sheer determination and application, they started to trouble Preston's back four.

Steve Tilson saw his effort from an acute angle well cleared off the line and Benjamin's looping header suffered the same fate.

Webb then rung the changes and introduced Andy Ansah for Locke and John Cornwell for the suffering Peter Butler.

The substitutions paid off when Blues got a goal back with only two minutes remaining on the clock. The goal had a stroke of luck about it after Chris Powell's ball forward was fortunately headed onto Brett Angell by Flynn and it fell nicely into the path of Ansah.

The substitute's speed took him away from his man and he showed a cool head to finish neatly under the body of Alan Kelly in the home goal.

Unfortunately, it was too little too late for Southend as Preston were able to see out the remaining two minutes to seal their second win in seven.

After the match, a distraught Locke blamed himself and his shocking miss for the 2-1 defeat. "I'm really sick. I won't get an easier chance than that to score my first league goal – my Granny would have stuck it away," groaned Locke. "I've got no excuses, I flapped at it and that miss cost us dear because had I scored it would have rattled Preston and we might have gone on to win or at least earned a point."

For Webb, the performance did little to persuade him otherwise about the need to add to his team. "We exploded to the top of the table by scoring goals and still have players capable of hitting the net – I'm sure some team is going to be on the wrong end of a hammering soon, but at the same time I feel the time is right to bring at least one player in to strengthen the squad and keep one or two players on their toes. Perhaps providing much needed competition to spark them off."

The loss for Southend brought an end to a disappointing January that saw a return of only three points from the four league games they played. There were also the games at the tail end of December that had to be taken into account where successive home draws had followed a 1-0 defeat away at Chester. Overall, it meant that Blues had won just a solitary league game in their last seven – anything but the form of promotion contenders.

Results elsewhere meant that defeat at Preston saw The Shrimpers relinquish top spot as Grimsby climbed above them on goals scored after The Mariners won 2-0 against Bradford. Both teams were now on forty-nine points, but Grimsby had played a game more than Blues.

Of the other teams closest to the top two, only Brentford featured in action, winning 2-0 at home against Swansea to move within seven points of David Webb's men. Both Cambridge and Bolton didn't have games due to the F.A. Cup fourth round, but were no doubt delighted to see Preston's win over Southend.

So far during the campaign, Webb had been incredibly loyal to his first choice eleven. This was no doubt partly down to his lack of options in his squad, but the form they had shown offered no reason for him to change too much.

Now, after a dismal run that started following the win over Grimsby in the middle of December, questions were being asked and it was even being suggested that now they would begin fall away. From some quarters of the media it was now very much a case of 'it was never going to last' when talking up Southend's promotion challenge.

Webb's desire to bring in new faces was confirmation that he felt he needed to freshen things up in certain areas as the concern amongst the fans that the main group of players were beginning to run out of steam.

The run of form had cast fresh doubts in many supporters' minds and as there was no let-up in the games ahead it meant Southend could not afford to feel sorry for themselves. It was the mangers job to now lift his team and get them playing with the belief, conviction and authority they had displayed throughout the season…starting with an away trip at Shrewsbury Town and the difficult home game versus Stoke City just three days later.

Division Three Table, January 26th 1990

	TEAM	P	W	D	L	F	A	PTS	GD
1	Grimsby Town	26	15	4	7	43	23	49	20
2	Southend United	25	15	4	6	42	32	49	10
3	Cambridge United	24	12	7	5	42	28	43	14
4	Brentford	25	11	9	5	34	25	42	9
5	Bolton Wanderers	24	12	6	6	34	27	42	7
6	Tranmere Rovers	25	11	7	7	40	29	40	11
7	Reading	24	12	4	8	38	32	40	6
8	Leyton Orient	23	12	3	8	30	27	39	3
9	Stoke City	24	10	8	6	32	25	38	7
10	Huddersfield Town	25	11	4	10	29	30	37	-1
11	Bury	25	10	6	9	37	35	36	2
12	Bournemouth	24	9	9	6	32	30	36	2
13	**Swansea City**	24	10	5	9	33	31	35	2
14	Birmingham City	26	8	11	7	26	31	35	-5
15	Bradford City	26	9	7	10	30	32	34	-2
16	Exeter City	25	8	7	10	30	28	31	2
17	Wigan Athletic	25	9	4	12	35	39	31	-4
18	Preston North End	25	7	7	11	29	40	28	-11
19	Chester City	24	7	5	12	23	29	26	-6
20	Fulham	25	5	8	12	25	33	23	-8
21	Mansfield Town	25	4	8	13	22	35	20	-13
22	Shrewsbury Town	23	4	7	12	33	42	19	-9
23	Crewe Alexandra	24	4	7	13	34	46	19	-12
24	Rotherham United	24	3	7	14	22	46	16	-24

'Up The Blues!'
Photographs & Illustrations

Ian Benjamin's sensational strike at Roots Hall v Crewe

David Martin celebrates scoring v Preston

'Up The Blues!'

Benji showing his skill in front of the West Stand

*David Webb with his manager
of the month award for September*

'Up The Blues!'

Brett Angell with another clinical finish – this time v Bury

The goal scorers in the 10-1 win over Aldershot
(left to right) Prior, Tilson, Angell, Ansah, Benjamin

'Up The Blues!'

Andy Ansah scoring the decisive goal at Leyton Orient

The goal that clinched promotion. Benji nets to make history.

'Up The Blues!'

Seconds later: Benji is mobbed by his team mates

*'The Blues are going up': the players celebrate
their unbelievable achievement*

'Up The Blues!'

Steve Tilson tries in vain to break through a resolute Brentford defence in the season finale

Jubilant fans invade the pitch after the final game of the season

'Up The Blues!'

The open top bus parade about to begin its journey from Roots Hall

Skipper Paul Clark enjoying the celebrations

'Up The Blues!'

February 1991

"There is six inches of snow on the pitch"
– John Adams, Southend United Vice-Chairman.

The first month of the New Year had not been too kind to Southend United. Whilst the dream of a historic promotion was still very much on, they had ended January by losing their position at the top of the league after a disappointing run of results. The task was now to not only reignite the promotion push, but to also try and regain pole position in the Division Three table.

The defeat at Preston had proved to have more repercussions than just the manner of the loss. Struggling with a persistent injury, Peter Butler had tried to play through the pain on Deeepdale's artificial surface and it had done him more harm than good.

It had emerged that Butler had been suffering for a few weeks with his knee problem and the pitch at Preston had only aggravated it further. After examining the complaint, the club doctor suggested that he should see a specialist to try and resolve any underlying issues that may have yet come to light.

The Shrimpers manager David Webb was hoping for some positive news regarding the player, "We must keep our fingers crossed that it's not too serious. Peter has bravely continued to play despite a niggling knee problem which has failed to respond to normal treatment from our physio. He saw our club doctor who recommended a visit to a specialist and made and appointment for him to see an expert in Romford last night."

"Hopefully it won't be anything too serious because it would be a blow to lose Peter for any real length of time as he has been a vital cog in our promotion wheel this season. The main thing is to ensure that the problem is nothing too dramatic and to ease any worry Peter may have himself."

However, whatever the outcome of the specialist's report, the influential midfielder would be missing for two games regardless after yet another booking he received at Preston that culminated in an automatic two match suspension. That ban would commence for the games following the big home clash with Cambridge United on February 8th. Whether it was because of suspension or a troublesome knee, Butler would certainly be missed during his enforced absence from the first team.

Webb also confirmed that he had failed to make any significant progress in his attempts to add some new faces to the squad and he was keen to point out that he wouldn't be forced into any spending money just for the sake of it.

"I've said all along that I don't want to make panic signings because we have had a poor run of results – anyone I bring in would have to be an improvement on what we've got otherwise there would be no point. At the moment the players who interest me are either not available or the clubs are demanding crazy prices," he revealed, before reluctantly admitting defeat for the time being, "I have decided for the time being to stop chasing my tail and stick by the lads we've got who, after all, have not done too badly so far this season."

The manager was also keen to reassure supporters that the poor sequence of results required a degree of calm from the terraces. "I want our fans to be patient both with me and the team," said Webb. "Every team, even Liverpool and Arsenal, hits a bad run at some stage in the season. The important thing is not to start taking panic measures and trying to change the style which has proved so effective."

"We have the players who can get us out of it and back on the winning trail. A win at Shrewsbury and then victories in our two home games next week would quickly dispel any crisis talk and that's what we must aim for."

"The lads have built up a good spirit and it's important to maintain that togetherness. If we run into trouble through injury or suspension I can always go out and bring someone in on loan. In the meantime, I want to give the current players a vote of confidence and send them into the second half of the season in a determined mood not to throw away all that they have achieved so far - we are still second in the table, level on points with leaders Grimsby and with a game in hand. There is little wrong here that a win won't put right."

The first opportunity of the month to get that win and back on track was with that away trip at Gay Meadow, home of Shrewsbury Town. Prior to the game there was good news surrounding Peter Butler's knee problem after it having been diagnosed as tendonitis. In the last few days leading up to Shrewsbury, Butler had followed doctor's orders and stayed away from training after having an injection to numb the pain. This gave the knee the opportunity to settle down and with a couple of days rest being all that was required, he was able to declare himself fit for the match versus The Shrews.

The Shrews had only won four league games at Gay Meadow all season, but despite this The Shrimpers would have to be on their game to avoid adding to the poor run they had recently suffered. Only the previous week, Town, bossed by John Bond, had defeated 1988 F.A. Cup winners Wimbledon by a single goal to nil in the same competition. That result would obviously have buoyed the whole club and they would be more than ready for the visit of Southend United.

Perhaps one of the reasons for the cup upset seven days earlier was the heavy mud that covered the Gay Meadow pitch making it more suitable to sides in the lower leagues as opposed to teams in the First Division – even though it was Wimbledon and not Liverpool!

As the game got under way, it was clear that the pitch was having an effect on the game. The ball struggled to run true all afternoon and players had a battle on their hands just to get any passes to their intended targets.

In fact, there was only one piece of quality on show throughout the match and that came as early as the eighth minute when Southend scored a goal that would not have looked out of place in England's top flight.

Peter Butler's role for the goal proved crucial and he underlined the desire needed in a promotion chasing team. He won the ball in a boggy centre circle before playing the ball hard into the feet of Benjamin. With his first touch, Benji played the ball back to Butler who had spotted the run of Angell and played an inch perfect ball through the heart of The Shrews defence for the striker to latch onto and calmly place his first time shot past Ken Hughes in goal for the early lead.

Blues almost immediately added to their advantage when Andy Ansah's fine work on the wing presented Angell with a chance to convert, but the forward was unable to connect properly as he searched for his twenty-second goal of the campaign.

Southend continued to try and add a second goal, but they were denied by some good defending that saw a Steve Tilson shot well blocked. Moments later, Dave Martin went close with a free kick that failed to find the target from twenty yards out.

Midway through the half, John Bond's side managed to raise their game and they then had a spell where Blues were unable to get out of their half for any real length of time.

It was scrappy and untidy in places, but Shrewsbury began to work Paul Sansome and, thankfully for the visitors, Sammy was in great form between the sticks.

In particular, midfielder Tony Kelly was left to rue the acrobatics of Southend's number one when Sansome wonderfully covered the ground to tip over his clever chip that looked to be a certain goal.

There was no further action in the first forty-five and as the second began it was more backs to the wall for Southend as Shrewsbury continued to get the ball into their opponent's penalty area.

Again though, it was untidy and ugly to watch, but with Blues defending their one goal lead, every ball that was cleared to safety and every shot that was blocked was greeted with determined cheers from the travelling fans behind the goal.

Still, whenever the home side managed to find themselves with a clear shooting opportunity they were denied by the superb Sansome time and time again – the pick of the bunch was his full length stop to deny a dismayed Mick Heathcote an equaliser and a share of the spoils.

It was a classic example of a side 'winning ugly' that secured three valuable points for the Essex side, something that was not lost on David Webb. "The result was the important thing today after one or two spluttering displays recently. It's ironic that we played better against both Huddersfield and Preston in the previous two games and lost," he pointed out.

The winner came from Brett Angell's cool finish that won the game, yet he was in no doubt as to whom the real hero of the hour was. "Forget my goal – Sammy was the one who earned us three points, he was magnificent," Angell exclaimed, before perfectly summing up the afternoon. "Perhaps we did not play as well as we have done for most of the season, but you could not fault the whole team for the way they battled and fought for every ball."

Indeed, the man Southend had to thank for the win was their goalkeeper who revealed he almost had to sit out the match due to a back problem that had prevented him for taking part in training the day before the match.

"Luckily it (the back) eased itself during Saturday morning, but I honestly thought there was a real doubt about my being able to play. It appears that my back goes into spasm and the muscles contract. I felt it gradually stiffening up during the game, but luckily I came through okay, although there's no way I could go out and play ninety minutes (right) now. I have an appointment with the club doctor to see if he can clear it up – it's not fair on the other lads if I cannot go into a game one hundred per cent confident of doing my best and not letting anyone down."

After the 1-0 triumph over Shrewsbury, Webb chose to elaborate on the situation surrounding Spencer Prior's future and the youngster's decision to regret the offer that the club had put on the table - a decision that would lead to Prior being placed on the transfer list.

"I am very disappointed because I obviously feel that Spencer has a bright future in the game otherwise I would not have offered him a new contract. His contract is up at the end of the season and I don't want us to be in the same situation we found ourselves in last term over David Crown when we lost out by having to go to a transfer tribunal."

It was unclear as to exactly why Prior had turned down a new deal, but he possibly could have felt hard done by after losing his place to Pat Scully following the Irishman's arrival. His performances at the tail end of the calendar year had seen him make two costly errors – which cost him his position in the starting eleven - but there could be no complaints over his form in the first half of the season. For a player of such a young age, he had fitted in remarkably well alongside Paul Clark and, as Webb pointed out, looked like he could go on to bigger and better things.

The possibility of the reason being more money was spoken about amongst fans – there was no way Southend's wage budget was anywhere near the likes of Bolton, Birmingham, Stoke and Preston, but even so it was hard to believe Prior would be pricing himself out the club's reach at just nineteen years old. Whatever his reasoning, Webb had made the right decision and the fact that Prior was to be still involved in and around the first team offered hope that a resolution could be met.

For Southend and Prior, their next league action was back at Roots Hall with Stoke City as their opponents. It was Stoke who, back in September, had ruined The Blues unbeaten start in spectacular fashion when they crushed a stunned Shrimpers side 4-0 at Victoria Road.

The return fixture came just three days after the Shrewsbury match and the thoughts of manager David Webb centred on his team owing their opponents for that hammering suffered earlier in the season.

"It would certainly taste sweet to get one over Stoke…or even four," he quipped. "That result still hurts and is the one black mark on what has been a pretty good season so far, but it won't be easy because, make no mistake about it, they are a good side."

"Stoke are a big club and desperate to get back in the top flight again. We will need to be at our best if we are to get a good result, but the lads are in the right mood and if we play to our full potential then we should collect all three vital points."

There were no new concerns for Webb over injuries which meant that Paul Sansome's would continue in goal despite the obvious worries about his back complaint. Dave Martin was also given the all clear after he too was suffering with a back injury. Webb declaring that both players would be "one hundred per cent for the Stoke game."

With Martin and Sansome both fit to play, Blues fielded an unchanged team for the second successive match and, with revenge at the forefront of supporters minds too, kick off couldn't come quick enough for the crowd of just over five thousand that attended on a cold and frosty Tuesday night.

It was the first of two home games in the space of a few days with high flying Cambridge United due at The Hall on the forthcoming Friday, but it was a huge credit to Webb and his players that they only had eyes on Stoke and the performance reflected that.

From the opening minute, Southend didn't allow the visitors any time on the ball to get going and they worked extremely hard to keep the ball in their opponents half of the pitch. The reward for The Shrimpers was several corners they had won in the opening twenty minutes, but unfortunately they couldn't find a way passed a determined Peter Fox in goal.

Fox underlined this midway through the half when he somehow managed to turn a Brett Angell header onto the post and he denied the same player after thirty-four minutes with a smart save from close range.

Despite Fox's performance, a breakthrough did come with only four minutes of the opening half remaining. The goal was as route one as you could get, starting with a drop kick from Paul Sansome that was flicked on by Angell and then helped on further by Ian Benjamin's clever hooked pass.

The chase was now on and it was being led by Steve Tilson and Andy Ansah as the ball travelled into the penalty area. Both Blues players got in each other's way and, as Fox narrowed the angle, the ball fortunately found a way behind the keeper and at the feet of Tilson whose cross cum shot deflected off Angell and into the empty net.

That was goal number twenty-two for Angell and it was the luckiest of all his previous strikes, but that didn't matter one little bit. It was an important goal at an important time of the match and the celebrations amongst the players underlined as much.

After the interval – and with conditions now making the ground very hard under foot - it was very much more of the same as Southend continued to pepper Peter Fox's goal in the attempts to add to their lead. The keeper first denied Angell's close range header before thwarting Benjamin's long range effort with a save right out of the top drawer.

Chris Powell, who was having a fine game at left back, joined in the attack soon after and sent over a deep cross that was headed down by Angell for Ansah who saw his goal bound effort turned away by the sharp reflexes of Fox once more.

It was fast becoming Southend v Peter Fox - such was his excellent display between the sticks for his side. He had made several great saves to deny Blues a second goal and even when he was beaten by David Martin's thunderous half volley, the crossbar came to his rescue, keeping the score at 1-0 and that was how it stayed.

A delighted David Webb couldn't speak highly enough of his players post-match and was quick with his praise. "Our lads were magnificent. The boys were certainly fired up tonight, they desperately wanted revenge for that 4-0 defeat at Stoke last September and with any luck we could have won by an even bigger margin that that. Both teams deserve tremendous credit for the way they mastered those very difficult conditions, but I felt we always looked a side who wanted to win more than they did."

Scorer of the winning goal echoed his manager's sentiments. "There's no doubt we were by far the better side. We adapted to the conditions much better than they did and but for their keeper we would undoubtedly have won by a bigger margin. He robbed me of a hat-trick and how he got to a second half shot from Andy Ansah I'll never know. In the end, my goal ensured that justice was done," Angell said.

Justice was well and truly done as Southend had played like a team with a point to prove all over the pitch. In defence, Paul Clark was outstanding at centre back in not allowing Stoke to gather an impetus in the game and it was a second clean sheet in three days. Chris Powell also had another impressive game as the young left back was growing in stature with each match. Such was his self-confidence, he was also now becoming an attacking threat when he got into advanced positions.

But, perhaps the man of the match was Ansah. The winger gave Stoke full back, Cliff Carr, a torrid time with his pace and trickery and that played a huge part in Blues attacking prowess.

Those back to back wins for Southend saw them return to the top of the table as Grimsby dropped points away at Huddersfield with a score draw. Blues also still had a game in hand over The Mariners, but they were also casting a concerned eye over Cambridge United who had played one game less than Southend and were now only six points behind them in third. It set up the forthcoming Friday night clash between the two sides perfectly and a win for Webb's side would increase their gap over The U's.

However, the cold weather that had been evident in the match versus Stoke was to get worse and the day before Cambridge United was due in town. Heavy snowfall had covered Roots Hall and the match therefore had to be postponed. In fact, the weather was so bad that the pitch was deemed unplayable without the opinion of the referee necessary to verify such a decision.

Momentum had seemingly come back to The Shrimpers and so it was with huge disappointment to everyone that the match had fallen foul to the weather, but there was really no other option.

John Adams explained the decision to call off the much anticipated fixture. "Conditions are absolutely appalling and the forecast is that things are going to get even worse. There was no point in trying to put off a decision until tomorrow. It's only fair to supporters of both teams to let them know of the situation and save them having to wait until the last minute."

When asked about whether a decision should have been delayed until the match official could inspect the ground, Adams replied, "I doubt if the match ref could have got Roots Hall and it would have been equally difficult for a local official to get here as well."

The following day, David Webb had a look at Roots Hall's playing surface for himself and was in no doubt that the correct decision had been made. "The pitch was much worse than on Tuesday for the Stoke game and it would not have been right that such an important match should have been reduced to a lottery."

"We want the best surface possible so that the better footballing side has the greater chance of success. Both Cambridge and ourselves are on course for promotion and nobody wants to risk losing vital points simply through a player making a mistake on an icy playing surface. (The) frozen ground (is) now covered by snow which is also freezing – it was merely a formality for the game to be put off."

Webb thought he could now start planning for the away trip to Leyton Orient on the 12th, which was only four days away. But, no sooner had Webb cast his attention towards that encounter did that to succumb to the freezing conditions.

This now presented two key members of the squad who had been struggling with slight injuries the chance for some extra recovery days. It was hoped that the back complaints that had been hampering both Dave Martin and Paul Sansome would hugely benefit from the sudden break in league fixtures.

The main problem now for the team was how they would stay in shape as the weather had also prevented them from training at Gloucester Park. Webb's answer to this problem was to use the indoor pitch at Grays Football Club – the facilities that were used in the build to the away game at Preston.

The Southend Chief was full of praise for quality on offer at the Thurrock club and it more than served its purpose. "The facilities at Grays are excellent and we have been able to get some five-a-sides going and generally keep the players toned up," Webb explained, but still hoped for some outside training as soon as possible. "Hopefully we will be able to get outdoors and do some running which will make sure that we don't lose any of our fitness. The main thing during this period of inactivity is to make sure the lads don't get bored. Variety is the keynote."

Weather wise, worse was to follow for Southend in the next few days as the conditions failed to improve sufficiently for the home game against Reading on Friday 16th and that was also reluctantly called off.

This was another blow to Southend who were keen to get back to action as soon as possible, but John Adams never really believed the match would get the green light. "(The) match is a non-starter," he said. "There is six inches of snow on the pitch, but that has done a good job by keeping the surface free of frost."

Adams revealed that the surrounding roads were a factor in the postponement as well as the safety of both sets of supporters had to be taken into consideration.

The following day there was at last some positive news on the horizon in terms of the weather forecast though and that meant the two clubs were looking at the possibility of a hastily rearranged date of 20th of February, just four days later.

"We are optimistic that providing the elements are kind to us then we should see some action next Tuesday. The police and the league have been very co-operative and we are ready to do all we can to get the game on," confirmed Adams.

That news was welcomed by Webb who was eager to see his side carry on their recent run of results. "The forecast is for the warmer weather to continue and I see no reason why the excellent Roots Hall drainage shouldn't be able to cope. We can't wait to get back into action again. The lads are desperate to continue where they left off in their previous two games – both victories over Shrewsbury and Stoke."

It was about to become a busy few days for the Southend and he was thankful for the bad weather so that he was able to devote his full attention to the pressing matters that surrounded his team.

First there was further developments regarding Sammy's back injury and the news was that of the good variety, although his keeper was not out the woods just yet.

Sansome had been given the thumbs up from the osteopath he saw to carry on playing and training as normal, but he must adhere to a strict programme to keep his back as supple as he possibly could to minimise the risk of repeating the injury.

An ever present between the sticks for Southend, Sammy was a key part to the team and Webb would want to keep it that way because in spite of the promise young reserve goalkeeper Jimmy Jones had shown, it would be a huge ask for the inexperienced youngster to fill Sansome's boots at this stage of the season.

There was also a decision to be made over Pat Scully's future as the Irish defender's initial loan deal was reaching its conclusion. In the end, there wasn't a lot to weigh up for Webb. Scully had been impressive in the games he had played in and had proved an instant hit with fans. The Shrimpers boss didn't think twice and set about putting the wheels in motion for the player to stay at Roots Hall for a second month.

"Results speak for themselves and the fact that we have won three out of the five games Pat has played in is testimony enough. Pat is a fine prospect who will get better with the more league experience he gains. He settled in very well at the club and has proved a popular addition to the squad. We are delighted that Arsenal have agreed to his staying a little longer," said an excited Webb.

The Blues manager was indeed a fan and was keen on taking Scully to Essex permanently, but wasn't sure how that would sit with his parent club. "Arsenal have been keeping close tabs on his progress while with us. We shall just have to see whether they would be interested in us buying him or whether they want to keep him on their staff."

It was also confirmed by the manager that there had been no new developments concerning the man Scully had replaced, Spencer Prior and the player's stance regarding the contract offer on the table.

The club had talked of getting the best possible fee for the centre back, but as had proved the case with the four players who had been in the same position during close season, the door would not be shut on anyone should things be resolved. It was hoped by all that Prior would sort his future out soon and preferably that future would lie with Southend United.

As the weekend came and went, so did the weather that had left Roots Hall under a blanket of snow that had resulted in two postponements. That then gave the all clear for the quickly rearranged Reading fixture to go ahead just four days after the original date was cancelled.

Reading would arrive in Essex bringing with them a real upturn in their fortunes having won five out of their six league games since Christmas. That run had left them within touching distance of fourth place and they came to Roots Hall looking to avenge the two defeats they had suffered at The Shrimpers hands at Elm Park where they had conceded eight goals in the process.

The Blues boss was sure that the 4-2 and 4-1 triumphs in the league and Leyland Daf Cup respectively would mean the result would be a formality for his team. "If anything those results have probably fired them up and made them keener for revenge," Webb said. "Reading have collected some good results lately and nobody in our team will be allowed to underestimate them. We will need to show the same passion and drive as in our two matches before the freeze. The lads have a great incentive tonight because they will know that three points will push us four points clear of Grimsby at the top with a game in hand."

The home side would have to do without the influential Peter Butler for the match who began his two match suspension for an accumulation of yellow cards. The ban was something that Blues could have done without, but on the flip side it would allow the player to get some rest from action that might result in his niggling knee injury clearing up.

In his place would be the returning John Cornwell who was to make his first start for the club since his ankle ligament injury back in November. It wasn't as straight forward a decision as it might have seemed as there were other options open to Webb with Jason Cook and Adam Locke also in his thoughts, but in the end, the manager had opted for the ex-Swindon player to partner Dave Martin in the middle of the park.

"I have given the matter a lot of thought and watched all three lads closely in training over the last few days. In the end I decided that John was probably the best bet to do the particular job I had in mind. It's John's chance to get himself back in contention having been out of the starting line-up for three months," reasoned The Blues chief.

"Mind you, it won't be easy for anyone taking over from Butler who has been one of our most consistent players this season, but it's no use bemoaning your fate. I am sure Cornwell can slot into the side and help keep us on the promotion road."

The promotion push had stagnated for almost two weeks, but it was through no fault of their own and Webb was not about to offer up the freezing weather and heavy snowfall as a reason for his players not to put in a good performance.

"Our boys are keen to get on the pitch again and have certainly looked sharp and eager in our restricted training sessions. But these (the weather) are things you have to overcome in our season – soccer is a winter sport and you must expect the odd hiccup in fixtures – players must be professional enough to adapt."

So, aside from Cornwell deputising for Butler there was no other changes from the starting eleven that beat Stoke nearly two weeks ago. As for the subs, there was a recall for the fit again Adam Locke who replaced Jason Cook to sit next to Andy Edwards on the bench.

Reading were also forced into making a change to their preferred line up due to Craig Maskell's suspension and he was replaced by Steve Moran who lined up with Trevor Senior in the two man attack.

It was the visitors who started better as the home side resembled exactly what they were – a team who hadn't kicked a ball in competitive action for thirteen days due to the snow which was still visible behind the goal in front of the South terrace.

In the early exchanges it was poor play from The Blues with their passing often misplaced, forwards failing to hold onto the ball and defenders who struggled to cope with a lively Reading forward line.

Twice in quick succession Michael Gilkes worked well on the left wing to create chances for Senior, but on both occasions the striker made a mess of the finish, but the warning signs were there for all to see.

The Shrimpers then managed to briefly improve their game and fashioned a half chance for Dave Martin who could only head over, but Blues gave their fans something to cheer about soon after.

With twenty-six minutes on the clock, Paul Clark took a free kick just inside the Reading half. Seemingly anticipating a huge push from the opposition in the attempt to leave several Southend players offside, Clark casually lofted the ball forwards for Ian Benjamin whose run from deep caught out The Royals and left him through on Steve Francis' goal.

Benji's first touch was uncharacteristically heavy, giving the keeper a chance to narrow the angle, but Benjamin still beat him to the ball and toe poked passed the advancing Francis for his first goal since the reverse fixture in December.

Regardless of the goal, Reading carried on looking the better team and the one that was more likely to score. Fortunately for Southend, they managed to hold out and take a one-nil lead into half time.

If supporters were hoping that some words from Dave Webb would galvanise the team for the second half then they were very much mistaken. The game continued in much the same vain, only this time Reading got a deserved equaliser just nine minutes after the restart.

It was a neat passage of play that brought Reading back level before the ball was centred and met first by Trevor Senior, then Stuart Lovell and it was the latter's touch that left Pat Scully off balance which allowed the unmarked Steve Moran to sweep the ball into the net.

This then spurred the Royals on further, now believing they could take all the points on offer. Gilkes was seeing a lot of the ball, but after a physically strong challenge from Dean Austin the winger was stretchered off with what turned out to be a broken leg. Gilkes left to applause from all four sides of the stadium and, although the tackle wasn't malicious, Austin was clearly shaken by the severity of Gilkes' injury.

The game was won with only ten minutes left to play and it came as no real surprise when it was Reading who got the game's third goal. The match winner was former Exeter midfielder, Danny Bailey, as he latched onto Moran's headed assist to place his left footed shot under Sammy to seal a deserved win.

The goal was scored right in front of the travelling Reading fans and they celebrated with Bailey as the win further strengthened their promotion push while damaging that of their hosts.

After the match a disappointed Webb confirmed his fears of the lack of football would harm his team. "My fear was that we would never pick up where we left off against Stoke two weeks ago and that proved to be the case. Seven or eight players turned in below par performances and you can't expect to win when that happens," he said.

However, skipper Paul Clark refused to site the enforced lay off as a reason for the poor display. "We would only be kidding ourselves to put that forward as an excuse. The truth is we were second best in everything and put what must rank as one of our poorest performances of the season. So it's now up to everyone to roll up their sleeves against Fulham on Saturday and get this result out of our system."

Fulham at Craven Cottage would not be an easy place to go in spite of their lowly league position and they had just won all of last three fixtures there with wins over Chester City, Crewe and Preston North End. But, before thoughts turned towards the trip to West London, right back Dean Austin was cleared of all blame over the challenge that left Michael Gilkes with a broken leg.

The injured party himself said, "I knew I had broken my leg as soon as it happened, but it was an accident and I don't blame Austin for the injury," Gilkes declared.

It was a freak injury from an innocuous tackle and it was important for the club that everyone recognised that fact. It wasn't in Austin's nature to deliberately injure an opponent and Gilkes' words were echoed by his manager Ian Porterfield who also exonerated The Shrimpers full back from any blame.

An incident like that can have an effect on players, but Austin trained well leading up to the weekends match with Fulham and would be mentally okay to take his place in the starting line-up.

However, there were other positions in the team that were up for grabs after Webb confirmed in the press that he would be looking at his options for the match, confirming at least one change and not ruling out the possibility of more.

Unhappy with his side's display against Reading, The Boss said, "I will definitely make one change which in turn will lead to a couple of positional switches. I would rather not go into my plans in detail because we don't want give Fulham any chance of gaining an advantage."

"There's no need to press the panic button, but at the same time we must make amends swiftly for the Reading setback which was a bitter disappointment to everyone. The lads looked very rusty after their two week lay-off, but I am hoping they have got it out their system and will be back to normal tomorrow."

It was unusual for Webb to make changes to his side that were not due to injury or suspension. In fact, it could easily be argued that a significant reason for the success up to that point was that he was able to field a settled side most weeks. It had meant that there were good, solid partnerships all over the pitch that had improved as they developed. Butler & Martin in midfield, Powell & Tilson on the left, Austin & Ansah on the right, Angell & Benjamin up front. That had proved to be successful and for Webb to make a change or two to the team underlined just how unhappy he was with the manner of the defeat at home to Reading.

The promised change came and it was utility man John Cornwell who made way and in his place came Adam Locke. Locke was to come into the side wearing the number eight shirt, but after a reshuffle to the team, would start on the right wing. Ian Benjamin would drop into the middle of midfield in place of Cornwell and little Andy Ansah partnered Brett Angell in attack.

Benji had featured in midfield only once before in a Southend shirt and that was in The Leyland Daf Cup versus Maidstone. It had been effective and had worked well on the night, but that was against opposition from the league below – Fulham would represent a much sterner test for the makeshift midfield.

In direct opposition to Benjamin in would be Justin Skinner and Peter Scott who were tough, solid players at Third Division level. Other players with pedigree within Fulham's team were strikers Gary Brazil and Phil Stant who, on their day, could prove a real handful for any defence in the league.

This was recognised by Webb and he was quick to pour water on the notion that the West Londoners would be easy pickings for his team, recalling how impressive they were when they two sides met at Roots Hall three months earlier.

"I cannot believe they are down near the bottom of the table. When they played us at Roots Hall last November I thought they were the best side we have played. To be honest we were lucky to get away with a one-one draw that day."

When it was put to Webb that Southend United had never won at Craven Cottage in their history - underlining the huge task ahead - he replied, "Well it has to happen sometime – tomorrow would suit us fine!"

Fulham started the game like a side not really believing they could upset the odds and, devoid of a game plan to hurt their opponents, foolishly kept hitting long balls up to the strike force of Brazil and Stant. This was even more baffling for everyone watching as they were battling against strong winds in the first half and that particular tactic never really looked like paying off.

In contrast, Southend looked like a side that were determined to get back to winning ways. Martin and Benjamin were collecting the ball from the central defenders and managed to find the time and space to get the ball wide where Blues would look to hurt their hosts from there.

Such was the difference in approach play, belief and determination that it paid dividends for Southend as early as the fourth minute.

After winning a corner on the right hand side, the penalty box was flooded with blue shirts as they awaited Steve Tilson's corner kick. Making the most of the swirling winds, Tilson cleverly teased his left footed delivery into the six yard box where former Fulham's former Shrimpers keeper Jim Stannard fumbled the ball at the feet of Ian Benjamin who couldn't believe his luck as he managed to knock the ball into the unguarded net.

There was no let up from a fired up Southend side as they continued to push forward in numbers. Full backs Powell and Austin were allowed the space to overlap Tilson and Locke respectively to add to a fast growing corner tally – each one causing Stannard problems as he struggled to judge the flight of the ball in the heavy wind.

Midway through the half, an inevitable second goal came and it was no surprise to anyone within the ground that it stemmed from yet another corner.

Again, Tilly took the kick and Stannard, a fan favourite during his time at Roots Hall, went some way to further enhance his reputation amongst The Blues supporters as his massive error in judgement saw the ball fly over his head and onto Martin's for a straight forward finish.

That goal sucked all life from Fulham who were struggling to battle, not only The Blues, but the conditions also. With the wind firmly behind Webb's men they had scored twice and amassed an impressive nine corners in a half they dominated for the most part. Fulham's only real chance of note was when Sansome brilliantly denied Brazil with an agile stop low to his left.

The second half began with the home side looking to get back into the game and they did come close through Phil Stant, but he too met the same fate as his strike partner as Sammy was more than equal to the shot. Peter Scott fared a little better minutes later when he saw his shot evade Sansome, but not the woodwork.

Now battling the elements, Southend still looked comfortable in controlling the football match. Chris Powell was managing to cause Fulham problems when breaking forwards and was continuing his good run of form with another impressive display.

Such was the ease in which The Blues seemed to be in control, they further underlined this by increasing the lead even further with eighty-three minutes played. A long ball from Austin caused confusion amongst the home defence and that was all Andy Ansah needed to race clear before firing a left foot shot under Stannard for three-nil.

There was no more score in the remaining seven minutes of action and the comprehensive score line was more than enough to send the seven hundred plus travelling fans home to Essex full of high spirits.

The smiles on Blues fans faces grew even wider when results from around the country were known. Grimsby had suffered a 1-0 home defeat at the hands of Tranmere meaning Southend had returned to the top of the league on fifty-eight points.

Grimsby's loss allowed Bolton to leapfrog them into second place – now only two points behind Blues - with a great away win at Reading, while Cambridge slipped up at Bury, going down 3-1 and leaving them nine points adrift from The Shrimpers.

The win for Southend was more than welcome, but the manner of the triumph in difficult weather conditions was exactly the response wanted following the set-back against Reading a few days earlier.

Webb revealed he was far from happy then, but it was a different story now, "The lads showed great character and discipline to come back from the Reading defeat," he said. "I gave them a bit of a rollicking after that game, but I have nothing but praise for the rolled their sleeves up and got stuck in on this occasion."

That was the last of league action for the month for Blues, but there was the small matter of a home tie against Division Four side Torquay United in The Leyland Daf Cup southern quarter-final three days later.

One player, who was eager for the games to come thick and fast following his two goals in as many games after having not scored in any competition since December 7^{th,} was Ian Benjamin.

"Not being able to find the net irritated me more than anything else, (but) I still felt I was I contributing something positive to the side," admitted Benji. "But I'm delighted to have scored in the last couple of games and hope I can keep the run going, but the important thing is for the side to keep on winning and Saturday's performance at Fulham has given all the lads a big boost. We looked very rusty when losing two-one against Reading last week. I put that down to the lay-off because of the bad weather but we really got it together at the weekend."

Looking towards the visit of Torquay, Benjamin was hoping to revert to his more familiar role of striker after doing a superb job in midfield at Fulham. "Although I had no complaints at all when I found myself in midfield at the weekend, I prefer to play up front so I'm looking forward to playing there again this evening."

It seemed as though the experienced forward had already got the nod, but Webb was still not giving anything away, instead he opted to keep everyone guessing by saying "you'll just have to wait and see."

Victory over Torquay, nicknamed The Gulls, would mean a dream trip to Wembley would only be two games away, but typically, Webb was keen to not entertain any talk of a visit to the famous Twin Towers.

"Certainly it would be great for the club and our supporters to get to Wembley, but our primary aim at the moment is simply to keep on winning matches. Torquay are the present hurdle and it's up to us to overcome them...let's not start talking about finals just yet."

The Gulls manager arrived at Roots Hall more than familiar with the surroundings of a club where he had experienced success as a manager a decade earlier.

Dave Smith guided Southend to promotion from Division Four and in the process oversaw his side remain unbeaten over the twenty-three home games played. In that remarkable run, they also conceded only six goals!

That outstanding home form, coupled with eleven wins on their travels, culminated in Smith's Southend side crowned league champions for the first time in the club's history.

Smith was quite rightly held in high regard by everyone connected with the club and upon his arrival at Roots Hall with Torquay United, he was greeted with the respect and adulation he so richly deserved.

In spite of his love affair with his onetime employers, Smith was coming to Roots Hall with the will to see his current side progress at Southend's expense. That desire to win the match would also be replicated by Dave Webb, his players and the 2,273 fans in attendance.

As usual, Webb selected a side that he felt would be best equipped to do the job on the night. There was one change to the back four that had to be made due to Pat Scully's involvement while on loan at Northampton during the earlier stages of the competition.

In place of the Irishman came Andy Edwards who was preferred to the transfer listed Spencer Prior. In midfield, Blues were able to welcome back Peter Butler from suspension and now pain free from his niggling knee injury. He resumed his partnership with Dave Martin which allowed Benjamin, as expected, to return to his more familiar striking role.

However, the shock was that Benji would not line up with Brett Angell in attack - instead he was paired with Andy Ansah which meant Adam Locke retained his place on the right wing. Top scorer Angell would have to make do with a place on the bench with John Cornwell in a very strong line-up that was clearly looking to progress to the Southern Area semi-finals where Brentford were already waiting.

The game was very slow to get going and with it being a tight and cagey affair for the opening forty-five minutes, it didn't really come as a surprise that the score at the interval was 0-0.

The game had been littered with little imagination from either side, The Shrimpers repeatedly opting to go route one in the attempts to make something happen with very little effect that had left the crowd scratching their heads with what they were witnessing.

If there had been a straw poll among the watching public, then there would not have been a single correct prediction about what was to follow in the second half. As much as the opening half had been dull, what the second forty-five served up had to be seen to be believed.

Southend started the second half by using the wingers more with the intent to get the opening goal as soon as they could. They were rewarded on fifty-five minutes when Locke caused problems on the right before his cross was cleared to the waiting Andy Edwards who controlled, then volleyed the ball over the keeper's head for his second goal of the season.

Ten minutes later and Locke again was at the heart of Blues attack and his trickery resulted in left back, Peter Whitson, fouling him inside the area for a penalty kick. Dave Martin gladly stepped up and sent Howell the wrong way for two-nil.

More was to quickly follow for the home side when Ansah ran onto Steve Tilson's assist and finished well under pressure for his first of the night.

Ansah's second goal came inside a minute when he benefited from Butler's run down the left flank, leaving him to control the midfielder's pass with his right, before driving the ball into the far corner of the net with his left for goal number four.

Remarkably, two minutes later Southend added yet another. A textbook Tilson delivery from a corner was perfect for Dave Martin to rise above the Torquay defence and head home from close range for the third goal in four amazing minutes.

Still hungry for more, Blues pushed forward and the quality of skipper Paul Clark's cross field pass to Locke sent the winger through on goal. But, rather than going alone he unselfishly looked up to see substitute Brett Angell alone in the penalty area and the striker just couldn't miss after having the hard work done for him.

At six –nil, the home fans had been treated to a goal feast in the second half, but there was still one more to cheer on an unforgettable night for the Essex side.

Free of defensive responsibility, Chris Powell galloped down the left wing before sending over a deep cross that was headed back across goal by Angell to Tilson, who in turn found Ansah at the near post and the little man couldn't miss for his hat-trick and goal number seven.

That's how the match finished and it was perhaps the most contrasting two halves of football ever witnessed at Roots Hall. Just how a team goes from such a disappointing first half with no efforts on target to speak of and then produce a seven goal blitz in the second was partially explained by hat-trick hero Andy Ansah.

"The gaffer told us to start playing the ball into feet instead of hitting it long and high. He stressed we could then make things happen rather than hope they would and he was proved absolutely right," he revealed. Simple really. And that simplicity was a major reason as to why the manager was working miracles at Southend. He had his beliefs, kept his instructions straight forwards and rarely strayed from that mantra.

As the season progressed, Webb's work was giving the suggestion that something special was on the horizon at Roots Hall. The seven goal haul over Torquay took their goal tally up to twenty-three in Leyland Daf competition alone. They had also returned to the top of the table and there was hope – no, belief - that momentum was with them as the season entered its last three months. So far the hard work had seen its rewards, but with the pressure intensifying, Webb and his players knew that they had achieved nothing yet.

Division Three Table end of February 1991

	TEAM	P	W	D	L	F	A	Pts
1	Southend United	29	18	4	7	48	34	58
2	Bolton Wanderers	30	16	8	6	40	29	56
3	Grimsby Town	30	16	6	8	45	25	54
4	Cambridge United	26	13	8	5	44	29	47
5	Tranmere Rovers	30	13	8	9	45	36	47
6	Bury	30	13	8	9	43	38	47
7	Huddersfield Town	31	13	8	10	34	33	47
8	Brentford	29	12	10	7	37	29	46
9	Birmingham City	31	11	12	8	31	34	45
10	Bradford City	29	12	7	10	38	32	43
11	Reading	27	13	4	10	40	35	43
12	Leyton Orient	27	13	4	10	34	30	43
13	Wigan Athletic	29	12	5	12	43	40	41
14	Bournemouth	28	10	10	8	36	37	40
15	Stoke City	28	10	9	9	36	35	39
16	Exeter City	31	10	7	14	36	34	37
17	**Swansea City**	27	10	5	12	34	37	35
18	Chester City	27	8	5	14	27	34	29
19	Preston North End	29	7	7	15	30	47	28
20	Fulham	29	6	9	14	27	39	27
21	Shrewsbury Town	27	5	8	14	35	45	23
22	Mansfield Town	28	5	8	15	25	39	23
23	Crewe Alexandra	27	5	7	15	36	50	22
24	Rotherham United	27	4	9	14	25	48	21

'Up The Blues!'

March 1991

"It's important not to start putting pressure on the players by saying 'we must win our next game.' Let's just relax and I'm sure we will regain the cutting edge we had a few matches ago." – David Webb

It was somewhat of a surprise when top scorer Brett Angell was dropped to the bench for the 7-0 demolishing of Torquay United in The Leyland Daf Cup. That decision from David Webb was considered to be just a temporary one and that come the return to league action on March 1st, Angell would be restored to the starting eleven.

However, as Webb mulled over his team selection for the Friday night visit of Rotherham United there was no doubt whatsoever that the performance of his team in that aforementioned cup game had given him plenty to think about.

"It's a bit of a headache, but one which most managers would be delighted to have," he said when asked about his striking options. "Ansah has the explosive pace to turn a game, but on the other hand Brett has proved himself with his goals this term. Locke played wide on the right against Torquay and absolutely destroyed them after the break – whoever has to step down will feel a little aggrieved, but that's a decision I am paid to make."

"I look on it as a squad situation and having to shuffle the pack as tactics demand. It's not a question of dropping people, but simply playing either those on form or those who you think will do the best job in a specific game."

Recent displays of both Ansah and Locke influenced Webb's decision in the end and so it was that Locke retained his place on the right, while Ansah got the nod to partner Ian Benjamin in attack following his three goal haul just a few days earlier.

That meant that Angell, with twenty-three goals to his name, had to be content with a place on the bench, which spoke volumes about the forward options the club had. The combination of Angell and Benji had been a huge success throughout the season, but as the manager stated, Ansah's pace through the middle would offer something totally different in the final third.

Opponents Rotherham United were, as they had been for most of the campaign, fighting at the bottom end of the table, but that made no difference to Webb who was keen to pay them the respect he felt they deserved.

"This is Rotherham's cup final and they will come here with absolutely nothing to lose – we will need to guard against complacency," Blues Boss pointed out. "They have picked up some good results lately and we will certainly need to show the same fire as we did in that amazing second half on Tuesday. The lads must treat Rotherham the same as they would if taking on Grimsby and Bolton at the other end of the table."

The manager of course was 100% right. Blues had to approach the game in the right manner or risk coming unstuck, but for all their decent results of late, they were rock bottom of the league and the Roots Hall faithful were turning up expecting their side to win another valuable three points.

The home side didn't take long to get into their groove as they opened The Millers up with some fine examples of attacking play that many a side in the league would have struggled to contend with.

The wide men in particular were at the forefront of the attacks and after eighteen minutes of one sided action, Adam Locke conjured up some magic as The Shrimpers went one-nil up. He cut in from the right flank, brilliantly evaded two challenges before delivering a cross with pin point accuracy to Ian Benjamin who guided his header past Kelham O'Hanlon in goal.

Blues continued to control the game, but it took a further twenty-one minutes of play before a second goal was added. The goal itself was another for Benjamin who sent his powerfully directed header into the opposite corner to his first strike - the passage of build-up play for the goal in particular was a joy to watch.

It started with Dean Austin who played the ball first time into the feet of Andy Ansah. The forward flicked the ball into Benji's path and it was immediately played back into Ansah's path who was able to look up, bide his time and send over a cross for Benjamin and goal number two. The majority of the move was all one touch football and served to underline just how cutting Southend could be when in full flow.

The first half ended at 2-0 and the decision to leave Brett Angell on the bench was proving the right one. Benji's brace had given Blues a cushion to take into the second half and his strike partner for the night, Ansah, had proved lively throughout the half despite himself not registering a shot on target.

Being behind at the interval meant one thing for Rotherham – they came out for the after the break chasing the game and, with nothing to lose, they dropped their defensive approach of the first half for a more attack minded one in the second.

It could have also been argued being two goals to the good, Southend took their foot off the pedal and that only encouraged Rotherham further. The differences in the way they went about their business in the early exchanges of the second half reaped rewards when the visitors clawed a goal back just eleven minutes after the re-start.

It was a left wing corner that led to the goal after Paul Sansome only managed to get one hand to the ball, pushing it only as far as Neil Richardson on the edge of the area. Richardson wasted no time in passing the ball to his right where Des Hazel was waiting unmarked and the winger drove an unstoppable shot passed the static Sammy and into the top corner.

It was a goal that breathed life into the away side and put fear and anxiety into Southend and their fans. From being comfortably in front, they were now clear signs of nerves among the players in blue.

Hazel screamed for a penalty after Paul Clark's robust challenge took both man and ball, but the referee waved away the protests. Not long after that, Richardson went close and his team-mate, Mark Dempsey, closer still as they looked like they would get the goal needed to pull level.

Webb sent on Brett Angell with ten minutes left for Steve Tilson in an attempt to use Angell's height to get his side further up the pitch as Rotherham just kept on attacking.

Fortunately, the minutes passed and as the final whistle sounded, there was huge relief within Roots Hall as everybody inside the ground knew only too well that the victory was not deserved. The bottom placed team in Division Three had more than matched the team at the top and yet still were to head home with nothing to show for their efforts.

A confused Rotherham manager, Phil Henson, raged after the game, "How on Earth did we lose that?! We were the better side...there's no justice!"

And, on reflection he was right, but when you're at the bottom of the table looking up, that's the way things can go. Compare Henson's comments to those of David Webb, who welcomed the win however that happened to have come about, and it didn't seem to bother him one bit. "We never got to grips with their style of play, but at the end of the day we got the most important thing – three points!"

It was the perfect example that football was all about getting the win – especially at the business end of the season. Rotherham played well and should have got more for their efforts, but left Roots Hall empty handed whereas Southend had turned out a below par display and still got the all important three points - sometimes that can be the difference that separates sides at opposite ends of the table.

The following Tuesday, Blues were in home action again against Brentford in the Southern Area semi-final of The Leyland Daf Cup. Wembley was now very much on the horizon and David Webb was keen to take his side to the famous old stadium for the competition's showpiece final.

One player in particular who was desperate to feature in the game was striker Brett Angell who understood the manager's reasoning for leaving him out for the Rotherham match, but wanted to force his way back into the side.

"It's the managers' decision who he picks and I appreciate he had a difficult task for the match," he said. "The boss made a tactical switch against Torquay earlier in the week, switching Andy Ansah inside and pushing Adam Locke wide and Andy responded with a hat-trick in a seven-nil win which made it a tough decision who to leave out. It happened to be me this time, but we are all members of the squad and hopefully it will be my turn to get the nod when the team-sheet goes up for The Leyland Daf Cup semi-final against Brentford."

David Webb confirmed that the conundrum surrounding his striking options was giving him plenty of food for thought as he pondered who to select for the match. "I had hoped to have a definite idea following yesterday's training sessions, but it's still very open and I doubt I will make a decision until just before kick-off."

The boss also admitted he wanted to win the tie and would be looking to do as such, but conceded it was still second in his list of priories. "While it would be great to get to Wembley I wouldn't want it at the expense of our league ambition. Promotion is our number one priority. If we can do it without disrupting our form or picking up unnecessary injuries then it would certainly be a wonderful climax to the season."

The manager was right, the league had to be the main goal for the season, but a trip to the famous old stadium was not something that fans and players alike would ever forget. Webb himself had played at Wembley during his career when he featured in the 1970 F.A. Cup final for Chelsea against Leeds United. He was well aware of what it would mean to the whole club, "It's every player's ambition to play there and this Cup gives lower division lads the rare chance to taste the atmosphere and glory. It all adds up to the prospect of an exciting clash – we are all looking forward to it."

The team was not announced until the day of the game and it was Brett Angell who was chosen at Andy Ansah's expense who only made the substitute's bench. It was an opportunity for Angell to cement his place in the team once more and it was hoped by the supporters he would thrive on the service provided by both Steve Tilson and Adam Locke.

The other change from the side that beat Rotherham was the usual enforced one for The Leyland Daf competition as Andy Edwards came in for the ineligible Pat Scully at centre back. It was a strong team that was to start and a look to the bench to see John Cornwell sitting alongside Ansah showed that there was good options for Webb should he need them over the course of the game.

It was a poor start to the match from the home side and one that left that left them with an uphill battle inside the first twenty-five minutes. Southend failed to match the tempo and desire from a Brentford side that came out of the traps very well from minute one.

In the fourteenth minute, Brentford made Blues pay for this failure by taking the lead from a right wing corner. Allan Cockram took the kick that was flicked on at the near post by Terry Evans and an unmarked Neil Smillie was able to arrive unmarked at the back post to head home from eight yards.

Southend's players looked around at each other, but in truth they were all culpable for what was a poor goal to concede. However, eight minutes later the lesson wasn't learned as they conceded from another corner, this time from the left. Again, the towering Evans won the initial header that caused chaos in the six yard area before Keith Jones forced the ball over the line for 0-2.

Roots Hall fell silent as their team uncharacteristically were falling apart in front of their eyes. The situation The Shrimpers found themselves in, though, got the sort of reaction required as they suddenly woke up and began to play.

As Southend pushed forwards, they began getting off some shots at goal, but found Bees number one Graham Benstead in good form to preserve his sides lead. The pick of the saves came on the half hour mark when he somehow got a hand to Benjamin's effort when it looked a certain goal.

Before the half ended, Benstead was at it once more. This time he was faced with left midfielder Tilson bearing down on his goal and the keeper won that duel too, stopping the shot with his legs.

Webb responded to his side's need for goals at the break by introducing Ansah for Locke in the hope that the pace now on the right wing would help unlock the Brentford defence.

The home side responded by really putting their opponents under pressure as soon as the game re-commenced. Benstead had to be at his best to deny Angell first, and then Ansah second. Even when the keeper was finally beaten, the post denied Blues after Ansah's drive looked to have been good enough to pull a goal back.

Still pushing forwards, Southend created their clearest chance of the night on sixty-two minutes when Tilson's cross found Angell free inside the penalty area, but somehow the top scorer's header inexplicably missed the target.

Brentford then had a period of containing Blues attacks and looked comfortable to see out the win that would take them through to the Southern Area Final.

Just to rub salt in the wound, they added a third goal two minutes from time and the scorer was no stranger to Roots Hall. Former Roots Hall favourite, Richard Cadette, showed his predatory instincts to be in the right place at the right time when he swept the ball home for an easy finish at the South Bank end of the ground.

'Up The Blues!'

It capped off a disappointing night for Southend and one where David Webb was fully aware of why his side were dumped out of the competition. "We paid the price for being sloppy and sleepy in the first half hour," he explained. "After that we played much better than we did in beating Rotherham last weekend and created plenty of clear cut chances. But, this game is all about taking them and that's something Brentford gave us a lesson in. They had four opportunities and took three of them – so good luck to them in their bid to reach Wembley."

Cadette - a transfer target for Southend earlier in the season – then echoed Webb's comments, "Southend had more opportunities than us, but didn't take them," he said, before adding a cheeky swipe at his former employers, "perhaps they need someone like me!"

It was a big defeat - a 0-3 reverse could hardly be anything but - however, there wasn't three goals between the sides and had Blues not found Benstead in fine form then maybe it would be they who were one step closer to the Twin Towers. The scale of the loss was down to the importance of the game and the club felt it.

It was imperative that the team bounced back from it immediately and that would be down to the manger to make sure his players were ready for the next fixture. But that too was a hugely important one as they faced a tough trip away at third placed Grimsby Town.

One thing that was clear was that the club's supporters were not dwelling too much on the Leyland Daf defeat as more than a thousand followers were making the trip up to Cleethorpes to give their team their unequivocal backing.

It was a tremendous effort from the fans, especially as the crunch game was coming just four days after the Brentford disappointment and the cost involved. This was to be Southend's third match of March already and there was still a further six games to play with a Saturday, Tuesday, Saturday, Tuesday scenario becoming the norm during this busy period of the season.

The travelling fans that would be in attendance at promotion rivals Grimsby was fully appreciated by the club, as David Webb stated the day before the match. "The support we've had away from home has been superb all season, playing a huge part in helping us chalk up a record nine away wins and it will be great to have a big following tomorrow," said the appreciative boss.

'Up The Blues!'

It was certainly going to be a big crowd for the game at Blundell Park and that was for one reason only...it was a massive match that could have a major bearing on the promotion shake up in Division Three. Of course, that wasn't something Webb had dismissed, but he wanted his team to approach the game in the normal way.

"The clash between the two sides at Southend earlier in the season was a great advert for lower division soccer and I am confident the standard will just as high tomorrow. While a draw would be an acceptable result for us, we shall go there looking for victory because I feel we are a better side when we attack and go out with a positive attitude."

If Blues were to return to Essex with all the points on offer then Webb would have to make the right call when it came down to selecting the right side for the match. At the back, it was fairly obvious that Pat Scully would return at Andy Edwards expense, but up front it wasn't as clear cut. Ian Benjamin was a certainty, but Angell, Ansah and Locke were all left hoping they would get the nod to play too.

In the end, Webb reverted back to his familiar faces and that meant Adam Locke was named as substitute with Brett Angell and Andy Ansah received the good news they wanted to hear. The other change of note was a change to the second substitute with John Cornwell missing out, his spot going to young Edwards.

Webb's comment alluding to the previous encounter between the two sides back in December being a standard bearer for the lower leagues was true. But, as much as that pulsating pre-Christmas meeting was a great game, the return game at Blundell Park was anything but.

It proved to be a tight, cagey affair that resembled such a fixture that was surrounded in pressure. There was pressure for Grimsby to close the six point gap to Blues and for Southend to come away and further enhance their promotion credentials.

As both sides cancelled each other out in the first half, it was only nail biting due to what was at stake.

The best chance of the opening half hour fell to Brett Angell after he fashioned a chance for himself when he rolled his marker from a Chris Powell throw in, but failed to hit the target and instead disappointingly dragged his shot well wide of Steve Sherwood's goal.

Grimsby came a little bit closer to breaking the deadlock when Tony Rees saw his effort cannon back off the crossbar with a shot from twenty yards, much to the relief of Southend and their superb support.

There was to be a goal in the first half though, and it came in the fortieth minute after Dave Gilbert's skilful run drew a foul when Peter Butler brought down the midfielder twenty-five yards from Paul Sansome's goal.

Gilbert dusted himself down, eyed up the shooting opportunity before smashing the ball into the net through a poor defensive wall that badly let Sansome down.

It was advantage to The Mariners, but there was a chance for The Shrimpers to pull level immediately. Unfortunately for The Shrimpers, Sherwood was equal to Angell's goal bound effort to keep his goal intact and his side one goal to the good.

The second half descended back into the familiar pattern of the first where the sheer intensity surrounding the match saw two very good teams cancel each other out.

As the game progressed, Blues opted to go long in their build up play, but Grimsby's two central defenders dominated Benjamin and Angell with relative ease aerially. It was a tactic that was destined to fail, but still the balls were hit long towards the forwards as opposed to keeping it short and getting Tilson and Ansah involved.

After eighty minutes there was a half-hearted penalty shout for Southend when Tom Watson's hand connected Benjamin's shot, but it was waved away by referee Neil Midgley.

Grimsby continued to shut out Blues and their defenders dropped even deeper with each passing minute which took them up to the final whistle and a valuable three points over the league leaders.

It had been a poor match with neither side deserving the win, but Gilbert's solitary goal five minutes before half time was good enough to seal a hugely important win for the home side.

Southend had failed to play to their potential and get any sort of result in a massive fixture. All in all, the uncharacteristic display was huge disappointment for the club and Webb voiced his concern about his side's mental approach to the game.

"We seemed to show a lot of fear and gave them far too much respect – some of our boys looked nervous and jittery. I want us to get back to playing with the freedom and flair we showed which got us in this lofty position," was his honest assessment. Webb also wasn't entirely happy about the goal that won the game for the home side, "We normally put five in the wall but one broke out this time – but full marks to the fellow (Gilbert) for a superb swerving strike through the gap."

In the post-match press conference it wasn't considered a smart move to suggest The Shrimpers were heading into a mini-slump at such a pivotal time of the season. Webb was short and sharp with his reply, "I expect most clubs in the country would like to be ten points clear of fourth place with two games in hand at this stage of the season," he said.

He then backed his players to get back to putting in the type of performance that wins games sooner rather than later. "It's important not to start putting pressure on the players by saying 'we must win our next game.' Let's just relax and I'm sure we will regain the cutting edge we had a few matches ago."

It was hoped that the 'cutting edge' would return in time for the next game, another away fixture, this time at Swansea City. The game came on the Tuesday evening, a mere three days on from Grimsby. Add to the hectic fixture schedule that Southend faced, Webb also had to try to do any further business in the transfer market before deadline day at the end of the month. The manager had his work cut out and there was little time to gather his thoughts inbetween matches, let alone finalise his squad for the season's finale.

Swansea was not having the greatest of seasons. The Welsh team had suffered heavy periods of inconsistency and as a result they occupied seventeenth spot in Division Three. However, an interesting statistic ahead of the game was that The Swans had only scored four goals less at home than the high flying Blues and they had conceded sixteen, the same amount as Southend.

That, perhaps, spoke more about Southend's inability to keep them out at Roots Hall than it did about Swansea's when taking into account their respective league positions. Either way, playing at Vetch Field was always a tough task for any side – especially The Shrimpers who had never won there in seventeen previous attempts.

That particular stat didn't concern Webb who spent more time deliberating who would start up front with Benji after revealing that Adam Locke would play on the right of a four man midfield.

"It's the usual dilemma I've faced lately of who to play alongside Ian Benjamin. Both Angell and Andy Ansah can put forward justifiable arguments for being included and I shall give it a lot of thought before announcing my line-up."

The selection dilemma was one that had cropped up over recent weeks and, in truth, it was one that many fans didn't understand. Angell was the top scorer, so surely he would be a guaranteed starter in the team? But, that wasn't the case due to Locke's good showings on the right and the pace threat that Ansah posed through the middle of the pitch. It was a good selection headache to have for any manager and whoever missed out would just have to wait for their opportunity to shine.

On the day of the game, Webb issued a plea to everyone connected with the club to 'stay calm' as the season entered its last fifteen games of the campaign with history in the making all to play for

"It's an old cliché, but we must take every game as it comes and not start getting too excited about what is ahead of us. There are several clubs all battling it out at the top of the table and it's a case of the team which keeps its nerve best will win the honours in May…it's as simple as that," Webb said, bluntly.

With speculation and opinion offered as to who would start in attack with Ian Benjamin, it was a little bit of a surprise when Webb went with Ansah's pace ahead of Angell's aerial threat. It meant that the latter would be wearing shirt number twelve as he sat on the bench next to John Cornwell who was named as the other substitute for the game.

Other than Adam Locke in for Angell, the team remained unchanged from the side that failed to turn up at Grimsby. It was hoped that the usual back four and central midfield two would excel in their attempts to right the many wrongs that reared their head at Blundell Park three days earlier.

That notion was severely put to the test immediately from the kick off when the home side came at their visitors with attack after relentless attack. In the opening twenty minutes they had forced an impressive six corners as Southend desperately tried to avoid conceding an early goal.

Unfortunately, it was the last of those six corners that proved too much for The Blues. Paul Clark lost Jimmy Gilligan and the striker couldn't fail to connect with Andy Legg's corner, powerfully heading Swansea into the lead.

That goal provoked the perfect reaction from Southend and within sixty seconds they had pulled themselves level. The equaliser too stemmed from a corner kick, won when Andy Ansah's effort was deflected wide after some good work from Benjamin.

Steve Tilson took the kick and sent over his trademark inswinger that proved too much for goalkeeper Lee Bracey in the wet conditions and Adam Locke was able to fire his shot past several bodies into the unguarded net.

Amid the celebrations of getting back on level terms immediately, both Peter Butler and Dave Martin were notable for their fist pumping gestures to their team mates. They knew only too well that to a man they had to be ready to match Swansea's dedication and, as far as they were concerned, the game started at that very moment.

Blues began to take control and, in reality, there was only ever going to be one winner from there on – such was Blues heart and desire. Butler, Martin, Tilson and Locke were relentless in their pursuit of the ball and when they managed to get hold of it, they opened the home side up with some superb football.

They thought they had taken a deserved lead when Tilly's ferocious strike found its way passed Bracey, but his celebrations were cut short when the lineman flagged for offside due to Benjamin having roamed beyond the last defender, cutting short Tilson's joy.

A second goal did eventually come, but they had to wait until eleven minutes after the interval. It was a flowing passage of play that was a fine example of how to play with pace and hurt the opposition.

Locke started the move on the right, beating the full back and running deep into Swansea's half. He looked up and fed the ball infield to Ansah who was only well aware of the space to his left that Ian Benjamin had taken up. Without hesitation, Ansah played the ball to Benji whose exquisite side foot finish found the far corner of the net for a 2-1 lead.

More was to follow when Ansah capitalised on Swans centre back, Paul Miller, losing his footing in the wet conditions. He carried the ball forwards before unselfishly squaring the ball for Locke who first beat Bracey with his eyes and then the ball for a deserved lead of 1-3.

It got better still when, with fourteen minutes remaining, right back Dean Austin hit a long ball over the top of Swansea's defence and into the path of Ansah whose pace took him away from all the white shirts who chased in vain. Bearing down on goal and with Bracey reluctant to commit, he beats the keeper at his near post for his first of the match and Blues fourth overall.

It capped a memorable display from Southend, one that made a little bit of history, but more importantly the result – and performance – cemented their position at the top of the table, putting paid to any talk of a mini-crisis.

Two goal hero, Adam Locke, was rightly delighted with getting a starting position in the team, as well as netting a brace. "It is something of a relief to find myself on the scoresheet at last. I'm the first to admit I've tended to freeze when easier chances than I had tonight came my way, so to put a couple of goals away was a great boost and hopefully it will give me the confidence to go and get more – providing I'm picked!"

"The fact that I came in for Brett highlights the quality of players fighting for places and emphasises that nothing can be taken for granted. I'd like to think I've done enough to keep my place, but I won't know that until the boss picks his next team. For the moment I'm just happy I played my part to sink Swans, but at the end of the day, this victory was down to great team work and team spirit. We were a bit down after Saturday's defeat at Grimsby, but this decisive victory has put us back in the groove."

The win had maintained their three point lead ahead of Grimsby and there was a result in midweek round of fixtures that raised an eyebrow or two when Southend's next opponents, struggling Mansfield Town, had destroyed high flying Bolton 4-0 at home.

The result got Blues attention and they were well aware that they needed to approach the tricky home fixture in a professional manner.

Helping The Shrimpers with their preparation was midfielder, Martin Ling. Ling had returned from a one month loan spell at Mansfield only two weeks earlier and was only too happy to dish the dirt on the team he made three appearances for in his time there.

"Mansfield will play five at the back and it's important that we stay patient and work at breaking them down – then our superior fire power should do the rest. Kevin (Kent) is a potential match winner who must be watched closely. He is a sharp and lively player who can perform on either flank," offered Ling.

As for Ling himself, he hadn't featured a great deal for Southend over the season and he was only too aware that the situation was unlikely to change in the foreseeable future.

"Obviously I face a tough task with the team doing so well, but I haven't given up hope of breaking in should the circumstances arise. I know the manager has not completely ruled me out, but it's hard for him to change a winning side and I must be patient and ready to grab my chance if it comes along," he said.

The team that would have the challenge of beating a side fighting for survival would be unchanged from that that handsomely beat Swansea. That meant there was no place for Brett Angell in the starting eleven, but the in form Locke would have the opportunity to build on his man of the match display at Vetch Field.

"Adam has the ability to be a match winner, not only by setting up chances for other people, but by getting into scoring positions himself – his performance at Swansea should be just the lift he needs," said an expectant Webb. "We must go out tonight and stamp our authority on the game from the start because Mansfield should have their tails up after that surprise win over Bolton. It's up to us to deaden their enthusiasm by imposing our own drive and passion."

There was another change to the team and that came as a result of Pat Scully's loan period due to expire the next day and the manager thought it would be best if Spencer Prior came into the side and get some much needed game time.

However, the Scully situation wasn't dead and there was a chance something could be resurrected – either on loan or a permanent transfer - but for now Prior was the man to partner Paul Clark in defence.

The young defender himself was facing an uncertain future what with still being on the transfer list and his return to action would be his first since the loss at Tranmere on New Year's Day.

The Friday night game was Southend's third in the space of six days and it would provide a test for Webb's small squad's energy levels. Never mind the thirty-six point difference between the two sides and the expectancy that it should be another easy win from The Roots Hall crowd, the manager would have not underestimated the opposition.

The players began the game in the correct manner by having a lot of the ball and pressurising Mansfield as they looked for an opening goal.

Blues fashioned a great chance for Ian Benjamin and when the number ten was through on goal, he was brilliantly denied by Stags goalkeeper, Andy Beasley.

Moments later, Southend were in the ascendency again and during this period of dominance, Locke was fouled as he threatened to make something happen for his side. From the rehearsed Tilson & Butler free-kick, it was the latter who found Dave Martin's head and his effort was cleared off the line by George Foster.

It was shaping up as being only a matter of time before the deadlock was broken and on twenty-five minutes, that was what happened. The goal though, came at the other end of the pitch and sent a stunned Roots Hall into silence.

On a rare foray forwards, Mansfield won a corner kick on the right hand side. Kevin Kent's cross was inadvertently flicked on by Dean Austin and was met by the head of Foster. His downward header caused confusion in the six yard box and as the fans in The North Bank looked on anxiously, Steve Wilkinson was first to the loose ball, hooking it into to the roof of the net for a shock lead.

The Shrimpers then fell a little flat as their passes failed to reach their intended targets and when they did work the ball into good areas, the forwards were left frustrated by Locke's insistence on delaying the cross a little too long, allowing Mansfield to get back in numbers and clear the danger.

At the beginning of the second half it was clear that Blues had come out with real intent to turn the game around as they attacked The North Bank. Benjamin was proving a key figure as his hold up play brought others around him into the game and allowed the play to develop.

The pressure was gathering momentum very early in the half and in the fifty-third minute Southend got back on level terms. It was another set play that brought them level when Steve Tilson's perfect corner kick found Martin who managed to jump higher than Beasley in goal to flick the ball over the line for the equaliser.

Not content with that, Blues went straight after their opponents from the re-start. Working hard and getting the ball into the final third and just three minutes after the leveller, Peter Butler broke through on goal after Benji's intelligent pass. One on one with the keeper, he calmly lifted the ball into the top corner of the net to send Roots Hall crazy at the dramatic turnaround.

Southend had the bit between their teeth and didn't let the tempo they had generated drop as they pushed on for more goals. Unfortunately, they were unable to add to the two they had scored – despite Tilly's best effort with a shot from distance that crashed against the post.

The same player then should have done better at the end of the match when he failed to hit the target when he had only the keeper to beat. It was a chance that should have been taken, but as the final whistle sounded the miss didn't prove costly. The comeback had been completed and the players had underlined their determination and desire to succeed in doing so. However, the role the manager had played at half-time could not be underplayed after he read his players the riot act at the interval.

"We were either giving the ball away in the final third of the field or failing to deliver it quickly enough so when they came in at half-time I gave them a bit of a rollicking," admitted Webb. "Thankfully the lads responded in the right way full marks to them. Once the second goal went in I honestly thought we would go on and get four or five. We had enough chances to have done so, but in the end we finished up getting the three points and that was the most important part of the mission."

The word 'mission' that Webb chose to use was significant as the season was approaching its conclusion. Winning with style, plenty of goals and entertaining the supporters was now considered secondary in his thoughts. Getting the job done and adding another three points as often as possible was the sole target now and as each win was achieved, he knew it was another step closer to achieving that historical promotion.

The hectic schedule of games that March was throwing at Blues gave them another mission that needed completing only three days later on a rare Monday night match against Birmingham City at Roots Hall.

Beating Mansfield had increased their lead over their nearest rivals Grimsby Town to six points, but only for twenty-four hours. The following day The Mariners two-nil win over Brentford reduced the gap back to three points, although Southend still had a game in hand.

There was thirteen games left to play for The Shrimpers and every win was greeted with the relief of being one step closer to promotion and – dare people say it – even the league title!

Birmingham would present another tough challenge for Blues and their opponent's position of ninth in the table was misleading as they were only two points away from fourth spot. It was another big night at Roots Hall and, despite the short break inbetween games, Webb kept the same eleven.

Obviously well aware of the threat Birmingham posed, The Blues boss remained undeterred and believed if he could keep getting his small pool of players to perform then he was doing the right thing by the club.

"All matches are tough and the fact we are top of the table provides teams with a little more incentive to put one over us. It's never been my habit to worry about the opposition. My concern is that I get the best out of my players. That is the job I am paid to do and if I succeed in achieving that then we should get the result our fans want," he said confidently.

A larger than normal crowd of 6,328 turned out to watch two teams with aspirations on promotion battle it out on the Essex coast. It wasn't a classic in respects of the football played, but the intensity and edge to the game elevated it to such status.

The visitors were fired up and worked hard all over the pitch denying Blues any time on the ball to impose their style of play on the game. Players like John Frain, Vince Overson and Trevor Matthewson were prepared to get in the faces of Southend's players, always looking to disrupt them and drag them into a battle.

Fortunately, Webb's wonders were not shy in the physical side of the game when it was required and the likes of Clark, Martin, Butler, Powell and Prior relished the battle just as much as the impressive football they were also capable of playing.

The tackles were flying in all over the pitch and both Powell and Martin suffered cuts to their mouth and head respectively as the game threatened to boil over. But, after half an hour of hard tackles and fouls, the physicality of the game took a back seat at last to some football.

Southend's closest chance of the half came when Dean Austin found some room in a rare forage forwards and he unleashed a shot from distance that was matched by Brum's Martin Thomas in goal.

Then, on thirty-seven minutes, and with their first effort of note on goal, Birmingham scored. The goal was a perfect mixture of route one football and some showpiece skill that sent the away fans dancing on the terrace.

Thomas drop kicked the ball deep into Blues half and it caused a terrible mix up between Austin and Paul Clark that allowed Nigel Gleghorn to collect the ball ahead of them both. He then showed two pieces of sheer quality – first, he turned Clark with a great drag with his in-step before curling the ball beyond Sammy's dive and into the top corner.

It was a great finish, underlining the class that Birmingham possessed and also now the size of the task Southend faced to get back into the game.

At half time, Webb was forced into making a change with Andy Ansah having to be replaced by Brett Angell due to a groin injury. It was a change that would offer more aerial threat in the final third because, up to that point, everything that had come their way was dealt with comfortably by central defenders Overson and Matthewson.

The early signs in the second half suggested that Angell's introduction was having the desired effect. His height made him an easy target for crosses and he was pumped and ready to take on the commanding duo charged with taking care of him.

Unbelievably, The Shrimpers did level the scores and it came in the same minute of the game as in the previous match versus Mansfield. Again it was the fifty-third minute when the equaliser went in and in even stranger twist of fate, it was Dave Martin who scored it after a Steve Tilson right sided corner kick.

The delivery was such that it only required the deftest of headers from the midfielder that somehow found its way past a cluster of bodies and into the far corner of the goal.

Scored right in front of The North Bank, The Blues cheered with delight at the prospect of a second successive comeback in the games at Roots Hall. And, within a minute, that prospect became a reality with a second goal within sixty seconds that turned the game around in Southend's favour.

Blues won the ball back from their opponents almost instantly from the restart and worked it to the right wing where Adam Locke was waiting. On the halfway line and with Frain in his face, he cut infield before releasing Chris Powell down the opposite flank with a pass using the outside of his right foot. Powell had space in front of him and had time to look up, spot the run of Angell before picking him out with superb accuracy. As the ball came over the head of Overson on its way to Angell, The North Bank drew breath in anticipation as the substitute striker left the ground. The timing of the jump was perfect, as was the power and direction he delivered in that beautiful moment. Thomas in goal was left stranded and could only watch as the ball sailed into the right hand corner of the goal to give Southend a 2-1 advantage.

As the ball settled in the net, Roots Hall exploded in a way that can only happen when witnessing such a quick turnaround of events - the players and supporters alike had never seemed closer as they raised they the roof on a cold Essex night.

The game had still over thirty-five minutes left to play and there was still work to do if the three points was to be obtained. However, this Southend side had character, belief and a determination to be successful. They weren't about to sit back and hope that Birmingham wouldn't' find a way through.

In fact, The Shrimpers carried on looking for a third goal and they believed they had got it on seventy minutes when Angell put the ball past Martin Thomas for a second time, only for the linesman to bring the celebrations to a halt with his flag - ruling Brett offside.

From there, the game was end to end but without any real substance that troubled either keeper. If anything the game had descended back into the scrap that was on show at the beginning of the game.

But, as time was running out for the visitors, they launched one last attack and managed to work the ball wide to Robert Hopkins. The left winger steadied himself before firing off a shot that Sansome was equal to, ensuring his side gained all three points and increasing their lead to six at the summit of Division Three.

The one blot on yet another memorable night was that Dave Martin had picked up another yellow card for dissent in the first half and that would mean yet another suspension for the uncompromising midfielder.

Martin's latest ban – his third in all – meant he would not be available for the away games at Bournemouth and promotion rivals Bolton Wanderers. However, he optimistically believed that by winning those two games could well be enough for a very early promotion party. "I have looked at the fixtures all the top teams have left and reckon seventy-six points will definitely take third place because they are all cutting each other's throats," was his rationale.

"Of course we want to end up as champions but our first priority must be to make sure we go up and I am convinced that six more points will ensure that happens. We are all fast running out of matches and the teams below third place are going to have to put together an incredible run if they hope to stop us and, as most of them are playing each other, it's becoming an impossible task."

It was certainly big talk from Martin, but there was an element of possibility to his argument. Sitting top on seventy points, Blues had a twelve point cushion over fourth place, but there was still twelve fixtures left to play and the task of gaining six points from their next two games was going to be hard enough on its own.

Perhaps Martin's comments were made in the heat of the moment because promotion at the end of March was highly unlikely, in spite of his thoughtful reasoning behind them.

Talking to the press post-match, the man who effectively changed the game after coming on at half time revealed he felt under no extra pressure after being overlooked for a starting place in the team.

"The manager felt I had gone off the boil and perhaps being left out was just the spark I needed. Obviously I didn't like being on the bench, but I certainly had nothing to prove tonight and was just delighted to get on and score to crown what I felt was a magnificent fighting display by our lads," said Angell.

That Monday night game allowed a vital extra days rest for the players in what had already been a hectic schedule throughout the month. So, as the players received so much needed R & R, David Webb got stuck into possible transfer targets with the deadline day twelve days away.

There were unconfirmed rumours that Scully was still a target for the club, but the suggestions were that the player was hesitant about the wages being offered. One new face that Webb was able to reveal that had joined The Blues on a month's loan was forward Paul Moran from Division One side, Tottenham Hotspur.

Moran, twenty-two, had previously been on loan at Newcastle, but returned to London with his question marks over his professionalism after rumours of a drinking session the night before a game with a certain Paul Gascoigne.

However, Webb spoke of the assurances given from both Moran and his club manage that these stories were vastly exaggerated. "Both Moran and Spurs manager Terry Venables have told me these stories were blown out of all proportion and he wants to put it all behind him. He (Moran) sees this move as a chance to prove one or two people wrong and is certainly looking forward to his spell with us. The lad is very quick and looks sharp around goal. We have signed him for a month with an option to extend that if we both agree. It's all up to Moran himself – he has been thrown a lifeline and I am confident he will grab it with both hands."

The chance for Moran to kick-start his career looked like it would come as soon as Blues next game at Bournemouth. The reason being was that winger Andy Ansah was not going to recover from a groin injury that was sustained against Birmingham in time.

In previous games, when Ansah had been missing because of injury or suspension Adam Locke would come into the side, but that option was unavailable to Webb as he was struck down by a nasty flu virus.

It meant that when Southend took to the field at Dean Court on Saturday March 23rd, there was an unfamiliar look to the eleven that started. The back four and goalkeeper remained the same, but a reshuffled midfield and attack saw Martin Ling, Ian Benjamin, Peter Butler & Steve Tilson make up the four in the middle with Brett Angell and debutant Paul Moran in attack. The two on the bench were utility man John Cornwell and left back Christian Hyslop.

The absence of Ansah, Locke and Martin had had an obvious effect on the strength of the team. If anything, it highlighted the need for a fresh face or two before the transfer deadline passed as the squad looked a little threadbare with those three missing.

Webb, though, remained in confident mood despite being fully aware of the threat that the club he once managed posed. "They tend to win one and lose one, but have the potential to be a very dangerous outfit if it happens to be their day. But we have the best away record in the division having chalked up ten wins on our travels and need have nothing to fear. In fact, the way we have performed in our last three matches we will go into action brimming with confidence."

The boss' confidence in his team proved worthy when his makeshift side took the lead after thirty-two minutes in a game that had started very slowly for both sides.

Steve Tilson increased his assist tally for the season with an intelligent ball through to Angell who had pulled away from Shaun Teale to give himself the room to beat Gerry Peyton in goal with an impressive finish.

From there though, The Shrimpers inexplicably stopped playing and allowed Bournemouth to come back into the game.

As the tide slowly turned, it was clear that Martin Ling was struggling and his lack of first team games showed. The same had to be said for Paul Moran who was having very little impact on proceedings as he seemed to be struggling with the pace of the game.

The home side, picking up on Blues performance starting to wain as the game wore on, began building some pressure that Southend's back four were doing their utmost to repel and hold on to their solitary goal lead. That they were almost hanging on as the first half drew to a close was cause for concern with so long of the game left, too many in the team were struggling and it looked like a home goal would be coming eventually.

And that inevitably proved the case when Luther Blissett levelled the score with five minutes left to play of the first half. The goal was as straight forward as the former England striker would ever score.

A free-kick was awarded just outside the area and was taken by Andy Jones. His effort was initially blocked by Spencer Prior, but then the ball then ricocheted off Peter Butler and fell to an unmarked Blissett who poked the ball passed Sansome from eight yards out. Blissett, who had been on the receiving end of some stick from Blues fans, felt the need to celebrate in front of them – which didn't go down well with those supporters behind the goal.

After the break, it was all one way traffic. Blissett was giving young Prior a real torrid time, while Jones and Matthew Holmes were relishing the time and space they were gifted by an out of sorts Southend side.

A second goal was somehow delayed in coming by the excellent Sansome in The Blues goal. He made two great saves to thwart Blissett and deny him a second before again being at his best to stop Jones with a full length stop that earned him some grateful pats on the back from his team mates.

A second goal did eventually come for the hosts and the finish left Sansome with absolutely no chance after a diving header left him rooted to the spot. Unfortunately, the player who scored the goal was Spencer Prior who tried in vain to steer the ball away from goal and failed miserably.

On seventy-two minutes things got even worse when Captain Paul Clark had to be replaced by John Cornwell because of a groin injury. That signalled a further collapse from the boys in blue and they had Sammy to thank yet again after he made a tidy stop to deny Holmes.

A third goal was coming and it was no more than Bournemouth deserved. Southend were now at sixes and sevens and when Wayne Fereday's left wing corner was only half cleared by Tilson, Teale was able to work it back into the penalty area for Alec Watson who steadied himself with a cushion header before volleying the ball passed Sammy for the final goal of the match.

It was a poor performance from a Southend side that clearly missed some big players, yet that wasn't what rattled Webb once the final whistle had sounded. The Blues manager spoke of his disappointment at the yellow card Peter Butler was awarded for dissent before warning his players about their future discipline.

"A fortnight ago David Martin fell foul of the ref because he didn't know when to keep quiet and picked up a booking which carried him to twenty-eight penalty points and a two match ban. Now Butler has gone over the top and faces the possibility of a similar suspension for trying to have the last word," he moaned.

"I accept players are always likely to get to get booked for competing hard but it is sheer stupidity for anyone to try and have the last word with the ref. There's only ever going to be one winner in that situation – and it won't be the player. I can only hope Martin, Butler and everyone else now realises that talking back doesn't do them or the team any favours."

By choosing to go public with his warning, Webb had let everybody know how he felt about his side's sudden ill-discipline. He was well aware how costly suspensions could be to the team and with the dream of promotion in their own hands, he was determined not to see the success they craved derailed by moments of madness.

The loss gave the chasing pack a chance to close the gap on the leaders but it came as a relief when second placed Grimsby only drew at Swansea while Bolton, in third spot, also drew in their match away at Stoke City.

Those results of the weekend of 23rd March saw Southend remain top with a two point cushion and a game in hand over Grimsby. Third placed Bolton was now looking to make up six points on The Shrimpers having also played a game more. That added more pressure for the next match that pitted third vs. first in the following weekends game of the day.

It was rare for there to be no midweek fixture for Southend in March and before Webb had to turn his full attention towards Bolton, he was keen to bring a new face into his squad ahead of the trip to Lancashire.

Webb admitted that he was looking at the defence as an area he wanted to strengthen. He made no secret of the fact that he had made enquiries about Exeter City's Shaun Taylor as well as Reading's Keith McPherson when a surprising turn of events led to a phone call from Pat Scully to Webb about resurrecting the proposed deal that he had turned down only a week previous.

The deal was to see Scully re-join the club, only this time on a permanent deal for a transfer fee of a £100,000 and it seemed the young Irishman had sought the advice of an Arsenal legend.

"I am delighted that Scully has had a change of heart," smiled Webb. "It seems that when he turned us down originally he was wrongly advised on the terms he should expect. But yesterday he spoke to his Irish and Arsenal team-mate David O'Leary who said that what we had offered was more than fair and contacted me again."

"Pat proved during his time with us that he is a very good player with the potential to get even better. I see him not only as a vital signing for now but for the club's future."

"Our need (to add a centre back) was made urgent because our own Spencer Prior has made it clear that he wants to leave us at the end of the season and I didn't want to be in the position of having to chase around desperately looking for a replacement during the summer."

The speed in which the Scully deal was concluded allowed the player to go straight into the squad for Bolton, but there was still more activity as Webb battled hard to beat the deadline and get his transfer dealings done.

There were unsuccessful approaches for strikers Shaun Close of Swindon and Mark Loram of Torquay United, while he also looked to bring in a backup goalkeeper to Paul Sansome. Knocked back by his first target, Tottenham reserve keeper Kevin Dearden, Webb was then alerted to the availability of Spurs teenage stopper, John Cheesewright.

Cheesewright was loaned to Southend for the rest of the season and that left Webb content with his squad for the run in, although he would have welcomed either of the strikers to add to those he already had at the club.

One player that left the club on loan for the second time that season was midfielder Martin Ling. Swindon Town was the player's preference when presented with the option of moving to The Robins or Maidstone United.

That was all the transfer business done for the season and it left the manager able to focus fully on the tough task ahead at Burnden Park, home of Bolton Wanderers.

Ahead of the game there was a concern that Paul Clark's groin injury wouldn't clear up in time for the match, but any fears were allayed when he declared himself fit to lead the side out the day before the match.

However, David Martin was still missing as he served the last of his two match suspension, while Adam Locke was still absent due to illness. There was some good news though - forward Andy Ansah had shown up no effects from his groin complaint after starring in the 5-1 thrashing of Aldershot's second string.

Ansah netted a hat-trick in that game and that certainly gave Webb food for thought in what was expected to be a red hot atmosphere with a bumper crowd in attendance.

"The prospect of them being cheered on by one of their biggest crowds of the season will provide them with additional encouragement and incentive. We know what we are up against, Bolton proved what a difficult side they are when they earned a share of the points at Roots Hall at the end of December. They have plenty of good players in their ranks, but that is something I am not going to lose any sleep over...I never worry about the opposition. As is the case in every match, my main concern is that my players perform to the

'Up The Blues!'

best of their ability. If they do, then our fans will have plenty to shout about."

Despite being in third position, Wanderers had gone into the game in relatively poor form having recorded two losses and a draw in their previous three matches. Roared on by a passionate home crowd though, they would surely look to start the game fast and not give their opponents anytime to settle.

The team chosen by Webb had a more familiar look to it with Ansah getting the nod to start ahead of on loan Paul Moran. He came back into the team on the right with Benji moving back up front with Brett Angell. Into the midfield came John Cornwell instead of Swindon bound Ling which left Moran and Spencer Prior as the two substitutes.

The game started at a ferocious pace with the home side getting the ball forwards for Jamaican born Tony Cunningham and Tony Philliskirk at every opportunity.

Early on in the game, Blues were fortunate not to concede when Philliskirk's header narrowly missed the target after a Julian Darby corner kick.

Southend were struggling to get a foothold in the match, particularly in midfield and on the flanks which was unusual as that had been a huge part of their success throughout the campaign.

Bolton kept on probing and pushing for the goal that would break the deadlock, but Scully & Clark marshalled the men in front of them well and managed to hold out for half time with their goal still intact.

The start of the second period was very much in the same vain as the first with the home side having a lot of the ball in Blues half, but still they could not find a way through.

On the hour mark, Sansome was called into action and did well to keep out Cunningham's snapshot but in truth, it was just a matter of time before the majority of the 10,666 crowd got what they were waiting for.

It came on sixty-three minutes and it originated from a long ball into the channel where Cunningham was able to get inbetween Chris Powell and Pat Scully. The powerful striker used his strength before delivering the perfect ball across the face of goal to where an unmarked Darby was on hand to knock the ball into the net.

Both the crowd and players went crazy, fully aware at the importance of the goal. There was little coming back from the league leaders and the home side felt this was a great chance to close the gap to just three points between the two sides.

The Shrimpers supporters were hoping for a response, but still there was nothing. Angell and Benjamin were getting very little service from the teammates, but even so, both managed to work David Felgate in goal inside the last ten minutes.

The only real positive to come from the game was that Southend had not suffered a heavier defeat because in all but the score line, it was a very one sided game that could have been a lot worse.

The performance wasn't that of potential promotion candidates, let alone a side that had aspirations of winning the title. It was back to back defeats for David Webb's side for only the second time in the league of the season. But aside from the losses, the lack of cutting edge going forwards and the inability for the midfield to stamp their authority on the game was a cause for real concern.

What made the trip home to Essex even harder was that Grimsby had beaten Reading 3-0 to leapfrog Southend into top spot. Although still with a game in hand, Blues were now looking over their shoulders at Bolton who were a win from clawing level with them on seventy points and even more worrying was their lead over Tranmere in fourth position was cut to four points.

The Shrimpers boss tried to remain upbeat, despite the disappointment, "We were desperately unlucky to go down one-nil – it was one of those games when the ball just wouldn't run for us. It's rare for us not to score in a match this season but I'm not too worried about the setback because I know we will play worse than that and still win."

March ended with the Bolton fixture and that rounded off the busiest month of the season with an unwelcomed defeat. Over the seven league fixtures played, Blues had won four of them and lost the other three. It spelt out an indifferent month and one that had fans feasting on their fingernails with ten games left to play.

They had seen their team surrender top spot with back to back defeats and the fear was that their promotion dream that would make the season the most successful in their eight-five year history was in danger of imploding.

It was a bad time to start to falter and whilst David Webb remained calm, the supporters certainly didn't. As for the players, it was not yet known how they would respond, but in the last full month of the season that question was going to be answered one way or another. Southend fans were now praying that the answer that would be forthcoming would see the club over the finish line and into the unheralded world of Division Two for the first time ever.

Division Three Table March 30th 1991

	TEAM	P	W	D	L	F	A	Pts	GD
1	Grimsby Town	37	21	8	8	58	27	71	31
2	Southend United	36	22	4	10	59	43	70	16
3	Bolton Wanderers	38	19	10	9	51	42	67	9
4	Tranmere Rovers	38	19	9	10	55	39	66	16
5	Huddersfield Town	39	17	11	11	50	42	62	8
6	Bury	38	17	10	11	58	48	61	10
7	Cambridge United	33	16	9	8	52	37	57	15
8	Brentford	36	15	12	9	49	39	57	10
9	Bournemouth	37	15	12	10	49	46	57	3
10	Stoke City	38	15	11	12	51	46	56	5
11	Bradford City	36	15	9	12	52	44	54	8
12	Birmingham City	38	13	15	10	40	42	54	-2
13	Wigan Athletic	37	15	7	15	54	48	52	6
14	Reading	35	15	6	14	46	45	51	1
15	Exeter City	39	14	8	17	48	43	50	5
16	Leyton Orient	34	15	4	15	38	44	49	-6
17	Preston North End	37	13	7	17	45	56	46	-11
18	Chester City	36	11	6	19	35	46	39	-11
19	**Swansea City**	35	11	6	18	39	53	39	-14
20	Mansfield Town	37	7	11	19	36	51	32	-15
21	Shrewsbury Town	35	7	9	19	45	55	30	-10
22	Fulham	36	6	12	18	30	50	30	-20
23	Crewe Alexandra	35	7	8	20	46	65	29	-19
24	Rotherham United	36	6	10	20	33	68	28	-35

'Up The Blues!'

April 1991

"It makes a huge difference to the players to know there are people out there who really care." – David Webb

There was suddenly a scepticism born through anxiety surrounding Roots Hall as the season entered its penultimate month. Back to back defeats at the end of March had supporters convinced that their team going were to 'blow it' as Blues die hards cursed their rotten luck at the timing of this apparent bad run of form.

However, there was little time for David Webb and his team to feel sorry for themselves because there was seven league fixtures to play throughout April which would have a huge bearing on which way the season would go.

Their approach to the games had to right if they were to get back to winning ways and home in on the promotion that everyone connected with the club wanted so bad. Having led the in the table for so long throughout the campaign, to falter now would be a very bitter pill to swallow and so the most important game of the year was now the April 2nd home clash with Chester City.

Chester had defeated Blues 1-0 back in December, but had since stuttered in the league and was only nine points above relegation. That didn't matter at all for Webb who was fully aware that his team had to turn up or else.

"Chester will probably be like a lot of sides and save their best performance for games against teams at the top – we must be really professional and adopt a positive attitude right from the start. Hopefully our fans, who have been magnificent all season, will continue their one hundred per cent support – that little bit of extra backing from the terraces can sometimes just tip the balance."

To make sure the team approached the game in the right manner, Webb wasted no time in recalling David Martin to the side after he had missed the previous two through suspension. He was a massive miss in the games at Bournemouth and Bolton and it came as no surprise that he would come into the midfield at the expense of John Cornwell, who dropped to the bench.

The other substitute for the match was Adam Locke who was also welcomed straight back into the fold after being absent with a flu virus. In all honesty, the game came too soon for Locke who was still struggling a little, but his inclusion was a must due to on loan Spurs forward Paul Moran suffering with a back injury – a problem that was severe enough to cut short his loan spell.

On the day of the match, Webb spoke once more about the evening's crucial fixture and what a win could do for his side. "Tonight's game is the most vital of the season if we hope to have title aspirations," he underlined. "All our promotion rivals have tough games tonight and three points against Chester could make a big difference to our hopes of tasting champagne next month. I know we still have plenty of games left and matches in hand, but I want to ensure we win all our remaining home games…starting tonight," was his final rallying cry.

Webb's mention of their promotion rivals all being in action put a little more pressure on his team. All three of Grimsby, Tranmere and Bolton were playing away from home at Bournemouth, Birmingham and Cambridge respectively – none of which were the easiest of places to go and get a result. But, before attentions could turn elsewhere, Southend had to beat Chester and get the win that a nervous crowd of 6,190 hoped they would.

The anxiety that had crept into the terraces found its way onto the pitch and it became obvious that the players were not firing on all cylinders.

Still in control of the football for longer periods than Chester, the players were lacking the spark that had been so evident over the course of the season. Hardly helped by the windy conditions, Blues final ball was poor and in particular Steve Tilson's normally pinpoint crosses were more than a little wayward as they sailed well away from their intended target.

The half drifted into one of little action worthy of note. Chester was happy to allow Southend grow increasingly frustrated at their lack of success and let the importance of the game get to them. As the half progressed, frustration could now be heard from the terraces as fans bemoaned their team's inability to find the breakthrough.

Then disaster struck when, on thirty- nine minutes, there was a real cause for some disgruntled Shrimpers supporters to voice their anger when Chester mounted their first attack of note and scored.

The build-up to the goal started with a long pass forwards from Neil Ellis into the feet Barry Butler who proved too strong and skilful for Dean Austin. Butler's intelligence rolled the young full back on the edge of the area and, in desperation, Austin brought him to the ground. Instead of awarding a penalty kick, the referee rightly waved play on allowing Eddie Bishop to latch onto the loose ball and smash his powerful shot into the roof of the net for the lead.

The onus was now on Southend to up their game and try to turn a losing position into a winning one as they had done in their previous two home games. However, buoyed by their shock lead, Chester broke through with the last piece of action of the half.

A counter attack had presented Neil Morton with an opportunity to put the away team further in front, but as he took time to steady himself, Pat Scully was able to make a last ditch tackle to deflect the ball away from Sammy's goal to safety.

Heads went down as the half-time whistle went, afraid of exactly what their vocal manager had to say to them over the course of the fifteen minute interval.

Whatever was said by Webb it obviously had an effect on his team. Having resisted the temptation of making an early sub, the players began the second period in a more positive fashion.

The passing - still not up to the high standards in previous games - was better and Blues began to cause clear panic amongst Chester's back four.

The upturn in performance all started from Clark, Martin and Butler who constantly barked at their team-mates in order to get them going.

In fact, it was Martin set the tempo when his fierce drive from distance worked Fred Barber in the City goal.

Brett Angell then also went close with a header, while Andy Ansah's skilful approach play was let down by his cross which failed to pick out a blue shirt.

There was a sense on inevitably that an equaliser wouldn't be too long in coming. That was proved correct midway through the half when Ansah's pace left centre back David Brightwell dead. The winger was now one on one with Barber in goal and that proved little problem for Ansah who confidently beat the eccentric keeper from close range with a tidy finish.

The goal was celebrated wildly in the stands as though it had sealed promotion and not been an equaliser at home against un-fancied Chester City – such was the enormity of Ansah's strike.

Unfortunately, the goal failed to spur on Webb's side and instead it took something out of the player's legs and they then reverted to a performance that resembled the disappointing first half.

In fact, Chester grew in stature once more and very nearly timed their resurgence to perfection when the lively Morton played in Butler who could only hit the post, much to the delight of a relieved Roots Hall.

The final score was a disappointing one-one draw for Southend, but manager David Webb refused to be negative when talking to the press afterwards despite the players feeling it was two points dropped, rather than one gained, while also sending out a message to the fans.

"They (the players) came in at the end feeling very dejected and I had to try and lift them," he revealed. "I told them there was no need to feel down in the dumps. Having lost our two previous games my main concern was to stop the rot and get something out of the match. This the lads managed to do. Okay, it wasn't one of our more impressive displays but the fans are going to see many more scraps like this as club's battle for points over the remaining weeks of the season."

"Chester did not make things easy for us and the swirling wind also posed plenty of problems. So, taking both these factors into account I'm well satisfied with collecting a point - particularly after the way the other results went."

And what of the other results from the teams chasing promotion? All of Grimsby, Bolton and Tranmere Rovers missed the opportunity to capitalise on Blues home draw as they all suffered defeats. That meant that Southend had pulled level on points with leaders Grimsby, but were still in second spot due to an inferior goal difference. However, The Shrimpers still had a game in hand over The Mariners and even better still was that they now had a three and four point cushion over promotion rivals Bolton and Tranmere respectively, with two games in hand on both clubs.

It left Southend in a very good position, but it is always considered better to have the points in the bag, rather than games in hand. To maximise their advantage and at least cement their place in the promotion positions then those games in hand simply had to be turned into wins.

The following Saturday, April 6th, Blues travelled north to Yorkshire and faced Bradford City at Valley Parade. Under Scotsman John Docherty, The Bantams were having an inconsistent season that had them lying in twelfth place. They were coming off a 1-0 loss at Shrewsbury Town as they prepared for the visit of The Shrimpers, but more concerning for David Webb was their recent home record that has seen them go undefeated in their last six games at Valley Parade.

"They have proved a very inconsistent side but are more than capable of giving any team a shock on their day. If we perform with the same spirit and drive as we showed in our last away game at Bolton then I won't complain – providing we get a little more luck this time."

Giving Webb plenty to think about on the journey from Essex was the suspension of Peter Butler for the game and the injury that had definitely ruled out Steve Tilson and threatened to do the same to Paul Clark as well as utility man, John Cornwell.

Tilly had been suffering with a groin strain in recent matches and now the injury had finally gotten the better of the Essex man who didn't even travel to Yorkshire with the rest of the squad as a result. Favouring a balanced look to his team, Webb didn't hesitate in calling up left footed Christian Hyslop to play at left back and that allowed him to push Chris Powell further forward into the left side of midfield.

Butler's absence would likely be filled by Cornwell and it was hoped both he and Clark would be fit after some intensive treatment for their knee injuries. Both players travelled with the squad, but as a precaution Paul Smith, Spencer Prior and Andy Edwards were put on standby.

Injuries and suspensions were always a concern and there was never a good time to see your team suffer from both, but it was deemed even worse as the campaign drew to its conclusion. Webb though, remained positive as always and felt his squad were more than ready to cope.

'Up The Blues!'

"Obviously these are problems we don't want at this stage of the season, but it's no good being negative and bemoaning your fate. This is a time when our squad system may have to be tested and I am sure those who come in won't let us down."

"We have been pretty lucky with injuries for most of the season and it's just unfortunate that they have all come at once...and on top of Butler's suspension. Tilson has been troubled with a groin strain in several matches recently but has played through the pain – it may now be time to see a specialist to get the problem cleared up."

That would mean some time out of action for Tilly and Webb would have to do without one of his first choice midfield players.

There was some good prior to kick off with both Clark and Cornwell having come through their fitness tests to be given the green light to feature in the game.

Clark captained the team and lined up in defence with Pat Scully as his centre back partner. Dean Austin lined up at right full back, Hyslop on the left. In midfield Powell deputised for Tilson, with Martin lining up with Cornwell in the middle and, rather surprisingly, Adam Locke earned a recall at the expense of Andy Ansah on the right. Up front was the tried and tested duo of Ian Benjamin and Brett Angell. The two players selected for the bench was Ansah and Spencer Prior.

Southend, well backed by their fans that had all paid the rather odd £4.95 entrance fee, began the game well and immediately put their hosts on the back foot.

As early as the second minute The Bantams goalkeeper, Mark Evans was called into action and he did well to get down and stop Dave Martin's effort from distance, denying The Blues the perfect start

The pressure on Bradford's goal didn't show any signs of letting up as Webb's men looked to capitalise on their early dominance. Even an early enforced change by Webb didn't hinder The Shrimpers when Adam Locke was forced off with a dead leg to be replaced by Ansah.

On sixteen minutes a concise attacking move sent Dean Austin marauding forwards on the right hand side. Running at full speed, Austin broke into the penalty area and was thwarted by a desperate lunge from midfielder, Wesley Reid that sent him tumbling to the ground. But as the Southend players looked for the ref to point to the spot, unbelievably he didn't – instead signalling for play to continue.

That proved to be the all the impetus the home side needed and they then began to push forward as Blues players struggled to comprehend referee, Tom Fitzharris' decision a few minutes earlier.

They were still clearly reeling with twenty minutes on the clock Bradford scored the game's first goal.

The ball was worked down Southend's left hand side with far too much ease as Powell and Hyslop failed to cut out Sean McCarthy's cross which evaded everyone but Paul Jewell. He controlled the ball before sending it low, back across goal where striker Steve Torpey managed to finish for the home side.

Such was the speed in which the ball was worked from right to left and then back centrally that Southend's defence simply couldn't deal with it. It now needed a response from the away side and within sixty seconds they almost got the perfect one.

A Chris Powell free kick was sent over in the direction of Angell who rose highest in the crowded penalty box to meet the ball with a deft header that left Evans rooted to the spot. Fortunately for The Bantams, the keeper was saved by his far post before he was able to gratefully collect the loose ball.

The Blues kept looking for an equaliser and with only a minute left of the first half, Ian Benjamin fired in a snapshot from the edge of the area that failed to beat Evans once more.

After the break it was hoped Southend would manage to carry on and pressurise the home side until an equaliser came. Unfortunately, it was Bradford who came out with more purpose and endeavour and duly doubled their advantage four minutes after the re-start.

Again it was a goal that could, and should, have been dealt with better by the defence. Scully would have been disappointed at just how easily he was turned by Lee Duxbury before the City midfielder centred for Torpey to apply the finish for goal number two.

It was a terrible time to concede a second goal, but there was no sign of heads dropping from The Shrimpers as they battled hard to get back into the game.

Angell went close when he saw his deflected shot drop narrowly over the crossbar and from the resultant corner kick Scully's header looped over Evans, but was cleared off the line to keep Bradford's two goal lead in check.

'Up The Blues!'

Still The Shrimpers searched for the goal that would get them back into the game and on seventy-five minutes they finally found a breakthrough.

Austin collected the ball from John Cornwell wide on the right and sent over a cross that Benjamin cleverly helped on towards Angell. The tall striker managed to get a shot away – albeit via a deflection – and see the ball fortunately drop the right side if the crossbar for his twenty-sixth goal of the season.

With time against them, Southend to their credit never gave up on grabbing an equaliser. They pushed forward in numbers, but Bradford stood firm and combined an impressive display of defending with some blatant time wasting to see out a win over the league leaders.

Afterwards, Webb was left to rue circumstances that went against his team and cost them dear in their quest for three vital points. "This was a bitterly disappointing result because I felt the three points were there for the taking but luck and some of the decisions conspired to go against us."

However, full back Dean Austin wasn't quite as diplomatic as his manager when asked for his thoughts on the crucial sixteenth minute decision not to award Blues a spot kick. "I went past the player and the next thing he (Reid) whipped my legs from under me, but the ref told our lads who protested that I dived – something I would never do. I'm not a cheat," he fumed.

Results elsewhere around the country saw Grimsby return to Division Three's summit with a 1-0 triumph over Cambridge and their lead over Southend was now three points, albeit still having played a game more.

Bolton managed a 3-1 win over Birmingham to make up some ground on The Blues and was now only four points behind them in third place while Tranmere failed to beat Rotherham at home, suffering a surprise 2-1 loss that left them a point behind Bolton in fourth.

The fixtures continued to come thick and fast and Southend were once again in action midweek with a tough away match at near neighbours, Leyton Orient.

They were already going to be missing Peter Butler through the second of his two match suspension and it had been confirmed that Steve Tilson would be unavailable due to his groin problem. The injury was quite a bad one and after further tests it was confirmed that it was worse than first feared and Tilly would unlikely to feature again during the season.

"Apparently the only real treatment for this type of injury is rest and he has been advised not to play or train for at least six weeks," David Webb said of Tilson's injury. "This will effectively side-line him almost until we are due back for pre-season training. This obviously puts him out for the season which is a real blow to the lad as he has been a vital member to the side. Up until now had played through a lot of pain, but things go to the stage where he simply couldn't carry on."

Losing Tilly was a big blow at a very important stage of the season, but there was no use crying over spilt milk as far as Webb was concerned. He still had to prepare his team as best he could for the trip to East London and, rather boldly, pledged to continue to attack teams whether playing at home or away despite no wins in their last four outings.

"We always look better when we take the game to the other team and gamble on our own attacking ability, hence only one away draw this term. There's nothing wrong with our adventurous style, it's just that we need a change of luck at the moment. I reckon we have played better in our last three away games than in a lot of matches earlier in the season when we were winning. It just needs a bit of lady luck to smile on us a bit."

It was refreshing to hear that Blues would continue to go for the win each and every game, but it was going to be hard to maintain the same quality going forwards without Tilly on the left hand side of midfield. His eleven goals, as well as his creativity were clearly going to be missed.

In his place for match with Orient was Chris Powell who would continue in an advanced role with Christian Hyslop starting at left back. It wasn't an ideal situation, but for Webb it was the only option to keep the balance within the team.

"To be honest, we don't have an automatic replacement if Tilson is out of the side and I feel that Powell is probably best suited for that job, "he conceded before giving his backing to Hyslop's inclusion being based on merit, rather than lack of options. "Young left back Hyslop gave a fine performance on Saturday and deserves another chance."

The other key decision that Webb went with was to drop Brett Angell to the bench, even though the club's top scorer had scored in three of his last five games. The decision came about due to Adam Locke's recovery from his dead leg and that enabled him to start on the right of midfield with Andy Ansah once again switching to the middle of the attack as Ian Benjamin's striking partner.

Making the short trip to Brisbane Road for the second time of the season was an awesome following of over 2,000 Blues supporters who were in fine voice before the game had even kicked off.

That support certainly got the players in the mood as they totally outplayed The O's - a side who had won fourteen of the nineteen home fixtures played prior to this one.

John Cornwell, who was again deputising in Butler's absence, had his best game for the club, dominating his younger opponent, Chris Bart-Williams. Not allowing the highly rated Bart-Williams any time on the ball, Cornwell was able to break up play and set his side on the front foot throughout the contest.

On nineteen minutes, Southend got what their impressive start warranted – a goal. The Shrimpers were defending their penalty box as the home side managed a rare attack and the ball found its way to Cornwell who drove an accurate forty yard pass to Benjamin. Benji, as cool as ever, set Ansah away with a beautiful first time pass that allowed the number nine to utilise his pace to take him beyond Adrian Whitbread's challenge before firing his shot under goalkeeper Paul Heald for 0-1.

The goal sent the outstanding travelling army of Blues fans wild as they danced, cheered and roared with delight. The chant of 'Oo...Andy Ansah...' carried high into the East London night sky from the thousands packed into the away terrace.

Southend then carried on in an extremely professional manner by continuing to control the action. They didn't allow any complacency to creep into their game, looking as focused as ever throughout proceedings.

Orient's preferred form of attack was to get Greg Berry - the man who tormented Blues in November's F.A. Cup tie – in a one on one situation with Hyslop, but each time a question was asked, the young full back answered with a maturity beyond his years.

The home side were growing increasingly frustrated as they continued to struggle in finding way through and work Paul Sansome.

Their only shot of note was when Steve Castle tried his luck from distance and that was never going to test Southend's number one.

In the second half, The O's came a little closer form a corner kick that was met by Howard's powerful header, but Sammy once again underlined his growing reputation in Division Three by turning the ball over the bar and out for another corner kick.

At the other end, Ansah was still causing problems with his pace and after some tidy link up play with Benji, went close with a well hit volley that strayed just inches over Heald's crossbar.

Then, with only minutes left to play, the impressive Locke fashioned an opening for himself as he cut inside from the wing to fire a shot that beat Heald but unfortunately not the woodwork as the post spared Orient from going further behind.

That was that, the game was won and won in style. It was as comprehensive as a single goal victory could be. After managing only a single point out of a possible twelve in their last four matches, Blues answered their critics and put themselves back in contention for automatic promotion. And when it was announced that Grimsby had gone down 3-2 at Bury, it signalled more celebrations on the terraces as Southend were now level with The Mariners and still with that game in hand.

Even more important was that the seventy-four points that David Webb's side had accumulated gave them an eight point cushion over fourth spot and the security of a place in the automatic promotion spots that that brought them. For club captain Paul Clark, this was the main priority for the season. Never mind that the title was a serious possibility, he wanted that historic promotion first and foremost.

"My only concern is putting as much daylight as possible between ourselves and the fourth placed club to ensure that we are automatically promoted. Getting to the Second Division is what our season has all been about and I'm not really bothered in what position we finish as long as we get there (and) three more victories from our remaining seven games should be enough to see us up. Following this result I've got to fancy our chances of achieving that goal," he confidently declared.

"After taking only one point from our previous four games we were under a bit of pressure to get a result against Orient, but all the lads responded magnificently as I thought they would. I didn't see any fear in their eyes when I looked around the dressing room before the match. Naturally there was a little bit of tension, but there was no shortage of confidence. We knew that things would come right sooner rather than later if we continued to believe in ourselves."

Clark, the two time former caretaker player-manager in the late 1980's, still had a manager's vocabulary. His current boss couldn't have put it better and all that Webb was left to do was to praise the travelling Blue Army whose tremendous support wasn't unappreciated. "Our fans were absolutely magnificent. You'd have thought we were the home side the way they got behind us – they gave the lads a bigger lift than any pep talk!"

After the dust had settled from the fine win at Orient, the talk around town wasn't just of promotion, but of going up into the Promised Land as Division Three champions. Five of Blues remaining seven fixtures were at Roots Hall and it was widely anticipated that the next game – a home clash against promotion rivals Tranmere Rovers – could well prove to be key in The Shrimpers promotion dream.

With a game in hand over Tranmere as well as an eight point lead, a win would really see Blues take a big step towards glory. Also, the game was to be played on a Friday night and with all other sides in the promotion shake up in action the following day, the opportunity to put those teams under pressure with another win only added to the excitement surrounded the match.

Webb was keen to state the size of the job his side faced and was determined that feet remained firmly on the floor. "The battle for the top three places is still wide open. No-one can afford to relax and think they've all but made it. As far as we are concerned, there's still an enormous amount of hard work ahead to secure promotion."

He was right, of course, nothing had been achieved yet and each game was now going to be bigger than the last. The pressure on the team was going to intensify and there was no chance whatsoever of starting the run in with an easy three points...Tranmere were coming to Essex to win and anything other than approaching the crunch game in the right frame of mind would result in a major setback for The Shrimpers. David Webb was only too aware of this and spoke on the day of the game about the magnitude of the occasion that faced the sides come kick off.

'Up The Blues!'

"Tonight will be a big game for both Tranmere and ourselves – a real Cup Final which is bound to be full of atmosphere and I want to make sure that we put out the best side tactically to produce the right result."

The return from suspension of midfield dynamo Peter Butler, gave Webb food for thought when considering his team selection. There was also the possibility of recalling Brett Angell who was dropped for the trip to Orient at the expense of either Andy Ansah or Adam Locke.

Webb said he would take his time to make the decisions over those two players, but he again confirmed well before naming the rest of the team that he would again stick with Hyslop and Powell to work Blues left side in the continued absence of Steve Tilson.

As for Tranmere, they came to Roots Hall safe in the knowledge that they had previously beaten Blues 3-1 at Prenton Park and were fully aware that they were capable of causing problems for David Webb's team.

Rovers had suffered defeats in both their last two fixtures, but before then had won six games in a row. As well as that, they had just beaten Preston over two legs to reach The Leyland Daf Cup final at Wembley where they would do battle with Birmingham City. However, Tranmere boss Johnny King pointed out that the crunch game with Southend was all his players were focused on despite their impending date at Wembley.

A crowd of 8,622 – the seasons largest up until that point - were in attendance for the Friday night fixture and amongst them was a respectable contingent from The Wirrall.

The talking point before the game between the home fans was Webb's team selection that saw Butler's return to the line-up at the expense of Cornwell and Angell remain on the bench with Ansah once again preferred to play with Benji up front.

The latter of those two decisions was hardly a surprise really. Ansah had scored two in his last two starts as a striker and was without doubt the man in form. As for Butler's inclusion over Cornwell, it could have been viewed as a little harsh on the former Swindon player, but Butler was the team's engine and he so often set the tempo. In big games, the big players usually get the nod and all through the season he had proved to be one of those.

Yet again, Blues set about their opponents from the kick-off and with the terrific backing from the stands; they rose to the occasion and barely allowed Rovers so much as a sniff at goal throughout the early exchanges.

As Southend pushed forwards, they could have considered themselves to be unlucky as Eric Nixon in Tranmere's goal was in great form. Twice he denied Ian Benjamin an opening goal with two very smart stops.

Undeterred, Blues continued to work the ball wide and look to hurt the visitors from there. Butler was instrumental in this as he covered every blade of grass, winning tackles and getting the ball out to Chris Powell and Adam Locke on the flanks whenever he could.

Whenever Rovers did manage to venture beyond the halfway line, their strikers were found to be brilliantly marshalled by Paul Clark and Pat Scully, while the man that had terrorised Blues back in January, Johnny Morrissey, wasn't allowed to even see the ball as Hyslop denied him at every opportunity.

Then, with forty-two minutes played, the home side found the breakthrough to send their fans into ecstasy.

A throw in was won deep into Rovers half and Christian Hyslop made his way forwards towards the South Bank to launch another of his extremely long throws. The target was Dave Martin and it was his presence alone that caused panic in Tranmere's defence as the ball was allowed to bounce over several heads before falling to Ansah who superbly shielded Steve Mungall from the ball before acrobatically hooking the ball into the far top corner leaving Nixon scrambling across his goal.

It was a very clever, improvised finish from a player who was not lacking in confidence and the young forward was mobbed by his team-mates who knew the significance of scoring first in a game of that magnitude.

There was no time for King's men to comeback at Southend and as the home side comfortably saw out the half. The supporters feverishly cheered at the prospect of being forty-five minutes away from a massive three points.

After the interval Tranmere began to throw caution to the wind in the search for an equaliser that they desperately needed to keep their promotion hopes alive.

'Up The Blues!'

They huffed and puffed as they sought a goal, but they struggled to create anything as The Shrimpers were working overtime in their desire to close down, deny space and keep their goal intact.

In fact, during that spell they managed their first and only shot on target all game when Jim Steele fired off a shot from twenty-five yards that was comfortably dealt with by Paul Sansome.

Whether it was Rovers growing tired at their inability to probe Southend's resolute defence or Blues confidence rising once more as the second half wore on was hard to say. What was clear was that Butler once again began to influence the game in advanced positions and it was his industrious work that led to his side winning a sixty-second minute right wing corner.

In Steve Tilson's absence, Powell came across to take it and sent over a cross from which Martin was adjudged to have been fouled in the area by Steve Vickers for a contentious spot-kick.

This incensed the visitors so much so that the referee, surrounded by Rovers players at the time, opted to issue full back Dave Higgins with a yellow card for his over the top protests. Then, as Martin readied himself for the penalty, Nixon began playing games by reluctantly to getting back on the line and delaying the kick further.

It must have seemed like forever for Martin as he waited patiently for the ref to regain control of the situation and signal for him to proceed. Once he did, Martin began his run up on the whistle, opened up his body and struck the ball well down to Nixon's left, but the keeper read it perfectly to turn the ball wide for a corner. Or so it seemed.

The referee immediately indicated that there had been and infringement on Nixon's part as he strayed off his line to make the save and this only infuriated Rovers even more. Again they surrounded the ref, but once order had been restored Martin stepped once more and after deciding to stick with his original placing of the ball, he was outdone for a second time by Nixon who brilliantly repeated his save moments earlier to keep his side in the game.

This setback didn't have the desired effect that Tranmere had hoped. There was no dropping of heads and falling into a shell from their hosts, not even for a moment. Southend kept their focus and didn't allow their rivals a foothold in the game. Instead, it was The Shrimpers who nearly added to their lead through Benjamin, but the forwards effort flashed inches wide of the post.

There was little other action in the game and there was a collective roar of delight as the final whistle was blown. It was another valuable three points in Blues quest for promotion and what was an all-round great team performance.

Webb, keeping his feet firmly on the ground, spoke after the match and confessed there was a certain forbidden word that wasn't mentioned around the club. "We don't even talk about promotion - the word is banned," he said. "There are still a lot of games to play and anything could happen. One thing we must not do is get carried away or relax and start to think it's all over. I want us to go out and win all our remaining six games. If we do we will definitely go up and win the Championship - that has to be our goal."

It was Webb's responsibility to speak in such a fashion and it hardly came as a surprise when he did so, but looking fans that looked at the league table on Teletext late that Friday night had every right to begin to get carried away. For Blues had now played the same number of games as Grimsby, but after back to back wins they had pulled three points clear at the top with seventy-seven points – a tally that afforded them the security of a nine point cushion above fourth place and the play off positions.

It seemed as though Southend were back in their groove at exactly the right time, not only were the wins coming but players were playing well. None more so than match-winner Andy Ansah whose goals had proved vital in the last two matches.

"That's my twelfth goal of the season, two better than the target I set myself when we kicked off in August and with a player like Brett Angell waiting in the wings I know I've got to keep producing the goods," beamed a proud Ansah. "We are a team who fight and scrap for each other – sure I've grabbed the headlines with my goals lately but we couldn't have won without everybody playing their part," he added.

And that was so evident, not just against Orient and Tranmere, but all throughout the season. Webb had installed a real togetherness at the club from day one and that had stood the team in good stead throughout. It was hoped that that mentality would help The Blues get over the finish line within the next six games

The following day's fixtures were watched with interest as all of the other promotion contenders were in action and as they results filtered through that afternoon there was jubilation when Grimsby had only drawn away at Fulham. It meant The Shrimpers were still top with a two point advantage and once again with a game in hand.

Elsewhere, third placed Bolton lost at Bournemouth while Bury only picked up a single point but the big movers were Cambridge United. Having had several games in hand for the past three months due to a good run in The F.A. Cup that saw them eventually lose a quarter final tie at Highbury 2-1 to Division One giants Arsenal, John Beck's side had forced their way into the play-off positions and they still had games in hand over every team around them. They were most definitely a team to watch and were causing the other contenders to look cautiously over their shoulders.

There was a seven day gap between fixtures for Southend with Wigan Athletic coming to Roots Hall the following Friday, April 19th. It allowed the focus to switch from the tense race for promotion and towards club captain, Paul Clark. The skipper had been in good form over the course of the season, particularly in recent outings and the thirty-two year-old spoke of his desire to stay at the club for a long while yet.

Having been offered only a one year deal back in the summer which Clark accepted, he felt his form and contribution warranted a new deal and was keen to put pen to paper on a new one, should that be forthcoming in the near future.

"There's nothing for me to prove but I'd like to think I've done enough for the club to come up with a decent enough contract to keep me at the club. Nothing would give me a bigger kick than pulling on a Southend shirt next season and hopefully stepping out with them in Division Two. That would be a dream come true but I will have to wait and see what sort of offer Blues come up with – that's if they want me – before I'm in a position to make a decision."

He then turned his attention towards the club and Clark was felt sure that the future boded well on the pitch, whatever his next move would be, "With or without me, I'm convinced the club can look forward to the future with enormous confidence," he predicted. "About half the team are only just around the twenty mark and the great thing is that they are willing to learn. It's often the case that a young lad feels he's made it once he's grabbed a place in the first team, but at Roots Hall none of the lads are walking around with stars in their eyes. They still realise they have much to learn and are only too willing to listen to advice. That's an attitude which can only stand them – and the club – in good stead and one reason why I'd like to think I'll still be here next season."

As the Wigan game approached, it was time for David Webb to cast his attentions to his side and the task of preparing them properly to what was going to be a very difficult fixture. The Latics had climbed into ninth spot in the table after recent triumphs over Crewe, Rotherham and Brentford at home as well as a remarkable 6-1 win over Swansea on their travels.

They had scored goals throughout the season and came to Roots Hall boasting the highest amount in the league with sixty-four strikes from their forty-one games played. Of that tally, four had gone past Paul Sansome back in October in the comprehensive 4-1 victory over Southend.

Webb, though, had done his homework and was keen to see his troops even the score once the game got under way. "We have something to settle with them for a beating we suffered on their ground earlier in the season," he said. "If we go about in the same professional way we tackled Orient and Tranmere then I shall be more than happy."

"They are the type of side which tries to suck you in and catch you on the break. Our defence will need to show the same concentration and steel as they did in keeping clean sheets in our last two games. The match will certainly give us one of our hardest tests, but it should be a cracker as both sides have proved themselves in the scoring stakes."

There were no new injury worries for Webb to contend with and so he was able to name the same side that defeated Tranmere the previous Friday. That meant Brett Angell had to again be content with a place on the bench.

It also allowed Christian Hyslop to continue his run in the first team at full back with Chris Powell continuing his advanced role due to Steve Tilson's injury. There had been initial question marks over Hyslop's ability to slot into the team at such a crucial time of the season, but Webb was happy and declared the young left back was doing a "man-sized job" for him in that position.

It was anticipated that another big crowd would be in attendance for the game after over 8,000 had turned for the visit of Tranmere and Webb spoke of the importance of the supporters backing and the lift it gave his players.

"Our fans have been tremendous all season but have really got behind the lads in the last few weeks. It makes a huge difference to the players to know there are people out there who really care."

And they certainly did care. It meant a lot to the fans who desperately wanted the season to end with the dream promotion that they all craved. Against Wigan it would be no different and 7,550 arrived at Roots Hall hoping for the win that would see them reach the magical eighty point mark and a giant step closer to promotion.

It was a frustrating start to the match for The Shrimpers as they found little joy through Locke or Powell on either flank. Both Wigan full backs more than matched their opponents, denying them space to play and therefore the ball kept on being worked back inside to the centre of the pitch.

From there, particularly when Clark and Scully were in possession, the visitors retreated and gave little other option to Blues centre backs other than to lift the ball towards the strikers. Wigan was more than happy to deal with this as defenders Kevin Langley and Alan Johnson were excellent in heading away any danger that came their way.

The crowd's nerves began to show as they saw their team continually draw a blank in their search for an opportunity to score. Then, midway through the half, it was disaster for The Blues when The Latics got the game's first goal.

From goalkeeper Phil Hughes drop kick the ball ended up in Blues net within a matter of seconds. Hughes' kick was flicked on by Phil Daley for Gary Worthington to collect. His quick feet gave him enough room to turn and put the ball into the far corner of the goal beyond the outstretched hand of Paul Sansome.

Roots Hall fell silent before individual rallying cries grew into chants backing their team. Unfortunately, as Southend rallied, they were unable to penetrate a stubborn Wigan back line for the equaliser.

The only time that Blues tested Hughes in goal was when Ansah's clever run earned his side a corner kick which Powell took. His delivery was met by Dave Martin but there was to be no goal for the midfielder this time as the keeper did well to deny him his fifteenth goal of the campaign.

As the half drew to a close there was little else in terms of action as Wigan were quite happy to sit and keep playing in the same way that had frustrated the home side. Blues had only registered one shot on target and there could be no doubt that improvement was needed after the break.

Blues piled on the pressure straight after the re-start and they forced an immediate corner. Once more Powell found the head of Dave Martin but this time he was to be denied by several Wigan limbs as they scrambled the ball to safety from beneath the crossbar.

Still unable to get the break through, Blues piled on the pressure without success and as a result of this Webb reacted by introducing Brett Angell at the expense of Adam Locke just after the hour mark.

In spite of his introduction, Blues continued to draw a blank and found no way through as Wigan continued to defend very well to protect their one goal lead.

Angell and Benjamin got little change from Langley and Johnson; while Ansah fared no better than Locke had on the wing with left back Allen Tankard dealing with the change in personnel with relative ease.

With time fast running out, Blues began to go for broke and pushed more and more men forwards. Still with no suggestion of an equaliser, the inevitable happened to compound a disappointing night when Wigan broke and added a second at the end of ninety minutes.

Hughes collected the ball and released it quickly from his hands up towards Neil Rimmer who had the freedom of half the pitch after Southend's back line went missing. Rimmer was now in a race for the ball with Sansome. He got there first and took it around the keeper before having the easiest of tasks to put it into the empty net for the killer goal that confirmed Wigan's win double for the season over David Webb's team.

Defeat was hard to take at such an important stage of the season but the performance was even harder for Blues manager to get his head round. "This was probably our worst performance of the season – the scene was set for the lads to stake a title claim and they blew it," he raged. "There was no cohesive pattern to our game at all. When they came in at the interval I stressed they had to try and play it to feet and inject width to their game. Instead they persisted with a hit and hope policy."

"Some of our more experienced players just didn't perform and we finished up getting just what we deserved – nothing. We were victims of our own complacency - it was as if the players were convinced that promotion had already been achieved. Well, it hasn't and the sooner they realise it the better. There's still plenty of hard work to be done if we are not to come unstuck."

It was unusual and out of character for Webb to publicly lambast his players which gave an idea of just how annoyed he was with the display. There can be no doubt that the players would have felt the full force of his tongue after the match as well as what was expected of them in the remaining fixtures.

The next day saw second placed Grimsby fail to overtake Southend at the top when they drew at home to Birmingham, but with Bolton and Cambridge both winning home games against Leyton Orient and Stoke respectively, it reduced the gap amongst the top four to just four points. Still not out of it were fifth placed Tranmere also kept alive their promotion hopes with a narrow victory over Exeter.

It was down Cambridge United's excellent form that the gap between the leading four clubs had been cut. The U's had accumulated thirteen points in five games to put themselves right in the promotion shake up. Even more impressive was that those five games were played in the short space of an eleven day period and they now had a game in hand on Southend whilst trailing them by four points. Everybody was now looking over their shoulder with concern at John Beck's in form team because they were now posing a very serious threat at the top end of Division Three.

For Southend though, it was once more feared that they had 'blown it' by their worried supporters. The next three games were all very tough with an away trip to Exeter on the 27th April followed by what promised to be a tense, edge of the seat thriller at Roots Hall versus Cambridge, before getting back on the road with a journey north where play-off hopefuls Bury would be waiting.

Defeat in two of those would seriously damage chances of automatic promotion and so, even with five left to play, nothing could be taken for granted. Southend United and guarantees didn't often go hand in hand and so, with great trepidation, all eyes turned towards Devon and Exeter City.

In the week building up to the match, Cambridge played their game in hand over Blues and duly despatched of Bournemouth at The Abbey Stadium with a crushing 4-0 victory. That pulled them level on seventy-six points with Grimsby and Bolton – all three now a solitary point behind leaders Southend.

As they had in recent weeks, tickets for The Shrimpers followers who wished to travel to see their team were quickly snapped up with all of the 760 available to supporters going extremely quickly. John Adams even said that double that amount could have been shifted but for safety reasons at St. James' Park that was all Exeter could issue for the away fans.

On the eve of the match, David Webb spoke of the importance of not looking past Exeter for in favour of the more mouth-watering game with Cambridge United three days later. One game at a time and that meant Exeter was the priority.

It was also announced that Blues would be travelling down to Devon by air on the day of the game, but there was one stand out problem that came with that chosen mode of transport, as Webb explained. "Clarky has a definite aversion to going up in the air while Benjamin gets air sick and so they will be travelling down (by car) and staying overnight in a hotel," he said, yet still remained happy with the prospect of the flight, "It will be great for the other lads – a different way of travelling and hopefully it will give them all a lift in more ways than one!"

When asked for his thoughts on the game itself, a more phlegmatic Webb didn't want to pay too much attention to the last performance and focused on what could be achieved at St. James' Park. "It is vital we that we don't make too much of the Wigan result. In my book it was just one of those games when we had an off day as a team – no individuals were to blame."

"Up until then we had performed well in beating Orient and Tranmere and there's no reason now to suppose we won't reproduced that form tomorrow. My job is to try and get the balance of the side right to face Exeter and send out those who I honestly feel are best equipped to do a particular job."

"Let's not start getting too pessimistic. We have got five games left and must set about trying to win them all and that means going out with a positive attitude. If anyone had said at the start of the season that we would be top of the table with five games left, I'm sure everyone connected with the club – fans, players and officials – would have been jumping up and down with glee and that's the way it should be now. We have got a good following of supporters going to Exeter and there is no reason why we cannot pull together to produce the right result."

Surprisingly, the team remained unchanged for the fourth consecutive game despite the Wigan performance. It was unfortunate for Brett Angell who remained on the outside yet again, but this was a big public backing from the manager to his players to go and get the right result.

The signs from the beginning were that Webb was right to stick with the same eleven as the pace of Ansah was proving to be a real outlet that continually stretched Exeter's back line. This got The Shrimpers further up the pitch and that's when they began to cause problems.

As early as five minutes played, a throw in was won midway in the home sides half after Ansah panicked The Grecian's centre back Shaun Taylor into kicking the ball into touch.

Christian Hyslop launched the ball deep into the box and onto the head of David Martin who was strong enough to flick the ball on towards Ansah. The number nine, under pressure, showed tremendous speed of thought to turn and volley the ball into the net, leaving Kevin Miller in goal stranded for a perfect start for the visitors.

It was such a well taken goal from a man in form and the execution of the finish was so impressive. The players celebrated the strike, as did the hundreds of supporters right down at the other end of the ground, but they did so with a focus. There was no danger of Southend suddenly thinking that it was job done – they meant business.

Butler and Martin were again industrious and fully committed in midfield which set the tempo as it so often did. At the back, Clark was every bit the leader that was required of him as he marshalled the troops superbly.

However, it was never going to be a case of Exeter allowing Southend to have things all their own way. They were a good side, better than their mid-table league position suggested and boasted quality within their ranks.

Darren Rowbotham on the wing was an example of that and the more he got on the ball the more he began to cause Hyslop some problems. His close control and quick feet, as well as his desire to cut inside, were a concern, but with thirty minutes on the clock Blues had something else to worry about.

Kevin Miller's drop kick travelled high in the air and as it came down inside Southend's half, Clark was adjudged to have been over physical with Darren Boughey and the referee awarded the home team a direct free-kick.

Mark Cooper stood over the ball before retreating for a long run up which suggested he was going to shoot from all of thirty-five yards. Sammy lined up only a two man wall, but that was not enough to deter Cooper from an ambitious effort. The shot came in low and hard, flying past the wall before nestling into the corner of the net in spite of Sammy's despairing dive.

It was a very good goal that had pulled Exeter level, but there was a steely determination about Southend and they went straight back to the task in hand.

They forced their way immediately back up the other end of the pitch and were desperately unlucky when Ansah saw an effort cleared off the line by Taylor. The little forward then should have done better with a close range header following on from Dean Austin's good work down the right flank.

Exeter managed to survive another period of Southend pressure to see out the half which ended all square on a scorching day down in Devon.

In the second half though, Blues would be attacking the goal in front of their fans and that would give added impetus to the players as they looked to grab all three points on offer.

In the opening minutes of it was again the electric Ansah who again went close for Blues when he fashioned enough room to get off a shot from the edge of the area that Miller managed to grab at the second attempt.

After that, Exeter then enjoyed their best spell of the game as they turned the tables on their opponents and went close to taking the lead on two occasions.

Dead ball specialist Cooper again showed his ability with a teasing cross from a free-kick that was powerfully met by Taylor whose header flew towards the goal. Sammy was beaten and could only watch as the ball looked destined for the net, but somehow a miraculous goal line saving header from Hyslop kept the scores locked at 1-1.

Hyslop then repeated the same act ten minutes later as he again denied Taylor with a clearance off the line after another Cooper set-play.

It was then Southend's turn to attack in what was fast becoming a really open contest. Adam Locke was played through by Benjamin on sixty-one minutes and his shot beat Miller, but Scott Hiley came to the rescue making the games fourth goal-line clearance.

Three minutes later Blues seized the opportunity to counter quickly from an Exeter free-kick. The ball found its way to Peter Butler on the edge of the area and he wasted no time in giving to Locke wide on the right. Running from his own half, Locke aggressively attacked the defender standing in his way; beat him with ease before making his way into the penalty area. There were few options for him to choose from as he looked up so he simply drilled the ball across the six-yard box beyond Miller's dive and as Hiley tried in vain to steer the ball to safety, he inadvertently sliced it into his own net.

The Southend fans in the open terrace behind the goal went wild as they celebrated regaining the lead in such an important game. Locke was mobbed for his part in the goal by his team-mates and all the time Hiley lay on his back with his hands across his face at the realisation of what had just happened.

That was to be Locke's last contribution to the match as he had to be withdrawn due to a shoulder problem. He was replaced by Brett Angell who took his place up front with Benji as Ansah switched to the wing.

Angell, eager to impress, almost added a third for The Blues with his first touch when he connected with Chris Powell's deep cross from the left to guide it towards the far corner of the goal, but Miller was equal to it and the score finished 1-2 with all the spoils going back to Essex.

Blues had played some good football at times, worked hard, dug in and rode their luck. They were also beneficiaries to some good fortune as well, but overall they had come away from Exeter with a return to winning ways and with that came three vital points.

Results around the country underlined the importance of Southend's win with all of Grimsby, Cambridge and Tranmere winning away from home while Bolton drew at Rotherham. Blues win took them to eighty points with four games remaining, Grimsby and Cambridge both were level on seventy-nine; however John Beck's side still had four to play compared to The Mariners two. Bolton – on seventy-seven points - also had just two games left, while fifth placed Tranmere had three to go, but were seven points behind Southend.

All that meant that Southend were now just four points away from achieving the unthinkable. Four points from four games and the impossible dream would become real. It was close now, very close and the games couldn't come quickly enough for fans that travelled back to Essex hardly able to comprehend the magnitude of what they were witnessing.

For the first goalscorer at Exeter, it was important that the players maintained their focus and not get swept up in all the hype. "We must not think in terms of just getting enough points to settle for third place but go all out to win all our remaining games and take the title," Ansah said. "We literally chiselled out three points today in what was a battling rather than spectacular performance and that's the type of resolve we must show in all the games we've got left."

The man of the match, Christian Hyslop, played down his role in the win after the match when asked about his two off the line clearances. "I was just in the right place at the right time. It was amazing how they were almost identical headers arrowed in just under the bar and luckily I managed to get in the way of them," he modestly explained.

As for Webb, even he was forced to admit it was real edge of the seat stuff. "It got a bit nervy out there but the lads showed tremendous character to bounce back after the disappointment of that home defeat by Wigan," he said, before rejecting the chance to talk up Blues chances of getting up, "I'm still not talking about promotion until it's a mathematical certainty."

The chance to get three of those four points required would come three days later when Cambridge United came to Essex for a match that was absolutely massive for both clubs – so much so there was extended highlights scheduled to be shown on local television!

There was never any question that The U's were the form team in the division and had stormed their way into the automatic promotion picture. However, how they went about getting those wins had come in for some heavy criticism from the media. Their style being typecast as physically over the top as Beck's team felt no shame in their effective brand of 'long ball' football.

'Up The Blues!'

Beck was a maverick football manager – always coming up with inventive and out of the ordinary ways for his team to get the edge over their opponents. It was common knowledge that he liked to soak his players with buckets of cold water before games as part of their preparation. He felt no shame in confessing to growing the grass longer in the corner of their pitch so the ball would hold up as it's repeatedly thumped into that area for his strikers to chase.

Whatever was thought of Beck and his Cambridge team, there could be little denying that what he did was working. They shared second place with Grimsby and now the prospect of upsetting Southend's promotion aspirations while cementing theirs made them a very dangerous side to play at such a crucial stage of the season. Their chosen way of playing the game made them the pantomime villains of Division Three, but Southend's Andy Ansah believed a focus had to be maintained so that Cambridge didn't force Blues into a long ball game too.

"It's so easy to get drawn into playing the same way as the opposition, but that's not what has brought us so much success so far this season. We are a better side when we knock the ball wide or into the channels rather than simply trying an aerial bombardment – we must play to our own strengths. Sure, there will be pressure on both sides - this is without doubt our biggest game of the season – but we must fancy our chances as we have already beaten them four-one on their ground earlier in the season."

There was a slight concern that the pre-match build up was being taken over by Cambridge's long ball tactics. The focus should have been centred more on what Southend are capable of, but it was all about the visitors and that was a concern.

Christian Hyslop talked of The U's tactical approach in a manner that did little to go against that trend. "We know exactly what to expect from Cambridge. They will hurl long balls at us all night but we have the men at the back to cope with that - Paul Clark and Pat Scully won't get ruffled or bullied out of their stride. Providing we stay tight at the back, especially from corners and free-kicks, then I am sure we a will be celebrating a magnificent win," was his take on the hot topic sweeping Southend.

Webb, though, didn't mention the words 'long' or 'ball' in his pre-match press conference. Of course he was fully aware the threat that Cambridge posed, but he was too experienced to fall into the trap of talking up the opposition. He hadn't done so all season and wasn't going to start now. Instead, he backed his boys to be more than capable of getting another home win.

"It's bound to be a real tense game but our record at home against the other top sides - wins over Grimsby and Tranmere and a draw with Bolton – proves that we do have players who rise to the big occasion."

"Providing we keep our discipline and shape at the back and don't allow Cambridge to dictate the way the game is played, then I know we are good enough to claim all three points," he said.

There was expected to be a bumper crowd at Roots Hall for the match with the visitors selling out their allocation of fifteen hundred tickets. With around eight thousand plus anticipated for The Blues, it wasn't unreasonable to expect over five figures for the first time in the campaign.

The team news for both teams featured around injuries to key players. For The Shrimpers, winger Adam Locke was unable to start the match due to his shoulder injury not having cleared up as well as was first hoped.

His place went to Brett Angell who resumed his partnership with Ian Benjamin up front and that pushed Andy Ansah to back to a role on the right wing.

For the visitors they were missing a big player for them in the shape of twenty-goal striker, John Taylor. He was absent due to a nasty head injury suffered the previous weekend that left him with four facial fractures. The loss would be felt by The U's, but they still had enough fire power to concern Southend with Dion Dublin and Steve Claridge leading their forward line.

As the teams were warming up for the match, it was announced that the game was to be delayed for a period of twenty minutes to allow for the larger than normal crowd to get into the stadium safely and without missing a kick.

That only served to heighten the tension around Roots Hall as supporters just kept on coming through the creaking turnstiles one after the other. The official attendance was given as 10,664 and when the game finally kicked off at 20.05, a thunderous roar went up from all four sides of the ground.

It was a tense and tight affair as the opening exchanges got underway with no quarter asked, nor given as Blues and Cambridge threw themselves into every tackle. In particular the midfield was proving to be an intriguing battlefield as Martin & Butler were relishing their tussle with their midfield counterparts Colin Bailie and Richard Wilkins.

The quality of football on display perhaps suffered due to the magnitude of the fixture as both sides continued to play at such a high tempo that neither of them was able to get their foot on the ball and play.

There were chances in a frantic first half and they all fell for a home side that were backed by a strong wind. The first notable effort on goal came from a Dean Austin free-kick that was crossed deep into the box and met by Martin. The midfielder's header was good enough to find an unmarked Ian Benjamin who, at full stretch, managed to force John Vaughan into tipping it over the bar for a corner kick.

Chris Powell took it and The U's Phil Chapple got his head to the ball, but unfortunately for him it bounced once on the way to Pat Scully whose acrobatic volley was scrambled off the line by Dion Dublin before Bailie hooked it away to safety.

Sensing Southend may well be turning the game into their favour, the home crowd responded with chants of 'yellows...yellows...' and the home team continued to have the advantage as they pushed forwards once more.

Blues won another corner and, again, Powell came across to the right to take the kick. This time his delivery was aimed for the near post run of Benjamin. The experienced striker beat his marker to turn his header goalwards, but was denied for a second time by the agility of Vaughan in Cambridge's goal.

With the half coming to an end, The Shrimpers were still huffing and puffing at their opponent's resolute defence. Andy Ansah managed wriggle free and unleash a ferocious shot that caught Andy Fensome square in the face. Undeterred, Fensome rose instantly, ready and willing to put his body on the line for his team once more.

The last action before the break was again in the Cambridge half. Powell carried the ball infield from the left and as he made further progress towards goal he was brought down by Chapple before he could pull the trigger and shoot.

The free-kick was dead centre of the goal and supporters waited in anticipation as Austin shaped up to take the kick. He approached the ball, looked to curl it up and over but the effort was tame and was easily blocked by the wall.

During half-time it was wondered amongst Blues fans if they had perhaps missed their chance to score against what had proven to be a very stubborn opposition.

Early into the second period those fears grew as The U's came out and began having some success of their own with Dublin and Claridge beginning to get some reward for their endeavour.

The long balls from back to front were now turning Blues defenders as the wind was now with the visitors. Dublin was outmuscling Scully and Clark and the busy Claridge was collecting the scraps before recycling them back for wide midfielders Mike Cheetham and Chris Leadbitter.

The visitor's best chance fell just after the hour mark when a long throw caused confusion in the box.

The throw-in had the backing of the strong wind and that certainly added to the mix up as the ball bounced perilously inside the penalty box. Sensing the danger, Southend quickly closed ranks as they charged towards the loose ball in a desperate bid to protect their goal. The ball ricocheted off several bodies from both sides before falling to the feet of Dublin who managed to get the ball out from under his feet to lift his shot narrowly over the crossbar.

As time ticked by with the score still goalless Lee Philpott, on as a sub for the visitors, found himself in the clear and one on one with Sansome, but quick as a flash Blues number one dived courageously at the winger's feet to safely collect the ball.

Despite seeing his players get overrun for the main in the second half, Webb resisted the temptation to introduce either of his subs, instead showing great faith in his starting eleven to see the job out. That, though, nearly didn't happen when Dublin should have done much better with a good chance that failed to test Sammy with the last kick of the game.

It was a game of two halves that saw it end in a draw – Blues taking the first, Cambridge the second. Afterwards, it was voiced by many fans that the result was the right one and the point apiece saw both sides inch a little bit closer to the total that would be required for automatic promotion.

After the game, Paul Clark echoed those feelings with the overall target of going up still being the bigger picture for Southend.

"Normally I'm not happy with anything less than victory but this was a night when you can say we won a point rather than lost two. It keeps us on top of the table but more important it puts us a step nearer our Second Division goal."

Cambridge skipper and former Blue, Danny O'Shea, echoed Clark's sentiments when he spoke after the floodlights had gone out at Roots Hall. "We've both got to be happy with the result and I can't see either of us missing out on promotion after this," he declared. "This season we've had cup wins over Wolves, Middlesbrough and Sheffield Wednesday so that shows what we are capable of. And I believe if Blues get two or three more players in during the close season they won't go into Division Two out of their depth."

O'Shea's opinion on his former club was pleasing to hear, but you couldn't help but wonder if there was an underlying bit of kidology involved. Both teams were in a very healthy position, no doubt about that, but Cambridge also wanted the title as well as promotion and perhaps by heaping praise on Southend then more pressure would come with that.

Either way, the fact remained that The Shrimpers had three games to get three points and make history. To come were back to back fixtures at Roots Hall starting with the rescheduled clash v Orient preceding the season finale against Brentford on May 11th and prior to those matches was the trip to play off candidates, Bury, seven days earlier.

Yet another large contingent of travelling Southend fans would be in attendance for what could possibly be **the** game that saw the dream realised. They would travel north full of anticipation but, more than that, they travelled with hope and at the end of the day that was all they could do – hope. It was once more over to David Webb and his players to deliver for Southend United Football Club and secure the unlikeliest of promotions to English football's second tier.

Division Three Table end of April 1991

	TEAM	P	W	D	L	F	A	Pts	GD
1	Southend United	43	25	6	12	65	49	81	16
2	Cambridge United	43	23	11	9	69	41	80	28
3	Grimsby Town	44	23	10	11	64	33	79	31
4	Bolton Wanderers	44	22	11	11	61	49	77	12
5	Brentford	44	20	13	11	58	45	73	13
6	Tranmere Rovers	43	21	9	13	59	43	72	16
7	Bury	44	19	13	12	65	54	70	11
8	Bournemouth	44	19	12	13	57	55	69	2
9	Wigan Athletic	44	19	9	16	67	52	66	15
10	Huddersfield Town	44	18	12	14	57	50	66	7
11	Bradford City	42	18	10	14	58	49	64	9
12	Birmingham City	44	15	17	12	44	48	62	-4
13	Stoke City	44	16	11	17	55	58	59	-3
14	Leyton Orient	43	17	8	18	49	56	59	-7
15	Exeter City	44	16	9	19	57	49	57	8
16	Reading	43	16	8	19	51	57	56	-6
17	Preston North End	43	14	10	19	51	64	52	-13
18	Chester City	44	13	9	22	43	56	48	-13
19	**Swansea City**	43	13	9	21	48	66	48	-18
20	Shrewsbury Town	43	11	10	22	52	66	43	-14
21	Fulham	44	9	15	20	39	55	42	-16
22	Crewe Alexandra	44	10	11	23	58	77	41	-19
23	Rotherham United	44	9	12	23	47	84	39	-37
24	Mansfield Town	44	8	13	23	42	60	37	-18

'Up The Blues!'

May 1991 - End of Season

"I knew it was a goal from the moment the ball left my boot." – Ian Benjamin

At times where people feel under pressure or are possibly on the verge of something big, they will often seek reassuring comfort by repeating anything that has worked on a previous occasion. Sportsmen are probably more superstitious than most and with promotion to Division Two only three points away, Southend opted to travel by air for the big match at Bury – just like they did in their 2-1 win at Exeter the previous week.

In truth, how they arrived in Bury would not matter one little bit, but if by replicating the travel arrangements from the triumph in Devon put the players at ease and in a more positive frame of mind, then it certainly would do no harm.

The mission at Gigg Lane was a simple one – get the win and Blues would get promotion; it was as straightforward as that. There was also a scenario where a point at Gigg Lane may well be enough as long as Bolton slipped up against Swansea City in Wales.

The Southend boss wanted to achieve promotion and do so with a win, but was only too aware of the size of the task. "We want to clinch things with a little bit of style – and that means getting something out of the match. Naturally the lads are bubbling and can't wait to get into action, but I don't regard promotion as a formality. It is still something which has to be worked for and Bury, aiming to figure in one of the play-off positions, won't exactly be sitting back."

"The match will be every bit as hard as any we've had this season and it's up to us not to get too excited. That means cool heads – maintaining our discipline. Remember, we've got a lot of young lads in the side who are still feeling their way into the game. It's asking a great deal of them to keep composed but they've done just that in the last couple of games against Exeter and Cambridge."

'Up The Blues!'

"In fact, they have been under pressure for most of the season. I don't think the lads have ever been out of the top two and that's meant opposing teams have been hell bent on knocking them down. But they have met the challenge with flying colours. I've been proud of the way they have responded and I feel convinced they will come up trumps again."

That was Webby trying to take the pressure of his team and surely it was the right thing to do taking into account the enormity of the occasion that was rapidly approaching. However, it was all too easy and very risky to forget about the other side in this match. It wasn't all about Southend, and as Webb had pointed out, if anybody was thinking that the home side would simply roll over and allow Blues an easy ride was very much mistaken.

Bury had featured in and around the play-offs most of the season and there was a real chance that they would finish there too. Unfortunately for them, their form had dipped and they had only managed two wins out of six games throughout April. It was the wrong time to hit a sticky patch, but in spite of the poor form lately an impressive season at Gigg Lane had seen them only lose three games and by no means would it be a walk in the park for Blues.

On the day of the game it was reported that Southend had an injury concern ahead of the trip north to right back Dean Austin. Apparently, he had been struggling with a knee injury in the days leading up to matchday and as a precaution Webb opted to take fifteen players to the game with Spencer Prior and Andy Edwards on standby should he not recover in time.

However, eager supporters who were desperate to know the team as the players began their pre-match warm up took the opportunity for an impromptu chant of 'Deano, Deano...show us your shirt' in the attempt to see the number on his back. When this didn't work the fans tried 'Deano are you playing...Deano are you playing?' A simple nod from Austin was all the confirmation that was required to put reassures the travelling army.

With Austin fit and available, it was expected that Webb would name an unchanged side from the one that drew with Cambridge. So it came as a big surprise that that wasn't the case as the manager underlined his desire to seal promotion that afternoon with a bold move.

'Up The Blues!'

Adam Locke was the man who came into the starting line-up and lined up on the right of midfield, but it was at the expense of Chris Powell who dropped to the bench as Webb kept faith with Christian Hyslop after a string of good displays at left back.

Locke's inclusion on the right led to a reshuffle of the forwards with Ansah joining Brett Angell in attack and Ian Benjamin starting on the left side of midfield.

The full side selected to take on Bury was as follows: Sansome, Austin, Scully, Clark, Hyslop, Locke, Butler, Martin, Benjamin, Ansah and Angell. Substitutes: Powell and Cornwell.

Minutes before three o'clock, both sets of players came out from the tunnel to vociferous backing from their fans which grew in crescendo right up until the referee's whistle signalled for Southend to kick off and get the game under way.

It began in a very cautious and nervy manner that was no doubt a result of the size of the occasion, although there was some decent approach play from both sides that forced early corners at either end. Locke took The Blues corner kick and David Lee Bury's, both had similar results that didn't trouble either defence.

Of the two teams it was the visitors who came closest to breaking the deadlock twice through livewire Andy Ansah. The little forward was found by Peter Butler on the right of the goal and, without hesitation; he fired in a shot that didn't match the high standards he had set himself over recent weeks, dragging his effort well wide.

That situation was replicated by Ansah minutes later as he again found himself in a similar position, but his effort again failed to hit the target and work Gary Kelly in the Bury goal.

As the game progressed, the midfield tussle resembled a battlefield as Martin and Butler were flying fully committed into challenges and refusing to give their opponents an inch of ground. If Blues couldn't manage to outplay their opponents from the outset, then they would look to win the fight first to earn the right to then do so.

As Southend began to get slightly on top of Bury, they managed to display the first piece of real quality after thirty-nine minutes of play. The ball was played wide for Hyslop who had advanced over the halfway line. He looked up and found Brett Angell with an accurate cross that Blues top scorer managed to meet with his head, but the effort went agonisingly just over the bar.

Moments later the game changed. It was the visitors who had managed to have a period of pressure in the final third of the pitch, earning a free kick in a decent position. Dean Austin lined up the ball and fired off a shot that went into the wall and all of a sudden Bury were away with the lightning quick David Lee leading the charge.

Lee carried it from the edge of his area and easily evaded Dave Martin's sliding tackle, but his touch was a bit heavy and that invited Pat Scully to attempt to get to the ball ahead of him. Unfortunately, Lee's pace didn't give Scully much of a chance and, already committed, the Irishman connected the flying winger, taking him out high across the knees.

Immediately, referee Paul Vane was surrounded by players from the home side demanding the ultimate punishment for Scully's foul. Southend's players responded to this unsporting behaviour by pleading with Vane to be lenient with their team mate.

There then followed a period of waiting as Scully was given a long talking to by the referee and the consensus amongst away fans was that that was a good thing. Surely a yellow card was to follow, but then Vane shocked everyone as he pulled out a red and gave the defender his marching orders.

The tackle was very late and warranted a card, but surely a yellow was more just than the red that was issued. The tackle took place inside Bury's half and could hardly be viewed as a professional foul, but it was too late to appeal to the referee. The decision had been made, but that didn't stop Benji telling the Mr Vane exactly what he thought of his decision.

The immediate reaction from Southend's bench was to put Dave Martin in at centre back in Scully's absence and bring Benjamin into the centre of midfield with Angell working from the left hand side. They then made sure that they saw out the half before they could get into the dressing room and regroup at the interval.

All of Martin, Angell and Benjamin carried on in their adopted roles after the break and even though the work rate did not drop from Southend, with ten men there was little doubt that the game had swung in Bury's favour.

It was clear that the home side would now look to make the most of their advantage and began to pile on the pressure. But, everything that they threw at their opponents, Southend managed to repel with brave headers, block tackles and sheer hard graft.

This was typified when Bury's Kevin Hume was played in on goal by Lee for a shooting chance just inside the area and just as he shaped to shoot, Paul Clark appeared out of nowhere, timing his tackle to perfection to avert the danger.

Moments later the home side were away again and in similar circumstances. Liam Robinson had managed to get away from Clark before getting caught in two minds as he considered his options. That moment of hesitation was all that Christian Hyslop needed to make a superb saving tackle by going to ground and taking the ball, much to Southend's relief.

Bury were now enjoying their best spell of the game and were awarded a free-kick when Martin upended Hume in a dangerous position. Mark Kearney and Charlie Bishop stood over the ball with the former taking the kick, but the delivery was below par and sailed straight into the grateful arms of Paul Sansome.

It was becoming real backs to the wall stuff for The Shrimpers. Every time they cleared their lines with a courageous header or volleyed clearance - the ball just came back into the danger areas, yet the home team still proved wasteful in front of goal.

Hume was found guilty of this with twenty minutes left to play when he managed to escape Clark's attentions before lining up a shot from twenty-five yards that did more damage to the roof of the stand rather than Southend's goal.

Minutes later, Bury twice went close to getting the game's opening goal in the space of sixty seconds. First, Robinson made room for a shot that looked a certainty to go in until somehow Sansome's agility managed to push the ball onto the bar and out for a corner kick.

Lee's accuracy from the resulting corner picked out centre back Peter Valentine whose header seemed destined for the net, but again Sammy pulled off a stunning reaction save to keep his goal intact.

Southend then managed to offer something in return as they hit a long ball forwards to utilise the pace of Ansah who tried at every attempt to stretch the home side's defence.

This time he collected the ball, turned and got away from Colin Green before hitting a speculative shot from distance that sailed well wide of the goal. That effort seemed to lift spirits and give Blues some belief that they could make use of Ansah's speed to take some of the pressure of the defence.

With nine minutes remaining, they did exactly that with outstanding results. Dave Martin won a header deep in his just inside his own half that dropped at the feet of Ansah. The Blues number nine carried the ball forward, twisting and turning as he went, leaving two Bury defenders in his wake. Then, faced with a third, he fortuitously beat his opponent and found himself wide on the right hand side. From there, Ansah then looked up and miss-hit a cross with his left foot that luckily found its way to the feet of Ian Benjamin.

Benji had his back to goal and his marker was touch tight behind him, but he knew exactly what he was going to do. Twelve yards from goal he controlled the ball with his right foot before feinting like he was going to go left. That dummy fooled his marker and gave him all the room he required to push the ball with the outside of his right to tee up a sweeping left foot shot that headed towards the goal.

As the ball left Benji's left boot and travelled towards the goal there was a deep intake of breath from Blues supporters. Time momentarily stood still...before eventually it crossed the line and came to rest perfectly in the corner of the net.

Pandemonium ensued on the away terrace as Southend's ecstatic fans went crazy! Fists clenched & screaming with delight, dancing with anyone they could find and jumping onto the fence that kept them away from the playing surface! The release of emotions at that moment was unbelievable...it was eighty five years in the making!

The players also celebrated the goal with as much joy as was being displayed on the terraces. They engulfed the goalscorer and knew they were now close, very close and all the while David Webb remained a figure of professionalism in the dugout by refusing to get caught up in the raw emotion that was unfolding right in front of him.

Southend were now defending for their lives as Bury were desperate to equalise in their quest for a play-off spot. Webb immediately threw on substitutes John Cornwell and Chris Powell in place of Locke & Angell to offer some much needed fresh legs out on the field.

Blues continued to hold on, but it was nail biting stuff and, at times, unbearable to watch for the fans away at the opposite end of the round.

The ball kept on being pumped into their area time and time again, but the colossus figures of Martin and Clark kept putting their bodies in the way of everything. It was a terrific example of giving your all when you're fighting to hold onto something you so desperately want.

As time ticked away, The Shrimpers supporters frantically checked their watches in the hope that full-time was approaching, but it seemed to take an eternity just for every single minute to pass.

Whistles were echoing around the away stand as the home fans willed their team on for one last push for an equaliser. Their hopes were raised when Roger Stanlislaus hit a high diagonal ball over towards Lee on the right but it never reached its intended target as Hyslop cut it out with his head and guided the ball back to Sammy.

The whistles from the Southend faithful for full-time were now getting desperate. Sansome drop kicked the ball forwards and with it travelling high into the air referee Paul Vane signalled for the end of ninety minutes meaning that history had been made. Southend United had won promotion to Division Two for the first time in their history!

Immediately after the final whistle had sounded the celebrations began and at first it was extremely raw as nobody really knew what to do, some of the players ran towards the fans while some of the other heroes embraced each other on the pitch.

On the terraces, there was an almighty cheer as hundreds of Blues fans climbed up on the fence so they could exchange handshakes with the players who had made their way over.

Chants of 'going up...going up' were coming from Southend's jubilant supporters while John Cornwell lifted man of the match Dave Martin upon his shoulders right in front of them. The players who weren't involved now made their way onto the pitch to join in the celebrations as did Pat Scully, showered and changed after his first half dismissal, and he was greeted by the welcoming arms of Peter Butler.

The players were then got together by the press photographers for a team picture that captured the moment perfectly. They huddled together in typical fashion, all full of smiles, bouncing up and down wearing the numerous scarves they had been given by fans while singing 'The Blues are going up...The Blues are going up...and now you're gonna believe us...and now you're gonna believe us....and now you're gonna believe uuuuusssss...The Blues are going up...'

'Up The Blues!'

When they broke away from the cameras they turned once more to their adoring supporters who were now calling for David Webb, but the Blues boss wasn't on the pitch having left his players to enjoy their moment. Webb had left for the dressing room at the final whistle and by this time he was enjoying a well-earned whisky as he lay in the bath.

"Let the lads who have done the job enjoy their moment of glory – I'll celebrate with the supporters once we have clinched the championship," he told the reporter who went to inform him of the fans request.

Back out on the pitch, the players began slowly filtering away and many of The Blue army had made their way down from the fencing and worked their way back to their family and friends who had stayed at the back of the stand.

It was such a magical feeling for many, a memory that would stay with them always. Grandfathers, Fathers and sons cuddled as they spoke in disbelief that the dream had finally been realised. It was heart-warming to see so many people share such a moment – beaming smiles on faces that were only broken to wipe away the tears that grown men cried that afternoon.

After even more celebrations in the dressing room, match winner Ian Benjamin spoke of his delight at being part of the promotion team. "It's great for me personally to have scored the goal to create history for Southend United – a real dream come true – but the other lads deserve credit for what they did. The young lads in the team were superb and showed that the club has a tremendous future. They can certainly do well in a higher grade of football – even an old man like me is looking forward to helping to play a vital role in Division Two," he smiled.

"We all felt the ref over-reacted on Pat's sending off, he seemed to be swayed by the crowd, but it only succeeded in making us even more determined. We said at half-time that we had to pull together and make sure we didn't lose our shape, discipline or pattern and it worked a treat."

He then went on to modestly describe the goal that won the game and clinched promotion for Blues and the satisfaction he felt for the travelling supporters, "I always felt we could nick it and when Andy's cross fell to my feet I just turned and hit it. I knew it was a goal from the moment the ball left my boot. It was wonderful for our fans

'Up The Blues!'

who were absolutely brilliant and helped keep us going when we faced a real uphill battle. They never stopped shouting and urging us on and we responded in the best way possible."

David Webb, now out the bath, spoke to underline the importance that his number ten has within the club. "I was pleased for Benjamin that he scored the all-important goal because he typifies what I am trying to develop here – one hundred per cent professional players. Not only has he contributed some vital goals this season but his value to the team has been immense. He holds the front line together – getting the ball and bringing others around him into the game. Even when we have gone through a dodgy spell of form, Benji would be the last person I would consider leaving on the sidelines."

"There were one or two who posed the question whether he would be a regular in our side this season or merely come in and out as a squad player, but Benji soon dispelled any thoughts of that. He has been a tremendous influence on the younger players, always ready to give advice and lead by example. Benji gives so much and asks for so little – he is the best player I have ever worked with...and to think we got him on a free transfer!"

High praise indeed and the Southend manager had admiration for the rest of the squad too who had all performed to such a high standard throughout to seal promotion, but he now wanted the championship too. "We had a magnificent bunch of players out there today who did the club proud – they had a mountain to climb and scaled the peak. This was our little Everest and now we must look to our home games against Leyton Orient on Tuesday and Brentford on Saturday to finish the season in style and take the title which we will have earned. We have been top or thereabouts for nearly the whole season - up there to be shot at. There have been one or two little dodgy spells but these players have proved so resilient, bouncing back and proving people who have written them off or doubted their credentials wrong time and time again. I feel so pleased for them and everyone at Roots Hall from the team lady to the hardest fanatic on the North Bank – Southend United has arrived at last and let's all savour and enjoy it."

One player whose relief matched his happiness at promotion being won was Pat Scully. "I was absolutely devastated when the ref brought out the red card, but the lads didn't let it affect them and if anything (they) got better and stronger in the second half. I just prayed that my sending off would not wreck all that the players have fought for this season – I would never have been able to forgive myself if it had," said the Irish defender.

Things slightly calmed down over the next couple of days and Southend rightly received many plaudits for what they had achieved. Going from a team that, for the main, spent many of their eighty-five year history in the bottom two divisions without ever really troubling the top of the table in Division Three to a side that had now taken it by storm without any prior warning deserved all the recognition they got.

It also had to be noted that the squad boasted a lot of young talent with many players in their early twenties. If Webb could keep them together and build on that then the likes of Chris Powell (21), Christian Hyslop (18), Adam Locke (20), Pat Scully (20), Andy Ansah (22), Brett Angell (22), Steve Tilson (24) and Dean Austin (21) then who knew what lay ahead for the club.

Certainly Paul Clark was pleased with the youngsters within the squad and backed the club to progress even further. "It's amazing when you look around the dressing room and see all those young faces. About half the team are only just around the twenty mark and the great thing is that they are willing to learn. That's an attitude which can only stand them and the club in good stead for the future. I am sure the club is in good hands and can look forward to even more success," he said.

It was easy for the fans to carry on smiling and celebrating throughout the beginning of the week and, to some extent, the pressure had been lifted. Promotion after forty-four games was reason to party, but for the players, they still had fixtures to play – and that meant that the attention would have to be now turned towards Leyton Orient's visit to Essex three days after Bury, Tuesday 7th May.

For David Webb, it was simple and straight forward; one win from the remaining two home games would secure the title as Blues now had a four point lead over Grimsby & Cambridge after both failed to win as The Shrimpers triumphed at Bury – and he wanted that trophy. Promotion was unbelievable, but that was in the bag so his focus was now to 'go for the Championship' and he refused to allow complacency to creep into his troops.

"It's a relief to go into tonight's game knowing that we are already up but we owe it to ourselves and our magnificent fans to finish on a high note and that means the Championship. We have two games left against Orient tonight and Brentford Saturday and three points will be enough to take the title, but I have set a target of ninety points for the season and that means winning them both," The Blues Chief said on the day of the game.

"I will not excuse any let up in that quest. I know it would be easy for the players to relax now but I want them to continue to show a real professional attitude just as they did in overcoming tremendous odds and winning at Bury despite being down to ten men for most of the match. We can have a party on Saturday after the Brentford match."

With the main goal having been reached, there was a personal target for striker Brett Angell who was keen to claim the golden boot for the division. He was tied with Bolton's Tony Philliskirk on twenty-six league goals apiece, but wanted his second top scorer award in as many seasons after his twenty-three goal haul in Division Four with Stockport the previous year.

It wasn't a given that he would start with both Benjamin and Ansah both pushing hard for a spot up front, but whatever Webb decided he would be demanding nothing less than the professional approach that he asked for all season from his team. That was the minimum Webb required and Andy Ansah was well aware that that was the case.

"I don't think the manager will allow us to sit back and take it easy. That win at Bury was magnificent and the lads will obviously take a little while to come back down to earth, but I am sure by the time we take to the field our attitude will be just right and the thought of sealing it all up in front of our own fans will be too much of an incentive for us to throw it away now," he assured supporters.

For the visit of Leyton Orient, there was a bumper crowd in attendance with 8,760 there to hopefully witness the title being won. There crowd was anxious once more, but it was a different kind of anxiousness that they felt this time. The stands were full of excited reverberations from the home supporters about promotion being in the bag, but also because of the prospect that they would be crowned as the best side in the league.

For the match, Webb made one change to the eleven that beat Bury and that was to recall Chris Powell to the left of midfield at the expense of Adam Locke who returned to the bench. That meant that Ansah lined up on the right of midfield with Angell partnering the hero of the hour Ian Benjamin in attack. Defender Pat Scully was eligible to play despite his red card at Gigg Lane and would not face suspension until the start of the following season.

It was a promising and energetic start for the home team who were clearly feeding off the crowd and the confidence that came from having already sealed promotion. Ansah was twice found with intelligent passes, first from Butler, then Benjamin but on both occasions he was thwarted by Orient keeper Paul Heald.

It was clear that Orient were intent on spoiling the game - as well as Southend's party. From very early on Heald was happy to collect the ball, roll it to his defenders before getting it straight back and which began to infuriate the home fans, while wasting precious minutes on the clock as well.

After half an hour had passed, Blues registered an effort on goal when Angell connected with Austin's deep cross, but the forward was unable to add to his season's tally, putting his header went tamely wide.

The first half came and went without any more action of worthy of note. Orient had a plan and was determined to stick with it. Time wasting, breaking up Shrimpers pattern of play with fouls and played a very well drilled offside trap that was working a treat.

Fans knew an improvement had to come in the second half if their side were to clinch the league title and it was expected that Webb would have told his players that they needed to come out and play like champions.

Whatever was said at the break failed to have an immediate effect as the visitors from East London continued to do exactly what they had in the first half. Their spoiling tactics were not easy on the eye, but they were hardly going to lie down and allow Southend an easy ride.

Then, a rare foray forwards broke the deadlock and the visitors now had something to hold on to.

The O's won a corner and as Blues were sorting themselves out and not paying full attention, Chris Bart-Williams played it short and it was rolled back into the path of oncoming right back Chris Zoricich whose driven effort was turned into the goal by Keith Day.

David Webb instantly responded to going a goal behind by taking off his top scorer for Adam Locke and switched Ansah inside alongside Benji in the striker's role. The change seemed to be the kick start his side needed as they began throwing everything at Orient.

Within minutes Southend were piling on the pressure. Hyslop strode forwards to launch his trademark long throw into the area, finding the head of Dave Martin whose flick on came to Ansah and the little man produced a breath taking overhead kick that was somehow saved by Heald.

The effort deserved a goal, but the ascendancy was now well and truly with Webby's wonders. They needed an equaliser as quickly as possible and they got one on seventy-two minutes. Peter Butler took control of the midfield to lift a beautifully weighted pass over the opposition defence for Locke to run onto.

Heald came off his line to narrow the angle, but all that did was help Locke to make up his mind to coolly lob the ball over the keeper before adjusting his viewpoint to see the ball bounce into the empty net in front of a euphoric North Bank.

While supporters went crazy, the players didn't. Instead they grabbed the ball from the net and looked to get the game re-started as soon as possible.

Southend were now throwing everything they had at a team that had players back in large numbers for the remainder of the match.

In the minutes that were left to play, Blues fashioned another two very good chances to turn the game around and take the league title. First, Butler's shot from distance was deflected into the path of Martin who, from ten yards out, somehow managed to put his shot into the grateful arms of Heald.

Then, as the game was entering injury time, Butler played a very precise ball through to Benjamin who easily side-stepped Warren Hackett to set up a clear shot at goal, but the hero of three days earlier fluffed his shot which rolled straight at the feet of the waiting goalkeeper.

That was the last action of a frustrating evening where Leyton Orient clearly had not read the script. It was a game where Southend were supposedly going to wrap up the title and celebrate long into the night. As it turned out, it was now going to the last day of the season due to Cambridge's 2-1 win over Bradford that confirmed it was now a shootout between them and Blues with Grimsby unable to catch The Shrimpers with just one game left to play.

The Shrimpers Boss was disappointed and he couldn't hide his frustration at the missed chances that had cost his team. "Our finishing has let us down badly in the last few games and tonight was no exception. We were through three times with only the keeper to beat and yet failed to find the net."

"It was nice to go into the match knowing we have already made it into the Second Division but in a way it possibly worked against us as we didn't seem to show the right clinical approach. I certainly couldn't fault anyone for lack of effort or simply sitting back on their laurels, but we did not produce the necessary sharpness in and around the area."

And so it all came down to Brentford's visit to Roots Hall on Saturday 11th May. In truth, whatever happened and wherever the title ended up, David Webb's work had been nothing short of remarkable. Nobody had backed Blues for promotion at the start of the year and to have delivered that in any capacity was a massive achievement.

The club's success had not gone unnoticed elsewhere and in the build-up to the Brentford game there was a story in the local press that David Webb was on Chelsea's shortlist as the man to replace Bobby Campbell who had resigned from Stamford Bridge days earlier.

Webb's connections with the club were obvious having featured in the famous F.A. Cup win over Leeds in 1970 in which he scored the winner in a replay at Old Trafford. He was still held in high regard by their supporters, but Webb refused to be drawn on the matter. "I have heard the rumours but there has certainly been no approaches made to me or, to my knowledge, Southend officials. Some people might say there's no smoke without fire, but let's say I haven't seen any flames yet!"

And that was all that Webb would say on the subject, preferring to switch topics and talk about the possible surprise inclusion of a player whose season had been pigeon holed for the treatment room for the rest of the season.

Steve Tilson had been written off due to a persistent groin injury that progressively got worse as he continued to play through the pain. His loss had been a blow having scored some very important goals as well as creating his fair share too. However, Tilly had responded a lot better than expected to treatment and managed to get himself way ahead of schedule in his rehabilitation. Now he was pencilled in a midweek reserve fixture away at Barnet to see if there would be any reaction.

He had been out for six weeks in total so Webb was keen not to rush him back into the first team action until he was convinced he was ready. "Let's just see how Tilly performs tonight," Webb said, refusing to commit either way. "There must be a question mark over his fitness, but I am certainly not ruling him out of my team plans yet – he could be just the man we need at the moment."

Tilson came through the game at Barnet unscathed and declared himself fit for consideration for the title decider. As ever, Webb was giving his team selection a lot of thought and would not name it until the day of the game.

"It would be great for Tilly and the team if he played in our last game of the season, one which could reap the golden title harvest, but I will not give in to sentimentality. Tilson will play only if I feel his inclusion will improve the team," he said.

There was a big carrot in front of the club for the game against Brentford. It was going to be another large crowd for a game that was made all ticket. It was hoped this time the championship trophy would crown a superb campaign, but as much as Blues boss wanted to finish on top of the pile, he still pointed out that there was already much to celebrate.

"We all know that three points will give us the championship, and that would be a wonderful achievement after being top of the table for most of the season, but win, lose or draw we will still have a lot to celebrate afterwards," Webb pointed out.

"Of course we shall be going all out for victory over Brentford but we can go into action relaxed and free of pressure because we have already earned our number one goal – promotion. The title is the candles on the cake but if someone forgets to light them we can still have a party, this is one occasion when we simply cannot lose!"

Blues had mixed experiences of their previous clashes with The Bees earlier in the season. They won 1-0 at Griffin Park in the league back in November and lost 3-0 at home in The Leyland Daf Cup in March. With one win apiece, Webb wanted a second victory in the third meeting between the clubs, but he also wanted to do it in style. However, Phil Holder's side would not be rolling over and were after the points to force their way into play-off contention.

"It's all nicely poised and hopefully we'll produce a good game of football, a treat for our fans who have been magnificent all season. That's what I want from our lads, to finish a memorable season by playing the sort of soccer which has taken us to the top of the table. If they do that then we need fear no-one."

While three points would guarantee a first place finish, there were two outcomes at The Abbey Stadium that would mean the title would be heading to Essex. Cambridge were entertaining Swansea City and should they draw or even lose then Blues would be crowned champions regardless of their own result. It was important, though, that it wasn't left down to Swansea doing them a favour and they made sure of title glory with a winning result themselves.

A crowd of 9,666 flocked to Roots Hall to hopefully witness Paul Clark get his hands on the trophy, but they were also there to pay homage to their team and the outstanding accomplishments they had already made.

Webb made two changes from the side that drew with Leyton Orient, handing Steve Tilson an immediate recall at the expense of Chris Powell and Adam Locke replacing Brett Angell.

The full team for the season's finale was: Sansome, Austin, Scully, Clark, Hyslop, Locke, Martin, Butler, Tilson, Benjamin and Ansah. Substitutes: Powell and Angell.

Southend began by putting the visitors under pressure from the start with particular joy coming from the flanks and this resulted in the award of a twelfth minute penalty kick in front of a packed North Bank.

Tilson sent over a cross that somehow found its way to Andy Ansah who tried an ambitious overhead kick. He made contact, but the ball was deflected off Terry Evans and into the path of Locke who pushed it past Jamie Bates just as the full back recklessly went to ground, thwarting the winger in full flight.

It was an obvious penalty for Southend and an expectant North Bank waited for Dave Martin's kick. He began his run up before side footing the ball to the left, sending Graham Benstead the wrong way...but the ball clipped the post and rolled out of play for a goal kick.

A full to capacity North Bank swayed in anticipation of the net bulging, but it wasn't to be for Martin who had been one of the players of the season. After the miss, he retreated immediately back into position to get on the game with Butler's words of encouragement ringing in his ears.

Blues continued to play and put pressure on Brentford. On twenty-seven minutes a clever piece of play from Benjamin, Locke and finally Ansah, set up Tilson for an opportunity to score with his head, but the effort was comfortably dealt with by Benstead.

From that point on, The Shrimpers stopped getting the ball wide and instead resorted to hitting direct balls up the field for Benji, which was playing into the hands of visiting centre backs, Evans and Keith Millen.

At half-time the game was goalless and it was hoped that Blues would start to play the ball wide and attack from there as they had throughout the season. Trying to find Benjamin with balls from front to back clearly wasn't working, especially with the diminutive Andy Ansah as his partner and not the taller Brett Angell who was left watching on from the bench.

Fans who were still queuing up for a half time bite to eat as the game re-started would have missed the goal that came within the first sixty seconds. Brentford won a free kick wide on the left that was taken by Keith Jones. He lifted the ball towards the centre of the goal which was only half cleared and the loose ball fell to Gary Blissett who was unfazed by the tight angle, lashing the ball back across Paul Sansome and into the far side of the net.

The away side then nearly added to their lead when Blissett was denied by Sammy and then a few minutes later, Blues number one was at full stretch to turn away a Neil Smillie shot from long range.

David Webb reacted to what he was seeing by making a double change and introducing Chris Powell and Brett Angell for Christian Hyslop and Steve Tilson.

Unfortunately the changes never really looked like paying off as Southend continued to look to go long which was comfortably lapped by Evans and Millen.

Not once in the second period did Southend really trouble Benstead, nor did they look like ever doing so. Brentford's defence stood strong, while their midfield was working hard to prevent Blues time to get any sort of rhythm going.

As the final few moments of the season were coming to an end, a premature mini-pitch invasion by the home fans causing the game to stop for a brief moment until the police and stewards cleared the playing area. Once they had, the referee blew his whistle for the end of the afternoon's play and the 1990/1991 season.

The Blues hadn't managed the win to get the three points required to seal the title and soon news filtered around the ground that Cambridge had beaten Swansea 2-0 to pip Southend to first place, while Grimsby's 2-1 triumph over Exeter saw them finish above Bolton in the final automatic spot.

However, this didn't dampen the mood within Roots Hall one little bit. The party began regardless of where the league trophy was heading and supporters invaded the pitch to celebrate their historic promotion.

Fans sang, danced and rejoiced with one another in numbers that almost covered the entire playing surface, finally gathering around the tunnel area in front of the East Stand.

They were waiting for their heroes to appear inside the director's box to thank them all for giving them all the best moments of their life supporting Southend United.

While this was going on, celebrity fan Jimmy Greaves, summed up the mood perfectly. "Okay, so it would have been great to win the title but the players and David Webb deserve the highest praise for getting the club into the Second Division," he said. "They were tipped by most experts at the start of the season to go back into Division Four but have proved them all wrong and no-one can take away what they have achieved. It's tremendous for everyone at Roots Hall and I am really proud of them all."

The emotional scenes that were still carrying on in front of the East Stand seemed like they could go on forever, especially when the roar went up at the sight of the boys in blue that had made it into the second division. The full repertoire of chants came out for all the players who had all given their all over the course of the forty-six game season. But, just like at Bury, there was still no sign of Webby and he was being called for...

"The backing form the supporters has been superb from the time we kicked off the season (and) it's not just at home that the fans have given the players their one hundred per cent support either – matches at Cambridge, Brentford, Fulham, Bradford City and Orient readily spring to mind," said The Blues Boss. "To hear non-stop chants of 'yellows' or 'David Webb's yellow army' gives everyone a lift and helps dredge up that little bit of extra energy when the going gets tough."

Webb then finally made his way out to finally give those Blues fans what they wanted. A magnificent cheer erupted and songs broke out for the man who had orchestrated and overseen the greatest ever season in the football club's eighty-five year history.

He stood and surveyed the thousands below him who were looking on at him like he was the second coming! They were showing the great man that he was forever in their hearts for what he had done and just how much it meant to them.

Then, as he applauded his followers, he underlined his ambition and belief in the squad of players he had assembled. The players that had done all he had asked and more. Not content with promotion to Division Two, Webby pointed upwards and looked towards the sky before mouthing the words 'we'll go up again…we'll go up again…' to mass approvals from the crowd below.

The 1990-91 campaign had been the best yet for Southend United. The supporters had dreamed of a day when history would be made and at Bury it had been. Yet, in truth Blues fans felt like they were daydreaming at the marvellous football team that David Webb had put together. Many times throughout the campaign they had left Roots Hall in awe at just how good they looked in destroying the opposition in the climb to legendary status.

As supporters exited the ground for the last time that season, they once more walked away in awe, but also in anticipation and full of excitement for what lay ahead. They couldn't get out of their heads David Webb's vision that saw no limit for their club's future after signalling his intent to push on yet again the following year and seeing just how far he could take this little team from Essex.

For now, it was mission accomplished and they deserved all the plaudits and fanfare that came with that. Part of those acknowledgements would follow the very next day with an open top bus parade starting at Roots Hall before moving onto Shoebury and then along the seafront. The bus journey was to finish at Aviation Way where a champagne reception would be waiting.

Pat Scully spoke as he boarded the bus at Roots Hall, underlining the type of day that lay ahead. "Win or lose we'll drink some booze and if we draw, we'll drink some more," said the grinning Irishman.

Once on the bus, Paul Sansome was blown away by the numbers that greeted the team as they slowly made their way around the fifteen mile route, saying: "I did not think it would be like this. It is a great turnout"

His manager was also taken aback by the many, many happy faces that looked up at their heroes whilst waving commemorative flags and scarves in jubilation. "This is wonderful and just shows the kind of support we have had throughout the season, and particularly in the final stages," he said in disbelief.

But, it wasn't just Webby and his team that were in disbelief – the fans were still pinching themselves at the chance to get photos, autographs and shake the hands of those players responsible for the unlikeliest of victory parades for a team that would go down in history. Division Two football was only ever considered a pipe dream, but now it was a reality.

It proved another memorable day which capped off a wonderful season that would live long in the memories of all who were there to be a part of it. Looking back over history, it shows that Southend United Football Club has had many days in the sun before and since that season of wonder, but on May 4th 1991 the seaside sun shone brightest of all.

'Up The Blues!'

Final Table May 1991

	TEAM	P	W	D	L	F	A	Pts	GD
1	Cambridge United	46	25	11	10	75	45	86	30
2	Southend United	46	26	7	13	67	51	85	16
3	Grimsby Town	46	24	11	11	66	34	83	32
4	Bolton Wanderers	46	24	11	11	64	50	83	14
5	Tranmere Rovers	46	23	9	14	64	46	78	18
6	Brentford	46	21	13	12	59	47	76	12
7	Bury	46	20	13	13	67	56	73	11
8	Bradford City	46	20	10	16	62	54	70	8
9	Bournemouth	46	19	13	14	58	58	70	0
10	Wigan Athletic	46	20	9	17	71	54	69	17
11	Huddersfield Town	46	18	13	15	57	51	67	6
12	Birmingham City	46	16	17	13	45	49	65	-4
13	Leyton Orient	46	18	10	18	55	58	64	-3
14	Stoke City	46	16	12	18	55	59	60	-4
15	Reading	46	17	8	21	53	66	59	-13
16	Exeter City	46	16	9	21	58	52	57	6
17	Preston North End	46	15	11	20	54	67	56	-13
18	Shrewsbury Town	46	14	10	22	61	68	52	-7
19	Chester City	46	14	9	23	46	58	51	-12
20	**Swansea City**	46	13	9	24	49	72	48	-23
21	Fulham	46	10	16	20	41	56	46	-15
22	Crewe Alexandra	46	11	11	24	62	80	44	-18
23	Rotherham United	46	10	12	24	50	87	42	-37
24	Mansfield Town	46	8	14	24	42	63	38	-21

'Up The Blues!'

What It Meant to Me

I was fourteen years old when the 1990/91 season began. In 1981 I attended Roots Hall for the first time and instantly became hooked. I was in awe at everything I witnessed that day – the players, the atmosphere, the noise and the sheer excitement of a live match. I went along to the game with my two Grandads, Dad and elder brother – it was the start of a love affair with the club I still have today.

A football life of supporting The Blues was hard at times. All of my friends throughout school, college and work have been fans of the 'bigger' teams such as Spurs, Arsenal, West Ham and Manchester United. A question I still get asked today was one that I was frequently met with when I wore my blue 'Laing' or 'Firholm' sponsored shirt around town as a kid: "yeah, but who's your team in the Division One?" My response is still the same as it ever was – "well, who's yours in the lower leagues?!"

I have experienced a lot of disappointment watching my team; numerous relegations, miserable displays and embarrassing defeats, but in my opinion, this all serves to make me relish the good times even more.

I have spent countless amounts of pounds travelling all over the country to support my team. From Exeter to Newcastle, Rochdale to Bournemouth – even a crazy two day trip to Florence to see The Blues play against a Gabriel Batistuta inspired Fiorentina in the Anglo Italian Cup! I do this because I want to. I love my club and I love watching them play.

I know the limits I'm likely to get supporting Southend United. I'm aware that as a small club we're always going to be forced into selling our best players and replace them with ones of lesser ability. I understand that my team will frustrate and disappoint more often than not. I guess it's something that Blues supporters inevitably grow accustomed to, but in 1990 David Webb set about to change that mind-set.

Nobody really believed Webby when he said we could push on in 1990 and look towards Division Two, but we started the season like house on fire. We were winning games by playing some exciting and attractive football. We were scoring lots of goals and soared to the top of the table very early on.

There had been a big shift in personnel during the summer with Webb replacing my favourite player David Crown with a younger model in Brett Angell. The manager also got rid of the elder statesmen with Roy McDonough, Paul Brush and Paul Roberts all leaving the club. They were replaced with younger, hungrier players like Angell, Adam Locke and Chris Powell.

All of the new arrivals hit the ground running and the results on the pitch reflected this. There was none of the squad rotation policy that is prevalent in today's game. Webb knew early on his best side and rarely ventured away from it. Even in all the cup games it was generally the same players that played and as a result, there was a tremendous understanding all over the field.

The new look Southend got people talking in a way they never had before. There was always an air of doubt from my family as to how long it would all last – when exactly the wheels would come falling off, etc. But, as the months went on they never did. Each month was as prosperous as the last and the belief in Webb and the players grew like never before for a team in the blue shirts of Southend.

Sammy in goal was as good as we'd ever seen at Roots Hall, while the two new arrivals at both full back positions were a breath of fresh air. It was clear that both Dean Austin and Chrissy Powell would go on to have great careers.

Up front, the goals just flowed from the opening game away at Huddersfield for Angell. He was just as prolific as his predecessor and its testament to the player that Crown wasn't missed at all.

Benji, Tilly and little Ansah all weighed in with goals, but the three offered more than that. They were outstanding over the course of the season and were integral parts to the team as well as being fan favourites amongst the supporters.

Clarky and Dave Martin provided the steel to the spine of the side, both having superb campaigns that surprised supporters who had doubted their ability to maintain such a high standard over forty-six games.

For me, though, there was one player who stood out just that little bit more than the excellence that surrounded him and that man was Peter Butler. So often he set the tempo by winning tackles and putting his body on the line for the side. His passing was underrated, but that shouldn't have been the case. In that season Butler was unbelievable and was now the player I'd try and replicate in the playground.

There was some jittery moments along the way but the consistency and class from the team never wavered as they stayed in the promotion places for the majority of the season.

Then, with all the nerves playing havoc with the watching crowds, it suddenly came down to Bury away where the first opportunity presented itself for Blues to make history. A win away at Gigg Lane would seal promotion with two still to play. It surely was a case of when and not if we went up, but to do it in game number forty-four of the season would be extra special.

I remember the day well. We travelled on the coach up to Bury and took our place on the away terrace with around fifteen hundred other Shrimpers. The atmosphere was great as song after song was sung with all our hearts in the efforts to cheer on the boys.

Scully's red card was harsh and really put us up against it. I recall feeling incredibly annoyed and disappointed that it now clearly wasn't going to happen. Down to ten men…away from home…needing the win…oh, come on, it's Southend for goodness sake! I said to my mate that 'we're gonna blow this and the whole season.' Even at my young age I'd already developed the perfect frame of mind to support this team!

The game carried on goalless and the minutes kept ticking down. When Benji put the ball in the Bury net I went mad. We all did. It was such a special moment. A beautiful moment that evoked such an outpour of joy! It was **the** moment that won promotion to Division Two!

That year I hold dear to my heart to this day and always will. It remains my favourite season of my life when my team had unimaginable success and did so in such style. It meant a lot then and it means even more now… I was always proud of my team that I supported, but now I had more reason than ever to feel such pride.

After the final whistle that day, I climbed down from the fence at the front of the terrace before making my way up towards the back of the stand to see my Dad who was with my Uncle.

Having almost reached them, I then saw something that will stay with me forever. It was something that I'd never recalled seeing before - my Dad was crying. He was crying tears of joy and my Uncle had one arm around him, squeezing him tight.

My Dad had always wanted to see his team play in Division Two and he just couldn't hold back the tears when the dream – his dream - became a reality. He had been following Southend United since the 1950's and always spoke of it happening 'one day...' now it had finally been achieved.

Life has a nasty habit of kicking you in the arse sometimes and my Dad never got to see his beloved Southend United play in Division Two after falling ill in the summer of 1991. He wasn't considered well enough to attend the historic opening match versus Bristol City at Roots Hall. He died four days later on August 21st.

1990-91 means a whole lot more to me and my family than seeing Blues win promotion in style. David Webb and his team will forever be held up as Southend United legends and rightly so. What they achieved that season deserves constant recognition for all their efforts in delivering something that had never been done ever before. David Webb had a dream and I'm delighted that I was there to witness it come true, but even more so for my Dad.

'Up The Blues!'

Southend United: Results & Stats 1990/1991

August 25th 1990 - Division Three
    Huddersfield Town   1 – 2   Southend United
    Wilson   Angell
    Att: 5,219   Edwards
Team: (442) Sansome, Edwards, Cornwell, Clark, Hyslop, Ansah, Butler, Martin, Tilson, Benjamin, Angell.
Subs not used: Cook & McDonough.

August 28th 1990 - Rumbelows Cup Round One (1st Leg)
    Southend United   2 – 1   Aldershot
    Butler
    Martin   Att: 2,254
Team: (442) Sansome, Edwards, Cornwell, Clark, Hyslop, Ansah, Butler, Martin, Tilson, Benjamin, Angell.
Subs not used: Cook & McDonough.

September 1st 1990 - Division Three
    Southend United   3 – 2   Crewe Alexandra
    Benjamin   Sussex
    Martin (pen)   Hignett
    Angell   Att: 2,994
Team: (442) Sansome, Edwards, Cornwell, Clark, Powell, Ansah, Butler, Martin, Tilson, Benjamin, Angell.
Subs not used: Cook & McDonough

September 4th 1990 - Rumbelows Cup Round One (2nd Leg)

    Aldershot   2 - 2   Southend United
Att: 2,400   Austin
                                 Angell

Team: (442) Sansome, Austin, Cornwell, Clark, Powell, Ansah, Butler, Martin, Tilson, Benjamin, Angell.
Subs not used: Cook & McDonough

September 9th 1990 - Division Three

    Cambridge United   1 – 4   Southend United
Cheetham   Angell, 2
Att: 4,790   Benjamin
                                 Butler

Team: (442) Sansome, Austin, Cornwell, Clark, Powell, Ansah, Butler, Martin, Tilson, Benjamin, Angell.
Subs not used: Cook & McDonough.

September 14th 1990 - Division Three

    Southend United   3 – 2   Preston North End
Martin   Joyce
Benjamin   Thomas (pen)
Cornwell   Att: 4,614

Team: (442) Sansome, Austin, Cornwell, Clark, Powell, Ansah, Butler, Martin, Tilson, Benjamin, Angell.
Subs not used: Cook & McDonough.

September 18th 1990 - Division Three

    Southend United   2 – 1   Shrewsbury Town
Tilson   Clark (O.G.)
Ansah   Att: 5,100

Team: (442) Sansome, Austin, Cornwell, Clark, Powell, Ansah, Butler, Martin, Tilson, Benjamin, Angell.
Subs not used: Cook & McDonough.

September 22nd 1990 - Division Three

    Stoke City   4 – 0   Southend United
    Ware   Att: 11,901
    Biggins, 2
    Cornwell (O.G.)

Team: (442) Sansome, Austin, Cornwell, Clark, Powell, Ansah, Butler, Martin, Tilson, Benjamin, Angell (Cook).
Subs not used: McDonough

September 25th 1990 - Rumbelows Cup Round Two (1st Leg)

    Crystal Palace   8 – 0   Southend United
    Bright, 3   Att: 9,653
    Wright, 3
    Hodges
    Thompson

Team: (442) Sansome, Austin, Cornwell (Cook), Clark, Powell, Ansah, Butler, Martin, Tilson, Benjamin, Angell.
Subs not used: McDonough.

September 29th 1990 Division Three

    Mansfield Town 0 – 1 Southend United
    Att: 2,210   Benjamin

Team: (442) Sansome, Austin, Prior, Clark, Powell, Ansah (Locke), Butler, Martin, Tilson, Benjamin, Angell.
Sub not used: Cornwell.

October 2nd 1990 – Division Three

    Southend United 4 – 1 Swansea City
    Martin, 2 (1 pen)   Gilligan
    Tilson, 2   Att: 3,635

Team: (442) Sansome, Austin, Prior, Clark, Powell, Ansah (Locke), Martin, Butler, Tilson, Benjamin, Angell.
Sub not used: Cornwell.

October 5th 1990 – Division Three
    Southend United 2 – 1 AFC Bournemouth
    Martin   Ekoku
    Angell   Att: 5,255

Team: (442) Sansome, Austin, Prior, Clark (Cawley), Powell, Ansah (Locke), Martin, Butler, Tilson, Benjamin, Angell.

October 9th 1990 – Rumbelows Cup Round Two (2nd leg)
    Southend United 1 – 2 Crystal Palace
    Angell   Young
    Att: 5,199   Salako

Team: (442) Sansome, Cornwell, Prior, Cawley, Powell, Locke, Martin, Butler, Tilson, Benjamin (Ansah), Angell.
Sub not used: Smith.

October 13th 1990 – Division Three
    Birmingham City 1 – 1 Southend United
    Sturridge   Ansah
    Att: 9,333

Team: (442) Sansome, Austin, Prior, Cawley, Powell, Ansah, Martin, Butler, Tilson (Cornwell), Benjamin, Angell (Locke)

October 20th 1990 – Division Three
    Wigan Athletic 4 – 1 Southend United
    Page   Cawley
    Daley   Att: 2,691
    Griffiths, 2 (1 pen)

Team: (442) Sansome, Austin, Prior, Cawley, Powell, Ansah (Ling), Martin (Cornwell), Butler, Tilson, Benjamin, Angell.

October 23rd 1990 – Division Three
    Southend United 2 – 1 Exeter City
    Powell   Taylor
    Benjamin   Att: 4,280

Team: (442) Sansome, Austin, Prior, Cawley, Powell, Ansah, Martin (Cornwell), Butler, Tilson, Benjamin, Angell.
Sub not used: Edwards.

October 27th 1990 – Division Three

  Southend United 2 – 1 Bury
  Angell   Parkinson
  Tilson   Att: 4,001

Team: (442) Sansome, Austin, Prior, Cawley, Powell, Ansah, Cornwell, Butler, Tilson, Benjamin, Angell.
Subs not used: Edwards & Locke

November 4th 1990 – Division Three

  Brentford 0 – 1 Southend United
  Att: 8,021 Benjamin

Team: (442) Sansome, Austin, Prior, Cawley, Powell, Ansah, Cornwell, Butler, Tilson, Benjamin, Angell (Locke).
Sub not used: Edwards

November 6th 1990 – Leyland Daf Cup

  Southend United 10 – 1 Aldershot
  Angell, 4   Banton
  Tilson, 3   Att: 1,281
  Prior
  Benjamin
  Ansah

Team: (442) Sansome, Austin, Prior, Cawley, Powell, Ansah, Cornwell, Butler, Tilson, Benjamin, Angell.
Subs not used: Locke, Edwards.

November 10th 1990 – Division Three

  Southend United 1 – 1 Fulham
  Cornwell   Brazil
  Att: 5,808

Team: (442) Sansome, Austin, Prior, Cawley, Powell, Ansah, Cornwell, Butler, Tilson (Martin), Benjamin, Angell (Locke).

November 17th 1990 – F.A. Cup

  Leyton Orient 3 – 2 Southend United
  Castle, 2   Angell, 2
  Nugent   Att: 6,095

Team: (442) Sansome, Austin, Prior, Cawley (Locke), Powell, Ansah, Cornwell (Martin), Butler, Tilson, Benjamin, Angell.

November 24th 1990 – Division Three

Reading 2 – 4 Southend United
Senior   Martin, 2
Moran   Tilson
Att: 3,927 Angell

Team: (442) Sansome, Austin, Prior, Clark, Powell, Locke, Martin, Butler, Tilson, Benjamin, Angell.
Subs not used: Hyslop, Ling.

December 1st 1990 – Division Three

Rotherham United 0 – 1 Southend United
Att: 3,465   Benjamin

Team: (442) Sansome, Austin, Prior, Clark, Powell, Smith, Martin, Butler, Tilson, Benjamin, Angell.
Subs not used: Ling, Hyslop.

December 7th 1990 – Leyland Daf Cup

Reading 1 – 4 Southend United
Gooding   Benjamin, 2
Att: 1,472   Butler
             Angell

Team: (442) Sansome, Austin, Prior, Clark, Powell, Locke, Martin, Butler, Tilson, Benjamin, Angell.
Subs not used; Hyslop, Smith.

December 15th 1990 – Division Three

Southend United 2 – 0 Grimsby Town
Tilson   Att: 8,126
Martin

Team: (442) Sansome, Austin, Prior, Clark, Powell, Locke, Martin, Butler, Tilson, Benjamin, Angell.
Subs not used: Ling, Hyslop.

December 22nd 1990 – Division Three

Chester City 1 – 0 Southend United
Dale   Att: 1,523

Team: (442) Sansome, Austin, Prior, Clark, Powell, Locke, Martin, Butler, Tilson, Benjamin, Angell.
Subs not used: Ansah, Edwards.

December 26th 1990 – Division Three
    Southend United 1 – 1 Bolton Wanderers
    Tilson   Green
    Att: 7, 539

Team: (442) Sansome, Austin, Prior, Clark, Powell, Locke, Martin, Butler, Tilson, Benjamin, Angell.
Subs not used: Ansah, Ling.

December 28th 1990 – Division Three
    Southend United 1 – 1 Bradford City
    Tilson   Jewell
    Att: 6,767

Team: (442) Sansome, Austin, Prior, Clark, Powell, Locke (Ansah), Martin, Butler, Tilson, Benjamin, Angell.
Sub not used: Ling.

January 1st 1991 – Division Three
    Tranmere Rovers 3 – 1 Southend United
    Thomas   Angell
    Muir   Att: 7,214
    Morrissey

Team: (442) Sansome, Austin, Prior, Clark, Powell, Ansah, Smith (Ling), Butler, Tilson, Benjamin, Angell.
Sub not used: Edwards.

January 8th 1991 – Leyland Daf Cup
    Southend United 2 – 0 Maidstone United
    Cooper (O.G.)   Att: 1,849
    Angell

Team: (442) Sansome, Austin, Prior, Clark, Powell, Ansah, Ling, Butler, Tilson, Benjamin, Angell.
Subs not used: Edwards, Hyslop.

January 12th 1991 – Division Three
    Crewe Alexandra 0 – 2 Southend United
    Att: 3,595   Angell, 2

Team: (442) Sansome, Austin, Scully, Clark, Powell, Ansah, Martin, Butler, Tilson, Benjamin, Angell.
Subs not used: Prior, Ling.

January 19th 1991 – Division Three
    Southend United 0 – 1 Huddersfield Town
    Att: 5,509   Smith
Team: (442) Sansome, Austin, Scully, Clark, Powell, Ansah, Martin, Butler, Tilson, Benjamin, Angell (Locke).
Sub not used: Prior.

January 26th 1991 – Division Three
    Preston North End 2 – 1 Southend United
    Swann   Ansah
    Wrightson   Att: 4,351
Team: (442) Sansome, Austin, Scully, Clark, Powell, Locke (Ansah), Martin, Butler (Cornwell), Tilson, Benjamin, Angell.

February 2nd 1991 – Division Three
    Shrewsbury Town 0 – 1 Southend United
    Att: 4,377   Angell
Team: (442) Sansome, Austin, Scully, Clark, Powell, Ansah, Martin, Butler, Tilson, Benjamin, Angell.
Subs not used: Cook, Edwards.

February 5th 1991 – Division Three
    Southend United 1 – 0 Stoke City
    Angell   Att: 5,164
Team: (442) Sansome, Austin, Scully, Clark, Powell, Ansah, Martin, Butler, Tilson, Benjamin, Angell.
Subs not used: Cook, Edwards.

February 19th 1991 – Division Three
    Southend United 1 – 2 Reading
    Benjamin   Moran
    Att: 4,588   Bailey
Team: (442) Sansome, Austin, Scully, Clark, Powell, Ansah, Martin, Cornwell (Locke), Tilson, Benjamin, Angell.
Sub not used: Edwards.

February 23rd 1991 – Division Three
    Fulham 0 – 3 Southend United
    Att: 5,113   Benjamin
                    Martin
                    Ansah
Team: (442) Sansome, Austin, Scully, Clark, Powell, Locke, Martin, Benjamin, Tilson, Ansah, Angell.
Subs not used: Edwards, Smith.

February 26th 1991 – Leyland Daf Cup
    Southend United 7 – 0 Torquay United
    Edwards   Att: 2,273
    Martin, 2 (1 pen)
    Ansah, 3
    Angell
Team: (442) Sansome, Austin, Edwards, Clark, Powell, Locke, Martin, Butler, Tilson, Benjamin (Angell), Ansah.
Sub not used: Cornwell.

March 1st 1991 – Division Three
    Southend United 2 – 1 Rotherham United
    Benjamin, 2   Hazel
    Att: 5,622
Team: (442) Sansome, Austin, Scully, Clark, Powell, Locke, Martin, Butler, Tilson (Angell), Benjamin, Ansah.
Sub not used: Edwards

March 5th 1991 – Leyland Daf Cup
    Southend United 0 – 3 Brentford
    Att: 3,937   Smillie
                        Jones
                        Cadette
Team: (442) Sansome, Austin, Edwards, Clark, Powell, Locke (Ansah), Martin, Butler, Tilson, Benjamin, Angell.
Sub not used: Cornwall

March 9th 1991 – Division Three

Grimsby Town 1 – 0 Southend United
Gilbert   Att: 9,689

Team: (442) Sansome, Austin, Scully, Clark, Powell, Ansah, Martin, Butler, Tilson, Benjamin, Angell (Locke).
Sub not used: Edwards

March 12th 1991 – Division Three

Swansea City 1 – 4 Southend United
Gilligan   Locke, 2
Att: 2,712   Benjamin
              Ansah

Team: (442) Sansome, Austin, Scully, Clark, Powell, Locke, Martin, Butler, Tilson, Benjamin, Ansah.
Subs not used: Angell and Cornwell.

March 15th 1991 – Division Three

Southend United 2 – 1 Mansfield Town
Martin   Wilkinson
Butler   Att: 5,400

Team: (442) Sansome, Austin, Scully, Clark, Powell, Locke, Martin, Butler, Tilson, Benjamin, Angell.
Subs not used: Angell and Cornwell.

March 18th 1991 – Division Three

Southend United 2 – 1 Birmingham City
Martin   Gleghorn
Angell   Att: 6,328

Team: (442) Sansome, Austin, Scully, Clark, Powell, Locke, Martin, Butler, Tilson, Benjamin, Ansah (Angell).
Sub not used: Cornwell.

March 23rd 1991 – Division Three

AFC Bournemouth 3 – 1 Southend United
Blissett   Angell
Prior (O.G.)   Att: 7,421
Watson

Team: (442) Sansome, Austin, Prior, Clark (Cornwell), Powell, Ling, Butler, Benjamin, Tilson, Moran (Hyslop), Angell.

March 30th 1991 – Division Three
    Bolton Wanderers 1 – 0 Southend United
    Darby   Att: 10,666

Team: (442) Sansome, Austin, Scully, Clark, Powell, Ansah, Cornwell, Butler, Tilson, Benjamin, Angell.
Subs not used: Moran and Prior.

April 2nd 1991 – Division Three
    Southend United 1 – 1 Chester City
    Ansah   Bishop
    Att: 6,190

Team: (442) Sansome, Austin, Scully, Clark, Powell, Ansah, Martin, Butler, Tilson, Benjamin, Angell.
Subs not used: Locke and Cornwell.

April 6th 1991 – Division Three
    Bradford City 2 – 1 Southend United
    Torpey   Angell
    McCarthy   Att: 5,846

Team: (442) Sansome, Austin, Scully, Clark, Hyslop, Locke (Ansah), Martin, Cornwell, Powell, Benjamin, Angell.
Sub not used: Prior.

April 9th 1991 – Division Three
    Leyton Orient 0 – 1 Southend United
    Att: 6,306   Ansah

Team: (442) Sansome, Austin, Scully, Clark, Hyslop, Locke, Martin, Cornwell, Powell, Benjamin, Ansah.
Subs not used: Angell and Smith.

April 12th 1991 – Division Three
    Southend United 1 – 0 Tranmere Rovers
    Ansah   Att: 8,622

Team: (442) Sansome, Austin, Scully, Clark, Hyslop, Locke, Martin, Butler, Powell, Benjamin, Ansah.
Subs not used: Angell and Cornwell.

April 19th 1991 – Division Three

    Southend United 0 – 2 Wigan Athletic
    Att: 7,550   Worthington
                        Rimmer

Team: (442) Sansome, Austin, Scully, Clark, Hyslop, Locke (Angell), Martin, Butler, Powell, Benjamin, Ansah.
Sub not used: Cornwell.

April 27th 1991 – Division Three

    Exeter City 1 – 2 Southend United
    Cooper   Ansah
    Att: 4,941   Hiley

Team: (442) Sansome, Austin, Scully, Clark, Hyslop, Locke (Angell), Martin, Butler, Powell, Benjamin, Ansah.
Sub not used: Cornwell.

April 30th 1991 – Division Three

    Southend United 0 – 0 Cambridge United
    Att: 10,664

Team: (442) Sansome, Austin, Scully, Clark, Hyslop, Ansah, Martin, Butler, Powell, Benjamin, Angell.
Subs not used: Cornwell and Locke.

May 4th 1991 – Division Three

    Bury 0 – 1 Southend United
    Att: 4, 254   Benjamin

Team: (442) Sansome, Austin, Scully, Clark, Hyslop, Locke (Cornwell), Martin, Butler, Benjamin, Angell (Powell), Ansah.

May 7th 1991 – Division Three

    Southend United 1 -1 Leyton Orient
    Locke   Day
    Att: 8,760

Team: (442) Sansome, Austin, Scully, Clark, Hyslop, Ansah, Martin, Butler, Powell, Benjamin, Angell (Locke).
Sub not used: Cornwell.

May 11th 1991 – Division Three
          Southend United 0 – 1 Brentford
          Att: 9,666   Blissett
Team: (442) Sansome, Austin, Scully, Clark, Hyslop (Powell), Locke, Martin, Butler, Tilson (Angell), Benjamin, Ansah.